Christianity in Brazil

Bloomsbury Studies in Religion, Space and Place

Series editors: Paul-François Tremlett, John Eade and Katy Soar

Religions, spiritualities and mysticisms are deeply implicated in processes of place-making. These include political and geopolitical spaces, local and national spaces, urban spaces, global and virtual spaces, contested spaces, spaces of performance, spaces of memory and spaces of confinement. At the leading edge of theoretical, methodological, and interdisciplinary innovation in the study of religion, Bloomsbury Studies in Religion, Space and Place brings together and gives shape to the study of such processes.
These places are not defined simply by the material or the physical but also by the sensual and the psychological, by the ways in which spaces are gendered, classified, stratified, moved through, seen, touched, heard, interpreted and occupied. Places are constituted through embodied practices that direct critical and analytical attention to the spatial production of insides, outsides, bodies, landscapes, cities, sovereignties, publics and interiorities.

Global Trajectories of Brazilian Religion, edited by Martijn Oosterbaan, Linda van de Kamp and Joana Bahia
Religion and the Global City, edited by David Garbin and Anna Strhan
Religious Pluralism and the City, edited by Helmuth Berking, Silke Steets and Jochen Schwenk
Singapore, Spirituality, and the Space of the State, Joanne Punzo Waghorne
Towards a New Theory of Religion and Social Change, Paul-François Tremlett
Urban Religious Events, edited by Paul Bramadat, Mar Griera, Julia Martinez-Ariño and Marian Burchardt

Christianity in Brazil

An Introduction from a Global Perspective

Sílvia Fernandes

BLOOMSBURY ACADEMIC
LONDON • NEW YORK • OXFORD • NEW DELHI • SYDNEY

BLOOMSBURY ACADEMIC
Bloomsbury Publishing Plc
50 Bedford Square, London, WC1B 3DP, UK
1385 Broadway, New York, NY 10018, USA
29 Earlsfort Terrace, Dublin 2, Ireland

BLOOMSBURY, BLOOMSBURY ACADEMIC and the Diana logo are trademarks of
Bloomsbury Publishing Plc

First published in Great Britain 2022
This paperback edition published 2023

Copyright © Sílvia Fernandes, 2022

Sílvia Fernandes has asserted her right under the Copyright, Designs and Patents Act,
1988, to be identified as Author of this work.

For legal purposes the Acknowledgments on pp. xii–xiii constitute an extension of
this copyright page.

Cover image © Thomas M. Scheer / EyeEm / gettyimages.co.uk

All rights reserved. No part of this publication may be reproduced or transmitted
in any form or by any means, electronic or mechanical, including photocopying,
recording, or any information storage or retrieval system, without prior
permission in writing from the publishers.

Bloomsbury Publishing Plc does not have any control over, or responsibility for, any
third-party websites referred to or in this book. All internet addresses given in this
book were correct at the time of going to press. The author and publisher regret any
inconvenience caused if addresses have changed or sites have ceased to exist,
but can accept no responsibility for any such changes.

A catalogue record for this book is available from the British Library.

Library of Congress Control Number: 2021942937

ISBN: HB: 978-1-3502-0499-7
PB: 978-1-3502-0499-7
ePDF: 978-1-3502-0496-6
eBook: 978-1-3502-0497-3

Series: Bloomsbury Studies in Religion, Space and Place

Typeset by Deanta Global Publishing Services, Chennai, India

To find out more about our authors and books visit www.bloomsbury.com and
sign up for our newsletters

Contents

List of Illustrations	vi
Acknowledgments	vii
Abbreviations	ix
Introduction: The Global Significance of Brazilian Christianity	1
1 Christianity Comes to Brazil: Hybridity, Domination, and Resistance	11
2 Competing and Cross-Fertilizing Structures of Feeling and Experience: Ways of Being Christian in Brazil	39
3 Religious Innovators and Entrepreneurs: Brazilian Christianity from a Micro Perspective	57
4 Regional, Urban, and Rural Diversity	101
5 A Multifaceted Christianity: A Denominational View	119
6 Brazilian Christianity, Politics, and Society	141
Conclusion: Quo Vadis Brazilian Christianity?	173
Notes	189
Bibliography	212
Index	236

Illustrations

Figures

1	Growth in absolute numbers—population, Catholics, Evangelicals, and those with no religion by Brazilian region, 2000–2010	114
2	Percentage of annual rate of growth, 2000–2010	115
3	Main religions by region in Brazil, 2000–2010	115
4	Percentages of religious affiliation by decade	128

Tables

1	Population and Religious Affiliation by Region of Brazil	104
2	Percentages of the Population that Self-Declares as Catholic and Protestant in 2000 and 2010 by Region	113
3	Religious Breakdown of Rural versus Urban Brazilians, 2010	116
4	Christian Churches/Denominations in Brazil According to the 2010 Census	129
5	Classification of Pentecostals According to Freston (1995)	130
6	Main Pentecostal Churches in Brazil According to the 2010 Census	131

Acknowledgments

This book was written over five years. Like every work that aims to address a multifaceted and *longue durée* historical process, it required many hours of research and dialogue with the literature that informs it. I thank my colleagues in different parts of the globe who inspired my analyses through their studies.

My trajectory as an associate professor at the Federal Rural University of Rio de Janeiro (UFRRJ) and the ongoing dialogue I have sustained with colleagues from the working group Religião e Modernidade (Religion and Modernity) of the Brazilian Society of Sociology (SBS) have been fundamental for the thickening of many of the ideas contained in this book. The first steps in this journey took place toward the end of the 1990s. I am very grateful to Cecília Loreto Mariz and Maria das Dores Campos Machado for initiating me into the rich and thought-provoking field of sociology of religion and the realm of academic research.

I would also like to recognize the conversations I established with undergraduate and postgraduate students, both in the classroom and through the Research Group on Territorial Dynamics, Culture, and Religion (Grupo de Pesquisa Dinâmicas Territoriais, Cultura e Religião—CRELIG) that have helped me to sharpen my understanding of Christianity in Brazil. Every work that I have supervised and every discussion table that we have held reoriented and expanded my gaze on the always-dynamic Brazilian religious field.

In a similar way, my experiences as a researcher and research coordinator at the Center for Religious Statistics and Social Investigations (CERIS) opened a universe of interpretative possibilities about the patterns, continuities, and transformations that mark Brazilian Catholicism. Moreover, they allowed me to concentrate my analytical gaze on the institutional logics and dilemmas of the Catholic Church in Brazil, especially when the institution is confronted with the advance of religious pluralism that has elevated (Neo-)Pentecostalism to a prominent place in society. At CERIS, Rogério Valle (in memoriam) and Marcelo Pitta taught me the most lessons in my métier as a social scientist. With them, I deepened my analytical sensitivity and learned to review the receive certainties about a complex field, expand the interdisciplinary dialogue, and exercise a measure of theoretical-methodological creativity to approach the different facets of Brazilian Christianity. I am also grateful to Lucia Pedrosa-Padua who greatly contributed to turning my attention to the theological work on the religious lives of women, an area that remains little explored in the social sciences.

I also thank my Latin American colleagues linked to the Association of Social Scientists of the Religion of the Mercosur—ACSRM. The workshops on religious alternatives in Latin America that they organized were essential in elucidating and problematizing the specificities of religion in Brazil while allowing us to establish relevant comparisons about regional and global Christianities. In particular, I thank Néstor Da Costa of the Catholic University of Uruguay for the different research opportunities and partnerships over these years.

My post-doctoral work at the University of Florida—Gainesville in 2013 was a particularly important moment of growth in the study of and research on religion. It was made possible thanks to a grant from the Coordenação de Aperfeiçoamento do Ensino Superior (Coordination for the Enhancement of Higher Education—CAPES). I wish to express my deepest gratitude to the Department of Religion and the Center for Latin American Studies at the University of Florida for hosting me as a postdoctoral fellow and giving me the perfect setting to conduct my research. The dialogue with Manuel Vásquez was fundamental in maturing and consolidating this work which I now offer to the readers.

Abbreviations

AC	Alternative Christianities.
AG	Assembléias de Deus (Assemblies of God).
CCR	Movimento de Renovação Carismática Católica (Catholic Charismatic Renewal Movement).
CEB	Comunidade eclesial de base (Base ecclesial community).
CELAM	Consejo Episcopal Latinoamericano (Latin American Episcopal Conference).
CIMI	Conselho Indigenista Missionário (Indigenous Missionary Council).
CNBB	Conferência Nacional dos Bispos do Brasil (National Conference of Brazilian Bishops).
CPT	Commissão Pastoral da Terra: (Pastoral Land Commission).
ENCRISTUS	Encontro Nacional de Cristãos em Busca de Unidade e Santidade (National Encounter of Christians in Search of Unity and Sanctity).
FPE	Frente Parlamentar Evangélica (Evangelical Parlamentary Front).
HP	Historic Protestantism.
ISAL	Iglesia y Sociedad en América Latina (Church and Society in Latin America).
ITER	Instituto Teológico do Recife (Recife Theological Institute).
JUC	Juventude Universitária Católica (Catholic University Youth Movement).
LDS	Church of Jesus Christ of Latter-Day Saints (The Mormons).

Abbreviations

LT	Liberation theology.
MEB	Movimento de Educação de Base (Base Education Movement).
MST	Movimento dos Trabalhadores Sem Terra (Landless Workers' Movement).
PC	Catolicismo Progressista (progressive Catholicism).
PCC	Pentecostalism and Charismatic Christianity.
PT	Partido dos Trabalhadores (Workers' Party).
TLC	Traditional Luso-Catholicism.
UCKG	Igreja Universal do Reino de Deus (Universal Church of the Kingdom of God).

Introduction

The Global Significance of Brazilian Christianity

On July 24, 2013, barely four months into his office, Pope Francis, the first Latin American Catholic pontiff,[1] arrived in Brazil, on what was his first trip overseas. Hundreds of thousands of adoring followers lined the streets of Rio de Janeiro, the first stop on his visit, to catch a glimpse of the pope or perhaps even touch him as he went by in his thinly protected motorcade, in what a journalist described as a "mob scene" (Romero 2013). Francis came to participate in World Youth Day, a yearly event inaugurated in 1985 by John Paul II, one of his predecessors and, arguably, one of the most influential figures of the twentieth century. World Youth Day is the largest international gathering of young Catholics, who come together to energize their faith and to renew their pledge to spearhead a worldwide "new evangelization," as called for by John Paul II. Francis's visit culminated with a gigantic open-air Sunday mass in the famous Copacabana Beach, bringing together an estimated three million exuberant worshippers. While most of those present were Catholic, Francis also attracted many Protestants and practitioners of other non-Christian religions, as well as people who were simply curious or not affiliated with any religion but who wanted to partake in his charisma. Momentarily setting aside the fierce historic rivalry between Brazil and Argentina not only in the politics of the Southern Cone but also on the soccer pitch, a young Brazilian Catholic commented: "I think this pope is very different . . . . He hugs people. He's from the people. This pope is a Brazilian." Another young Brazilian who participated in the various events added that the pope's visit "has been fantastic. Much bigger and better than carnival."[2] An important ingredient of Francis's appeal is his call to make the poor the church's central focus of pastoral work and theological reflection, a call that has once again elevated the global profile of Latin American liberation theology, of which Brazilian progressive Catholicism has been a major contributor.

That Pope Francis's first international trip was to Brazil is not surprising, given that with close to 127 million Catholics, Brazil is the country with the largest Catholic population in the world, well ahead of Mexico (96.5 million), the Philippines (75.6 million), the United States (75.4 million), and Italy (49.2 million). The tumultuous reception Francis received confirms the continued vibrancy of Brazilian Catholicism. Nevertheless, there are ongoing tectonic shifts in the landscape of Christianity in the country. From 1910 to 2010, the year of the last national census, the percentage of Brazilians who declare themselves Catholics has fallen from 98 percent to approximately 65 percent. During the same period, the percentage of Brazilian Protestants has soared from the low single digits to 22 percent. The bulk of this growth has taken place in the last couple of decades: in 1991, only 9 percent of the population declared themselves *evangélicos*, the term that both the census and the faithful themselves use to characterize a wide variety of Protestant churches. As I will discuss in the Conclusion, when I reflect on the future of Christianity in Brazil, statistical evidence since the last census points to Catholicism's further numerical decline and Protestantism's continued growth. The majority of Brazilian Protestants— between 60 and 70 percent—are Pentecostals, underlining the fact that the most dynamic sectors of Brazilian Christianity, particularly in terms of demographic growth, are strongly "pneuma-centric," built around the embodied and profoundly affective experience of the Holy Spirit and its charismas (gifts such as divine healing, exorcism, prophecy, and glossolalia). Thus, Brazil, a country long considered Catholic, has now the largest number of Pentecostals (25 million) in the world, far outnumbering not only the United States (6.3 million), the nation where Pentecostalism originated, but also emerging global Pentecostal nodes such as Nigeria (5 million) and Ghana (3.8 million) (Mariz and Gracino 2013; Johnson 2009).

Demonstrating Brazilian Pentecostalism's national and global visibility, on July 31, 2014, just a year after Pope Francis's visit, Pastor Edir Macedo, the founder and leader of the Neo-Pentecostal Igreja Universal do Reino de Deus (Universal Church of the Kingdom of God—UCKG), inaugurated the Templo de Salomão (Temple of Solomon) in São Paulo, the largest city in South America. Built at the cost of more than $300 million, covering an area of 100,000 square meters, and rising over eighteen stories high, this temple is meant to be a replica of the original one built by the Jewish king and destroyed by Nebuchadnezzar II in 586 BCE, as imagined by Macedo, with grand columns, massive gold-plated doors, and lavish gardens. Macedo went as far as spending $8 million to bring stones from Jerusalem to erect his temple. The inauguration of the Temple of Solomon was a veritable glittering affair, gathering all the most notable figures in politics, economics, entertainment, and media in Brazil, including the then-president Dilma Rousseff. Thus, in many ways, this event marked the UCKG's public entry into Brazil's religious and secular elite, a sharp turn of fate for a former lottery-agent-cum-pastor who had spent time in jail on charges of charlatanism and for a church that was consistently embroiled in controversy. For example, in 1995, in an episode popularly known as "*o chute na santa*" (the kick on the saint), Sérgio von Helder, a prominent bishop in the Universal Church, punched and kicked on national TV an image of Nossa Senhora Aparecida (Our Lady of Aparecida), the Catholic patron saint of Brazil, telling the audience: "This here is not holy at all [*não é santo coisa nenhuma*]! . . . could God, the creator of the universe, be compared with a doll so ugly, so horrible, so damned [*desgraçado*]?"[3] The episode, which highlights the UCKG's strongly sectarian outlook, led to national outrage not only among Catholics but also other Evangelical Protestants, prompting Macedo to transfer von Helder to a congregation in the United States, where the latter eventually broke with the Universal Church and formed his own.

In attendance at the opening of the Temple of Solomon were also "the twelve tribes of Israel": delegations from the more than 100 countries throughout the world, from the United States and Latin America to Europe and Africa, where the UCKG has temples. While the Temple of Solomon may be the most spectacular of the Universal Church's temples, the church has a reputation for building gargantuan structures, like the "Cathedral of Faith" in the middle of Soweto (the largest church building in South Africa), and buying large landmark buildings, including the Rainbow Theater in Finsbury Park, London and the Huggy Boy Theater in Los Angeles, which have fallen into disuse in the post-industrial cities. Since founding it in 1977, Macedo has built up the Universal Church to more than 6,000 temples, 12,000 pastors, and close to 2 million members in Brazil, in addition to acquiring vast radio and TV networks that allow him to beam the church's message globally to an estimated 12 million followers. The central dimension of this message is a gospel of health and wealth enshrined in the church's motto: "*Pare de sofrer!*" (Stop suffering!). This gospel involves dramatic, visceral spiritual warfare, in which UCKG pastors physically and rhetorically battle with and cast out possessing demonic spirits that cause people illness, addiction, economic misfortune, and domestic strife. In Brazil, followers of the Universal Church associate these spirits with the entities venerated and incorporated by practitioners of African-based religions like Candomblé and Umbanda. As a result, the spiritual warfare advanced by the UCKG has paradoxical effects. On the one hand, it seeks to delegitimize African-based religions that compete for followers among poor sectors of the Brazilian population by portraying them pejoratively as "*macumba*" (witchcraft); on the other hand, it reaffirms the efficacy of these religions by recognizing the power of their spirits, in effect, syncretically incorporating elements of Candomblé and Umbanda into the Neo-Pentecostal worldview (Engler 2011).

These two vignettes—Francis's visit to Brazil and the inauguration of the Temple of Solomon—demonstrate the richness and complexity of Brazilian Christianity. They tell a story of religious hegemony, ferocious competition, fractious diversification, and extensive hybridity that is compelling and instructive on its own merits. Beyond that, these two vignettes throw into high relief the importance of studying dynamics in Brazil in order to understand the future of world Christianity, for the tectonic shifts that we are witnessing in Brazil are harbingers of the changing face of Christianity not only in the Americas, but also in the Global South. And as scholars such as Philip Jenkins (2008, 2011) and Lamin Sanneh (2005, 2016) have written, after centuries of being exported from Europe by conquerors, missionaries, settlers, and traders, Christianity's center of gravity is shifting to the Global South, with highly visible transnational churches founded and/or based in countries like Brazil, Korea, Nigeria, Ghana, and India now taking the gospel back to secularized Europe and North America via religious entrepreneurs and immigrants. So, what happens in the Global South has crucial implications for Christianity worldwide. The UCKG is certainly hardly alone in carrying out the Great Commission, Jesus Christ's call to go and make disciples of all nations. It is joined by other dynamic Brazilian churches like the Igreja Mundial do Poder de Deus (World Church of God's Power), the Comunidade Evangélica Sara a Nossa Terra (Heal Our Land Evangelical Community), and the Igreja Renascer em Cristo (Reborn in Christ Church), which have wide-ranging transnational ministries, combining old-fashioned door-to-door proselytizing with grand structures and massive events that are heavily mediatized and involve dazzling entertainment.

We will see that Brazilian Pentecostal churches are playing a protagonistic role in shaping Christianity in the Americas, with vigorous outreach ministries in Central America, the Andes, and the Southern Cone, where they fiercely compete with Indigenous (and also transnational) mega-churches like Casa de Dios (of the famed televangelist Carlos "Cash" Luna in Guatemala), Misión Cristiana Elim Internacional (El Salvador), and Misión Agua Viva (Peru), as well as among Brazilian and Latino/a immigrants in the United States, Europe, and Japan (Barrera Rivera 2013; Ikeuchi 2017). Linda van de Kamp (2017) has referred to a rich, "multi-polar" "Luso-Pentecostal transnational landscape" established by Brazilian churches in African nations such as Angola and Mozambique, a

Introduction   5

"Lusosphere" that mirrors and builds upon the transatlantic connections that were established with the slave trade.[4] These networks and flows were central not only in the formation of African-based religions like Candomblé and Umbanda, but also creolized Brazilian Christianity. And Cristina Rocha (2013, 2017a) has drawn attention to the thickening south–south webs between Brazilian and Australian Pentecostals.

Although Christian ministries from and to Brazil are varied, a key stake is the swelling number of young people in the Global South and beyond who have grown up facing the opportunities and challenges of a globalized world, with the simultaneous connectivity and dislocation, the access to instant information and the uncertainty and insecurity produced by late capitalism.[5] These youths live in the midst of a world thoroughly imbued by electronic media and driven by consumerism, a world in which virtually everything, including culture, is heavily commodified. These restless and anxious young people are both vital carriers and targets of Christian evangelization. No wonder, then, Francis's presence and message during World Youth Day in Brazil. And no wonder too that Brazilian Catholicism is at the forefront in developing its own pneuma-centric strands to compete with Pentecostalism in the form of the Catholic Charismatic Renewal (CCR) movement, which also skillfully uses media, music, and entertainment to attract young people. In 2012, Father Marcelo Rossi, a famous "singing priest" (*padre cantor*) and a leading figure in the Brazilian CCR whom we will feature later in the book, inaugurated the Theotokos (*Mãe de Deus*—Mother of God) Sanctuary, whose dimensions (containing a cross 42 meters high) and capacity (for 100,000 people) rival those of the UCKG's Templo de Salomão. In addition, the "*novas comunidades de vida e aliança*," communities of priests, nuns, and laypersons who live and/or work together, share resources, and have pledged to lead a life of service to the gospel and the church, such as Canção Nova (New Song), Shalom, Toca de Assis, and Arautos do Evangelho (Heralds of the Gospel), are rapidly proliferating nationally (Carranza, Mariz, and Camurça 2009). They are also actively involved in transnational ministry, producing a Brazilian "Catholicism for Export" (Carranza and Mariz 2013). While these life and covenantal communities exhibit age-old patterns of monasticism and popular devotion, they are also strongly influenced by the Catholic Charismatic Movement. This combination of old and new is attracting many young, urban, and educated Brazilians who are seeking a meaning, stability, and authenticity that they cannot find in secular, "liquid" late modernity (Bauman 2000).

In this book, I explore Christianity in Brazil from a global perspective, seeking to understand not only local, regional, and national specificities, but linking

6   *Christianity in Brazil*

them with global processes in world Christianity. Rather than telling a linear story, I have built the book layer upon layer, approaching the complex maze that is Brazilian Christianity from different entry points and analytical scales, seeking to elucidate the connecting passageways and crisscrossing patterns. As a sociologist of religion, I am particularly interested in the contemporary dynamics behind our two vignettes and what they might portend for the future of Christianity in Brazil. However, I am mindful that to fully make sense of the present, we must understand the history of Christianity and of the religious field more generally in the country. As I weave in the various layers, I will come back to this formative history, highlighting continuities and ruptures. I, thus, start with a historical overview of the implantation and evolution of Christianity in Brazil, showing how it is, from the beginning, a story of domination and resistance, and of ultimately unsuccessful attempts to obliterate native religions and the religions brought by millions of African slaves, as well of cross-fertilization of Christianity with these religions. It is a story of innovation, both at the grassroots and institutional levels, in the face of concerted efforts to impose orthodoxy. And as recent postcolonial approaches to the history of Christianity have shown, despite suffering persistent and widespread oppression and exclusion, native, slave, and freed-slave communities have been creative agents in the forging of Brazilian Christianity. The result of their power-laden yet mutually transformative interactions with Iberian Catholicism is a hierarchical yet highly variegated Christianity, a dynamic Christianity in tension with itself and with the larger Brazilian culture and society it contributed to forming.

History will also reveal that to understand Brazilian Christianity we cannot limit ourselves to a self-contained national scope. This might seem like a trivial insight. However, we have to keep in mind that, as heirs of modernity, the social sciences have been dominated by a "methodological nationalism," a spatial gaze which takes the nation—often imagined as a territorialized, homogeneous community, with one language, one culture, one people, and one religion coterminous with the state—as the "natural social and political form in the modern world" and the taken-for-granted unit of analysis (Wimmer and Glick-Schiller 2003). Methodological nationalism has led to the uncritical search for the reified essence of "national exceptionalisms," American or Brazilian, rather than to the careful study of the complex and dynamic interaction of reciprocally constituting scales. The recent resurgence of populist nationalisms, including the "*Brasil acima de tudo*" variety,[6] continue to demonstrate the power of the idea of the world as a billiard table, where single, impervious nations of different valence dislocate each other. Paradoxically, these resurgent nationalisms are profoundly shaped by global forces, carried across the world by transnational and transregional vectors and animated by geopolitical visions, such as the construction of an all-encompassing Christian civilization.

Whether we speak of the making of traditional Luso-Catholicism, the Royal patronage, the slave trade, Romanization, the missionary work that accompanied the Second and Third Great Awakenings in the United States, or the emergence of liberation theology in light of the Second Vatican Council's *aggiornamento* (updating), Christianity in Brazil has been forged in interaction with transnational and global actors and forces. As such, we must zoom in and out of Spatio-temporal scales—from the personal (biographical) and local to the national and transnational—to capture more fully what gives Brazilian Christianity its specific character, with continuities and ruptures. Here I operate with a globalization framework, which *"interrelates multiple levels of analysis—* economics, politics, society, and culture . . . [and] thus elucidates *a coalescence of diverse transnational and domestic structures,* allowing the economy, polity, society, and culture of one locale to penetrate another" (Mittleman 2000: 7, emphasis in the original). In other words, we should not oppose the global to the national and local, as if increasingly prominent global and transnational processes simply flatten dynamics within Brazil, obliterating their specificity and agentic power.[7] Here, the case of Pentecostalism is illustrative, for it involves "glocalization": the localization of the global, as a movement that originated outside Brazil and traveled across the world became implanted in the country with its own characteristics, and the globalization of the local, with indigenized, Brazilian expressions of Pentecostalism now unbound across the globe.[8] Moreover, in spite of this hypermobility, or perhaps as a dialectical response to it, the nation and its borders continue to matter, but they must be properly historicized and nested in multiple scales. Therefore, the goal is to develop a multi-scalar approach to Brazilian Christianity that explores the complex, power-laden interaction of manifold spatiotemporal levels (Vásquez and Knott 2014).

In Chapter 2, I discuss this tensile and variegated Christianity from a theological-pastoral-experiential point of view, presenting the multiple and often contested worldviews and ways of being Christian in Brazil. I am particularly interested in conveying this multiplicity as it is lived on the ground by Brazilian Christians. Here, I borrow Raymond Williams's notion of "structures of feeling" to highlight the fact that these ways of being Christian are not just about ideas and beliefs, but are also strongly affective, inextricably visceral, and invariably tied to materiality. In Chapter 3, I take a more micro approach, focusing on the

8 *Christianity in Brazil*

biographies, words, and actions of some of the key makers of Christianity in Brazil. While I take care to place these biographies in their proper religious and sociopolitical contexts, the rest of the book concentrates on fleshing out these contexts. First, in Chapter 4, I zoom out of the personal to focus on the differences that give Brazilian Christianity regional inflections, while still maintaining relatively stable and binding crosscutting national patterns. A central part of the story is the tension between city and countryside, with the pressures of religious pluralization and secularization that accompany the movement of people and, more specifically, the often-disorderly process of urbanization. These processes generate complex, often contradictory life conditions that Brazilians address through their social, cultural, and religious resources, including their beliefs, practices, and organizations. In Chapter 5, we shall see that different ways of being Christian, here crystallized in various denominations, offer different affordances and constraints that may be in sync (or not) with life conditions, potentially making some varieties of Christianity more attractive at particular junctures and for particular populations.

Taking care not to reduce religious dynamics to social, economic, and political logics, I take up in the next chapter the relations of reciprocal determination between Christian denominations and churches and the larger Brazilian society. While the interactions between churches and the state have been ongoing since the inception of Christianity in Brazil, two important recent developments occupy most of my attention in Chapter 6. The first one is the role that progressive Catholicism, particularly liberation theology (LT) and Comunidades Eclesiais de Base (Base Christian Communities—CEBs) had in the transition to democratic rule and the expansion of a pluralistic civil society following years of military dictatorship (1964–85). We shall see that the rise of LT and CEBs and their contributions to the process of democratization in Brazil took place at the crossroads of global, regional, and national processes, including the reforms unleashed by Vatican II (1962–5), which were magnified by the Latin American bishops at their meeting in Medellín (1968), and the emergence of revolutionary movements (in the wake of the Cuban Revolution in 1959) and repressive military regimes to contain them throughout the Americas.

The second development that I will address is the influence that Evangelical Protestants and Charismatic Catholics have had on a potent drive to restore traditional, patriarchal values and a sharp turn toward conservative politics that culminated with the election of Jair Bolsonaro, until then a retired military officer in the far-right fringes of congress, as Brazil's president in 2018. While strongly conditioned by national factors, Bolsonaro's ascendency is also linked with the dramatic expansion of (social) electronic media and the growth of nationalist and populist movements across the world in response to the dislocations and contradictions of the recent episode of globalization.

As such, because of their entanglement with contemporary global and transnational processes, these two developments point to the future configuration of Brazilian Christianity nationally, as well as its place internationally. In the Conclusion, I complete the arc of my narrative, coming back to the contemporary vignettes with which I started in the introduction, now with a fuller understanding of the actors and forces behind them. With this understanding, I venture some potential scenarios for Brazilian Christianity. And I will argue that these potential scenarios not only provide an instructive window into the creativity and increasing protagonism of Christianity in the Global South, but also into the roles that the religion may play in the face of the uncertainties, risks, challenges, and fears generated by late modernity's hypermobility, multifariousness, and connectivity.

Far be it for me to claim that this is a comprehensive and definitive treatment of Christianity in Brazil. Entire books can be written, and in fact, have been written, as my bibliography will show, on just one historical period, church, or figure. Nevertheless, I am confident that I have fulfilled the goal of offering an accessible, well-informed, and analytically rigorous overview of the main events, players, trends, theological notions, schools of thought, movements, and organizations that have shaped Brazilian Christianity. I certainly wanted to introduce in a concise manner the basic elements to understand what is currently going on in Brazilian Christianity, as well as to highlight its important contributions to world Christianity and to venture some tentative hypotheses about the future. In my view, the single most important lesson is that the explosive expansion of Pentecostalism is but the most visible expression of the intensification of pluralism within Christianity and Brazil's religious field at large. While diversity, innovation, and global connections have been central features of Brazilian Christianity since its inception, late modernity, which is characterized by the accelerated mobility of peoples, ideas, images, capital, and commodities, has radically magnified religious pluralism, heightening processes like the circulation of believers among various traditions depending on the life cycle and in response to specific existent predicaments, multiple affiliation, (re)conversion, and non-institutional affiliation. If the current trends are any indication, the fragmentation of Brazilian Christianity does not necessarily portend the inexorable fading of Catholicism in the country. Rather, even when traditional Catholic identities at the individual and collective levels will undergo significant weakening, they are likely to persevere, revitalized or morphed into new viable—and even vibrant—forms and (re)located in a changing national map of faith. Therefore, it is more fitting to understand current dynamics not as a simplistic zero-sum game, in which you must always have "winners" and "losers," but as powerful signs of the tremendous innovativeness and adaptability of Brazilian Christianity, a creativity and vitality that will be increasingly expressed globally.

1

Christianity Comes to Brazil

Hybridity, Domination, and Resistance

The Portuguese Background

In order to understand the continuities and ruptures that characterize the development of Christianity in Brazil, one has to begin with Portugal. Moreover, we must start not just in the fifteenth and sixteenth centuries, the years immediately before the "discovery" and during the colonization of Brazil, but as far back as the first millennium BCE, when waves of Celts migrated from Central Europe to the Iberian Peninsula, intermarrying with Indigenous populations. This long arc of history shows that Portugal has been a quintessential place of encounter, conflict, and cultural and religious mixing. In fact, the name itself says it all, coming from the Latin *portus*, meaning port or harbor, and "Cale," an early Celtic settlement at the mouth of the Douro River that gives access to the Atlantic Ocean. In other words, the story that I am about to recount is, from the outset, all about "crossing" and "dwelling" (Tweed 2006).

Arriving early in the second century BCE, the Romans took almost 200 years to establish full control over the provinces of Lusitania (south of the Douro River) and Gallaecia (north of the Douro River), which would later become the nation of Portugal. Roman control enabled the spread of Christianity early on, following the death of Jesus, with Bracara Augusta—what is now the city of Braga—becoming a key episcopal and missionary center, rivaling Santiago de Compostela in the north, the city that would eventually become the site of the famous shrine containing the remains of St. James, one of Jesus's twelve apostles. There were also significant Sephardic Jewish populations throughout the area. With the decline of the Roman Empire at the turn of the fifth century CE, various Germanic groups, including Suebis, Vandals, and Visigoths, occupied the region, consolidating Christianity and blending it with their own beliefs and practices.

Another layer of religious cross-fertilization and conflict was added with the establishment of Al-Andalus—Muslim Iberia—beginning in 711 CE, which included the southern part of Portugal. Despite the fact that Porto was "reconquered" by Christians in 868 CE, the presence of Islam in the region shaped Iberian Christianity in important ways up until the end of the Reconquista in 1492, when Granada, the last Muslim foothold in the peninsula, fell. In that same year, Columbus landed in the Americas. For one thing, as "religions of the Book," Judaism and Christianity co-existed with Islam, enabling a measure of cross-fertilization that went hand in hand with intellectual and cultural flourishing. It is well known, for example, that Aristotle, whose thought was central to Thomistic Catholic theology, was made accessible to the West via Muslim (Al-Andalus) philosophers such as Averroes (1126–1198).

The battles of the Reconquista and their extension into the Crusades also gave rise to a particular form of Portuguese millenarianism called *Sebastianismo*: the fervent hope for the eventual return of King Sebastião I (1554–78), who presided over the country's colonial expansion until he disappeared during a battle against the advancing Ottomans in Alcácer-Quibir, in Morocco.[1] Like Jesus Christ, whose body disappeared after his martyrdom and who is expected to come back to usher in a new age of peace, happiness, abundance, and justice, Sebastião, popularly known as *o desejado* (the desired one), is a messianic figure who will return to restore the Portuguese empire to its former glory. Sebastianism would surface periodically in Brazil, from religious movements like Canudos to the widespread (though always unfulfilled) belief that Brazil is "the country of the future"[2] and, arguably, the recent election as president of Jair Bolsonaro, who presented himself as a "*mito*," a mythological embodiment of Luso-Brazilian virility who would come to protect and save Brazil from corruption, crime, decadent communism, and moral licentiousness. I will have more to say about this in Chapter 6.

The Reconquista (Reconquest) also marked Portuguese Catholicism with a strong concern for purity, which eventually led to the expulsion and forced conversion not only of Muslims but of Jews in 1497.[3] Moreover, the *conversos*, as the Jews who converted to Christianity in order not to be expelled were called, came under the watchful eye of the Holy Inquisition, which was officially established in Portugal in 1536. Under pressure from the Inquisition, many *conversos* sought refuge in places like Recife, in northeast Brazil, where the Dutch, who were more religiously tolerant, had an enclave.

As we will see in Chapter 2, the struggles around the Reconquista, the Inquisition, and the gathering Reformation made Luso-Catholicism at the official level particularly concerned with orthodoxy, seeking to carry out the conclusions of the Council of Trent (1545–63), which reaffirmed the seven sacraments as efficacious signs of divine grace, the justification by good works, the cult of the saints, and the veneration of relics. In elevating the sacraments, Trent made clerical power the centerpiece of religious life. In contrast to this drive for orthodoxy and centralization, at the grassroots level, the multiple waves of invaders, migrants, settlers, missionaries, and merchants made for an internally diverse Christianity, inflected by many sources, including local pre-Roman and Roman religions, Islam, and Judaism. This built-in openness and capacity for hybridization—in tension with the search for orthodoxy—would be further intensified and enriched by the religious and cultural exchanges that accompanied the colonization of Brazil.

One more feature of Christianity in Portugal worth highlighting—the Padroado Real (the Royal Patronage)—also comes from the Reconquista. During the reign of the first king of Portugal, Afonso Henriques (1139–1185), nicknamed "o Conquistador" (the Conqueror) and "o Fundador" (the Founder [of the empire]) in recognition of his successful campaigns against Muslims, the emerging state formed a close alliance with the papacy. In his 1179 bull *Manifestis Probatum*, Pope Alexander II officially recognized Afonso as the king of Portugal, lending legitimacy and stability to the regime. In exchange, Afonso granted the church large swaths of the conquered lands, making it the largest landowner in the kingdom. While the relation between the crown and papacy was not always harmonious, the arrangement between Afonso and Alexander II set the groundwork for the Padroado Real through which the Holy See recognized the right of the Portuguese kings to the newly discovered lands in the Americas. In 1493, Pope Alexander VI decreed through his bull *Inter caetera* that the Spanish Crown had rights over all lands 100 leagues west and south of the Azores and Cape Verde, both of which were held by Portugal. The demarcating line was later extended by the Treaty of Tordesillas (1494), protecting Portuguese access to the coast of Africa and rights over Brazil. This arrangement was ratified a few years later by Pope Julius II.

Papal recognition was critical given the competition that the Lusitanian and Castilian monarchs faced from other colonizing powers like the French, Dutch, and English. As mentioned above, the Dutch established a significant presence in northern Brazil between 1630 and 1654, centered around the cities of Recife (as the capital), Olinda, and Fortaleza. In exchange for papal recognition, the Portuguese Crown committed to the conversion of all inhabitants under their control and to the military protection of the church's interests. In effect, the

Portuguese and Spanish kings became the vicars of Christ in the Americas, meaning that, as part of the process of Christianization of the Natives, they were in charge of the building of churches, cathedrals, monasteries, and seminaries, as well as of the naming and payment of various ecclesiastical functionaries, from bishops to priests. The kings used agricultural tithes to support their patronage.

The Royal Patronage was key to the establishment of Christianity in Brazil and throughout Spanish America. With a papacy weakened by previous schisms and threatened by the Reformation, the Royal Patronage enabled the wealthy monarchs to spread and establish Christianity in the newly discovered lands. Nevertheless, the Royal Patronage had the net effect of placing the Catholic Church in a structurally dependent position. In fact, all decisions regarding the establishment of Christianity in Brazil were administered by the Mesa da Consciência e Ordens, a tribunal created by King João III in 1532 to deal with military, civilian, and religious matters in the colonies.

While initially, the interests of the crown and papacy coincided— the pacification and management of Native populations—once secular administrative institutions were in place, the incentive for the state to fund the church's expansion was greatly reduced. In fact, if ecclesial authorities became too influential, they could compete with secular powers. As a result, chronically underfunded, the Catholic Church in Brazil, as throughout the Americas, suffered from a persistent scarcity of priests. In turn, this scarcity resulted in a shallow evangelization, making it difficult for the papacy to implement fully the reforms advanced by the Council of Trent. As we will see in the next chapter, the generalized absence of priests to perform the sacraments and teach doctrine, particularly in remote areas of Brazil, generated the need and space for the emergence of a robust grassroots Catholicism that was not always in line with the official church's emphasis on orthodoxy.

Christianity in Brazil: The First Cycle

On April 22, 1500, Pedro Álvares Cabral reached the Brazilian coast, landing in Porto Seguro in the northeastern state of Bahia, encountering hunter-gatherer and fisher Tupi-Guaraní groups that had been present for thousands of years. This encounter set what historian Eduardo Hoornaert (1979) has called "cycles of Christianization." From the outset, it is necessary to state that the impact of these expansionary cycles on Indigenous people was devastating. Estimates of the Indigenous population in Brazil before the conquest and first cycle of

Christianization range from 2.5 to 8 million. Within the first hundred years of colonization, more than 90 percent of that population had perished, primarily due to epidemics of smallpox and other contagious diseases.[4] Beyond these mind-boggling numbers,

> [P]riests committed ethnocide by straightjacketing and even destroying Native culture. From the start they tried to undercut the authority of indigenous religious beliefs. They misunderstood the Natives and demonized their customs, using, for example, theatrical presentations in which Natives appeared as devils. Ironically, priests even presented themselves as substitutes for the *pajés*, or indigenous medicine men. (Serbin 2006: 33)

The Natives were not passive or utterly eradicated, becoming historically irrelevant. Along with the millions of African slaves forcibly brought to the country, they have played major roles in the forging of Brazilian Christianity, and society more generally. They responded to the conquest and colonization in a variety of ways, sometimes fighting back through uprisings and rebellions. A case in point was the movement called *Santidade*, which took place in the 1580s in the Jaguaripe region of Bahia among the Tupi. Blending Indigenous utopian beliefs and practices such as ritual dance with Christian millenarian symbols and an inversion of clerical hierarchies, *pajés* preached that they were the real bishops and saints and prophesized that a world without evil was imminent, setting slavery and the Jesuit missions straight.

> Santidade preachers urged the faithful to flee from whites and attack them, affirming that total triumph was at hand and with it would come a new era of prosperity and abundance. The Indians would no longer need to work because the arrows would hunt alone in the bush and the fruits would sprout from the land without anyone planting them. The old Indians would be young again and the men would become immortal. All the Portuguese would either be killed or become slaves to the same Indians who they enslaved. The triumph of Santidade was thus equivalent to finding the Land without Evil [*a Terra sem Males*], the Tupi paradise of which ethnologists speak, whose search had once brought this group to the Atlantic coast of South America. (Vainfas n.d.)

At other times, Indigenous people fled to the interior, where colonial power was intermittent, and re-articulated their communities there. There they also appropriated Christianity creatively, blending it with their own beliefs, symbols, and practices, and took advantage of the practices and institutions of the empire in their own process of ethnogenesis. I will have more to say about this a bit later.

16   *Christianity in Brazil*

In the first cycle, Brazilian Christianity's hold was very tenuous, focused on a narrow strip along the coast, particularly between Natal and Salvador in the northeast, owing to the inaccessibility of the country's interior. The years following Cabral's landing were marked by the activities of traders, pirates, and privateers interested in raw materials like brazilwood since Portugal's attention was directed to the more profitable India and the East Indies colonies. Without the financial resources to colonize and exploit the new lands in Brazil, the Portuguese Crown devised a system of hereditary *capitanias* (captaincies), essentially land grants given to noblemen who would be in charge of settling, developing, and administering these large territories. This system was unsuccessful and was eventually subsumed under the governorships. However, the captaincies set the rudiments of an economy and way of life that would be based around large *engenhos*—sugar cane plantations—which is why Hoornaert designates this period as the "sugar cane cycle," characterized by a "sugar-mill Christianity."

The structure of this Christianity was eminently feudal, with the lord and his family dwelling in the *casa grande* (literally the "big house") and the labor force segregated in horrific conditions in the *senzala* (slave quarters). The decimation of Indigenous populations due to war, exploitation, and illnesses, in addition to resistance to colonization from these groups and debates within the church about the unjust treatment and enslavement of Natives, led the Portuguese to begin importing African slaves to run the sugar mills as early as the 1530s. Eventually, it is estimated that of the ten to eleven million Africans who were brought forcibly to the New World, 3.6 million came to Brazil, a number that dwarfs the 650,000 who arrived in the North American colonies.[5] It is therefore not surprising that Africans shaped Brazilian Christianity in fundamental ways, particularly in places like Bahia, where close to two million slaves arrived up until the late 1880s when Brazil officially declared emancipation. By the 1820s, enslaved people made up about one-third of the population, with another third constituted by Blacks who had been able to purchase or win their freedom (Postma 2003: 78).

For sugar-mill Christianity, one strong pole of religious life centered around the *casa grande*. Usually located close to the mill at the center of the plantation and relatively luxurious, the big house was not only the residence of the enslaver and his family, but it often functioned as a school, infirmary, and bank; it even contained *capelas* (small chapels) where the *donas* (the ladies of the *engenhos*) would hold their daily prayers to the patron saints of their region in Portugal and where they could hear Mass and receive the sacraments when the priest was available. As such, the *casa grande* was the space where the dominant patriarchal Portuguese values were inculcated on the new generations.

The other strong generative pole in this first cycle was *senzala*, extremely rough constructions, often consisting of only thatched roofs without dividing walls, where enslaved people would sleep on straw or even the hard ground. Right outside the *senzala* would be a *pelourinho* (pillory), a stone or wooden column where they would be tied up and publicly flogged. In these crowded quarters, enslaved peoples from different parts of Africa jostled with each other, at times exchanging practices and beliefs and, at other times, seeking to connect with those in the same linguistic group or hailing from the same African region. The *senzala* was a crucial space of the development of Black lay brotherhoods (*irmandades*), which, as we will see in the next chapter, have played a central role in Brazilian traditional popular Catholicism, which is the core theological-praxical-experiential matrix of Brazilian Christianity, and in the rise of African-based traditions such as Candomblé and Umbanda. In a particularly poignant example of creative resistance and appropriation, slaves would use *pelourinhos* to dance and perform rituals to their African ancestors, even if under the guise of celebrating Catholic saints.

Runaway slaves also reconstructed and preserved African cultures, languages, and religions in independent, self-sustaining settlements in the hinterlands called *quilombos* or *mocambos*, both terms derived from the Congo-Angolan languages of the founding fugitives to designate armed encampments. The most famous *quilombo* was Palmares on the rugged border of the present-day states of Alagoas and Pernambuco. Established in the 1590s by Ganga Zumba, Palmares was in fact a confederation of eleven towns that functioned as an autonomous state with a diversified economy based on agriculture, hunting, gathering, fishing, trade, and incursions into the settlements and plantations established by the Portuguese. Just as in other *quilombos*, in Palmares, the runaway slaves from various parts of Africa mixed with local Amerindians and the white women they captured in their raids at plantations. This racial mixture was also accompanied by the creation of creole languages and a hybrid Christianity, in which saints like St. Brás and Our Lady of Immaculate Conception interacted with the *orixás* (the ancestral royal spirits of Africa). And owing to the fact that women were scarce, they had a very prominent role in polyandric arrangements. At its peak, Palmares had a population of between 20,000 and 30,000 inhabitants (Karash 2002). This *quilombo* endured multiple assaults by the Dutch and Portuguese, until its destruction in 1694. Its last leader was Zumbi, who had been born a free man in the *quilombo*, although he was captured by the Portuguese as a young boy and baptized by Antônio Mello, a Catholic priest who catechized him and taught him Portuguese and Latin. Keenly aware of the oppressive nature of the plantation system, Zumbi escaped and returned to Palmares, where he took power from Ganga Zumba, advocating a more uncompromising stance vis-à-vis the Portuguese. The latter saw him as a clear threat to their economic interests and persecuted him relentlessly. Finally, after many years of resistance, the Portuguese destroyed Palmares and captured Zumbi. They beheaded him and exhibited his head in a central plaza in Recife to make him an example of the consequences of revolting against the empire. Zumbi indeed became an example, but not in the way the Portuguese intended. Today, he has achieved the status of a mythical hero fighting against injustice and is a source of pride for Brazilians of African descent. But the legacy of Palmares goes beyond Zumbi's heroic leadership. For, as Karash (2002: 118–19) puts it, as a "society in which women organized the households, the people worked on communal basis, and elected black leaders governed a multiracial society that included tributary whites, [Palmares] was the opposite of the colonial society on the coast."

Even with their segregation of living quarters and their embeddedness in the transatlantic triangular trade (which brought slaves to the Americas; sugar, tobacco, and cotton to Europe; and textiles, rum, and manufactured goods to back to Africa and the Americas), the *casa grande* and the *senzala* operated as a fairly self-contained economic unit with moral underpinnings that resonated with the holistic and hierarchical worldview of Medieval Catholicism. The *casa grande* and *senzala* in effect constituted an extended family, with the *senhor da fazenda* (the lord of the manor) as the undisputed head and owner of his land, wife, children, and slaves, whom he was charged under the Padroado to Christianize and care for, just as the king was religiously sanctioned to oversee his domain. This unity characterized by drastic power asymmetries and exclusion gives Brazilian Christianity its blended yet conflictive character.[6] In Hoornaert's words: "Europe and Africa gathered in Brazil, white and black, free and slave, Christians and pagans [*gentios*]. The result of that long dwelling-together [*convivio*] of lords and slaves was an Africanized Christianity, as well as a Europeanized Christianity, a 'dark-skinned Christianity' [*cristianismo moreno*] anyhow" (1991: 42).

Institutionally, the church's presence in Brazil during this cycle was rather precarious. Between 1551 and 1676, there was only one diocese, that of Salvador da Bahia. In 1677, three more dioceses were created—Pernambuco, São Luiz de Maranhão, and Rio de Janeiro—extending the church's presence to the southeastern coast. Nevertheless, the presence of religious orders, particularly the

Society of Jesus, more commonly known as the Jesuits, demonstrated the vitality and creativity of Catholicism beyond the plantation. The first six Jesuits arrived in Brazil in 1549 under the leadership of Manoel da Nóbrega (see Chapter 3), the son of a prominent Portuguese judge who studied humanities at the University of Salamanca and University of Coimbra. Brought by Governor-General Tomé de Souza, the Jesuits' goal was to pacify the Natives through conversion and catechesis. The pastoral method they favored involved learning the Natives' culture and language—Jesuit novice José de Anchieta prepared and published the first grammar of the Tupi language in 1595—and founding *aldeias* (villages/ settlements), where the Natives would come to labor and be evangelized. In the process, the Jesuits were instrumental in the foundation of the cities of São Paulo (1554) and Rio de Janeiro (1565). The growth and "indigenization" of the Jesuit order in Brazil was swift. By 1574, there were 110 Jesuits, 14 percent of whom were Brazilian, and a century later, by 1698, that number had grown to 304 (37 percent Brazilian).[7]

Assessing the legacy of the Jesuits in Brazil is complicated: they have become central tropes in the process of imagining a humanistic, cosmopolitan, and progressive nation based on Eurocentric values. The Jesuits themselves have contributed to this narrative, with their own "Catholic Orientalism" (Xavier and Županov 2015), which produced a wealth of knowledge in the form of letters, missionary texts, administrative documents, grammars, and accounts and translations of Indigenous rituals and myths that circulated widely in the Portuguese empire and often informed and facilitated the activities of its agents. This orientalism was simultaneously an exercise of "impression management" (Županov 1999: 7), whereby the Jesuits presented themselves to European audiences as the builders of "Christianity as a universal religion," more specifically, of a "global salvific Catholicism" (Clossey 2008), bringing light to places and peoples engulfed in darkness.[8] More specifically, Županov (1999: 195–236) identifies in Jesuit missionary writings expressive modes of "saintly self-fashioning" and of proclaiming the fulfillment of utopia that helped the order to argue that its members were uniquely equipped to lead the Natives spiritually as well as politically. Hagiographies of the first Jesuit missionaries and those martyred as they sought to "harvest souls" were particularly popular, as the order built a public image and recruited more members. Invariably, these hagiographies glossed over the more ambivalent realities on the ground.

Nevertheless, even with these caveats, it is undeniable that the Jesuits contributed in significant ways to the consolidation of Brazilian Christianity and to the articulation of Brazil as an imagined national community, to borrow

20 *Christianity in Brazil*

from Benedict Anderson (1983). As historian Kenneth Serbin puts it: "Jesuits worked as physicians, botanists, soldiers, engineers, sailors, and statesmen. They wrote poetry too. The ability of the Jesuits and other clerics to communicate with the diverse Amerindian groups through the creation of a *língua geral* [general grammar], helped the Portuguese to consolidate their grip on Brazil and to build its economic foundations" (2006: 21). In Chapter 3, we will meet the Jesuit pioneers through their biographies and own words.

As Portuguese mistreatment of Indigenous people intensified in the context of the growing plantation economy and as gold and silver prospectors encroached upon the lands inhabited by Indigenous peoples in the interior of the country, the Jesuits began to speak against this cruelty.[9] At the same time, the villages set up by Jesuits, later known as *reduções*,[10] began to offer an alternative, relatively autonomous economy that allowed the Natives gathered in them a measure of protection, even within forms of organization that were authoritarian in their own right. As we shall see later, this divergence between the relentless logic of agrarian capitalism and the pastoral vision of the Jesuits set the stage for church-state conflicts in the eighteenth century, when the society was expelled from Brazil.[11]

The experience of the Jesuits shows the contradictions at the heart of Brazilian Christianity. On the one hand, Native populations were decimated by illness when they were brought to live side by side with Europeans and their evangelization often resulted in the loss of their culture and language. Drawing from Michel Foucault's work on the rise of modern disciplinary and surveillance practices, Gillermo Wilde (2015a: 177) argues that the Jesuit project of reductions was part of a "visual regime" that involved power-inflected mechanisms of differentiation, hierarchization, and place-making seeking to produce regimented Christian subjects. According to him, the Jesuits operated with a worldview "organized in terms of dichotomies that radically opposed 'Christian civility' to 'gentile chaos'" (177). In this dualistic world, Natives were the "Other," associated with the wilderness, a savage and chaotic realm that was populated by demons, cannibals, sorcerers, and sexually promiscuous women— an earthly version of hell. In contrast, missions were places of rational order, proper manners, and peace, where the new Christians worked and lived under a detailed spatial-temporal regiment that regulated their daily economic and religious activities, as they prepared for the coming of the kingdom of God.

> Jesuits constructed a radical opposition between the inner and the outer space of the mission town from both a material and a symbolic point of view. Jesuits regarded this series of overlapping dichotomies as an expression of the rational

Christianity Comes to Brazil

and natural ordering of the world. The rainforest, in the official discourse, was related not only to the infidels dwelling in it but also to the indigenous ancestors and memories that could always threaten the mission's stability. Mission history, as recounted by important seventeenth-century Jesuit chroniclers, was the story of an irreversible transformation in space-time categories. It was conceived as the gradual inscription of the marks of Christianity on "infidel" soil, the "domestication" of the "savage" mind, and the transformation of "lions" into "lambs." (Wilde 2015a: 179)

Paradoxically, the visibility regime advanced by the Jesuits generated spaces of heterodoxy, beginning with the wilderness that always marked the possibility of alterity and the fragility of order and civilization. In fact, scholars like Hal Langfur (2006), Fabricio Prado (2015), Cynthia Radding (2005), and Heather Roller (2014) have shown how Natives took advantage of outer, borderland spaces such as the southeastern edge of Minas Gerais and Espírito Santo (which later on, in the early nineteenth century, witnessed an uprising by the Botocudo people resisting attempts by the Portuguese Crown to exterminate them with the excuse that they were cannibals[12]), the Rio Plata region, and Amazonia to build extensive networks of circulation and mobility, "fluvial communities," as Roller characterizes them, that brought together various Indigenous groups in a process of ethnogenesis. These networks also enabled Indigenous groups to position themselves vis-à-vis competing imperial powers and trade advantageously with them. For example, Wilde (2015b) found that reductions in the River Plate region "traded products like yerba mate and leather hides throughout the entire region and had considerable influence in the policies of the colonial authorities. In turn, the Guarani natives participated in regional militia and helped the authorities in Buenos Aires and Asunción in different economic activities and in defense of the territory." Like the *quilombo* of Palmares for Brazilians of African descent, these networks carved out "spaces of indigenous collective action" that "proved surprisingly impervious to the imposition of external authority" (Harris and Espelt-Bombin 2018: 537). In other words, the narrative that "restive natives disappeared into the vast Brazilian interior, where they remained isolated and comfortably unaware of the political, social, and cultural transformations unfolding as a consequence of colonial rule" (Cagle 2018: 157) needs to be, at a very minimum, evaluated critically. Even in the context of sharp power asymmetries that constrained them, Natives remained important actors in the crafting of Brazilian Christianity and Brazil itself.

As the Jesuits organized various Indigenous groups according to their imagined hierarchies, they gave power to *caciques* (Indigenous chiefs), who

22 *Christianity in Brazil*

often turned the discourses and institutions set up by the Jesuits against them, affirming the relative autonomy of spaces like homes and gardens where Natives spent a great deal of their daily lives.

> the confrontation between Jesuits and Indians was not all about domination or resistance in the formation of mission space. A mission town was neither a Foucauldian Panopticon nor a free "land without evil," but rather the result of a tense process in which both Jesuits and Indians, as non-homogeneous actors, took part. It is important to remember that the Indians also participated in the construction of mission power. (Wilde 2015a: 197)

On the positive side, the Jesuits' defense of the Natives against abuses set in motion a prophetic strand within Brazilian Christianity that would inspire and dovetail with contemporary progressive Catholicism's preferential option for the poor.[13] Even then, Jesuit António Vieira's strong denunciation of enslaving the Natives did not extend to African slaves, toward whom the order had a more ambivalent attitude, often relying on plantations and African labor to support their monasteries and ministries. To the extent that the Jesuits denounced slavery and held the *senhores do engenho* accountable for abuses, it tended to be when the harsh treatment of the African slaves interfered with their evangelization or with their ability to attend Mass and receive the sacraments. Moreover, the Jesuits tended to espouse a "theology of transmigration," which justified slavery by comparing "Africa to hell, where blacks were slaves in body and soul, Brazil to purgatory, where blacks were liberated in soul by baptism, and death as entry to Heaven" (Hoornaert 1982: 76). In Vieira's words: "I persuade myself without doubt that the captivity of the first transmigration (from Africa to Brazil) is ordained by His Mercy for the freedom of the second (from Brazil to . . . Heaven)" (Hoornaert 1982: 76).

Until 1580, the Jesuits were the Portuguese Crown's official missionaries in Brazil. With the annexation of the Portuguese Crown by the Spanish (1580–1640), this monopoly was broken, and other religious orders came in. The Carmelites came to Olinda in 1580, the Benedictines to Bahia the year after, and the Franciscans landed, also in Olinda, in 1585. With more than 1,000 friars by 1767, the Franciscans achieved a presence and influence that would rival those of the Jesuits (Willeke 1974). In contrast to the Jesuits, however, the Franciscans, like the other religious orders, tended to have a more cooperative relationship with the secular authorities and be more open to the plantation system. The Franciscans founded reductions of their own, especially among the Guaraní in the greater Paraguay region, but they also ministered on *fazendas* and in convents, and sometimes even took over villages funded and run by Jesuits who were expelled by the crown. In that way,

Franciscans participated in the crown's efforts to assert its power and sideline the Jesuits, while, paradoxically, preserving the latter's pastoral experiments.[14] Here, we see once again the ambivalent nature of Christianity in Brazil, both challenging and buttressing the deeply unequal colonial power relations.

Riolando Azzi (1983: 25) has noted the strong resistance of the Portuguese Crown to found convents for women: while the Spanish created the first nunnery in Mexico in 1540, Brazil did not see its first convent until 1677, when there were already seventy such institutions in Hispanic America.[15] Nevertheless, Azzi highlights the fact that convents came to be prominent economic institutions with large endowments. As we shall see, women would come to play important roles as lay leaders in traditional popular Catholicism and, both as nuns and lay leaders, in the rise and proliferation of base Christian communities in progressive Catholicism.

Brazilian Christianity on the Move: Beyond the Coast

As the plantation economy expanded, there was a need to provide food for the growing populations on the coast. This need led to further exploration in the interior of the country, unleashing a series of reinforcing cycles. These explorations often followed navigable rivers like the San Francisco River, which flows from Minas Gerais in the south to Bahia and Pernambuco in the northeast and is known as the "national unity river," the Parnaíba in the north, and the Paranaíba in the southeast. Arguably, in terms of altering the landscape and shaping land tenure in Brazil in lasting ways, the most significant cycle involved the establishment of cattle ranches in what Hoornaert has termed the *ciclo sertanejo* or *ciclo do gado* (the backcountry or cattle cycle). According to Hoornaert (1982: 34–7), French and Italian Capuchins played a key role in this cycle, complementing the continuing work of Franciscan and Jesuit missionaries and building villages in the interior.

The cattle cycle was followed by other periods of Christian expansion, each further straining clerical resources. Building on their success in the coast, the Jesuits penetrated the interior following the Paraná River, creating between 1609 and 1630 a string of *reduções* that became highly successful in Christianizing and reorganizing the Tupi-Guaraní. Testimonies suggest that the Jesuits used music "to seduce the sensible souls of indigenous people and to achieve a more emotional consensus" (Hoornaert 1991: 58). Eventually, these self-sustaining villages came into conflict with expansions from the coast.

24 *Christianity in Brazil*

Early in the eighteenth century, the mining industry took hold in the states of Minas Gerais, Mato Grosso do Sul, and Goiás, attracting large numbers of people, who, without priests to minister to their religious needs, formed their own organizations. These organizations became known as "tertiary orders," groups structured hierarchically, mirroring the clerical orders, in which the laity sought to lead a life of piety through penance and the performance of charity.[16] We shall see in later chapters that there are contemporary efforts by the laity and clergy to recover the traditional piety of tertiary orders in the so-called *novas comunidades de vida consagrada* (new communities of consecrated life), such as Toca de Assis and Canção Nova, in response to the dislocation and instrumentalization of everyday life in late modern Brazil.

As the protagonists of the *ciclo mineiro* (mining cycle), these tertiary orders built ornate churches and shrines, often in honor of patron saints, with the riches accumulated through mining. They formed *irmandades* (lay brotherhoods) to administer these churches and their associated cemeteries and to oversee the veneration of the saint, including festivals and special Masses, for which the priest would be brought to celebrate. I shall have more to say about the worldview of lay *mineiro* Catholicism in Chapters 2 and 4, when I discuss theological and geographic diversity. However, it is important to stress here that its relative autonomy led to the development of a rich traditional popular Catholicism with its own beliefs, symbols, practices, institutions, and lay experts, which, although respectful of the official church's quest for orthodoxy, did not always see eye to eye with the clergy.

Typical of the mining cycle, as for most of Brazil's interior, was the practice of *desobriga* (literally "the unburdening," or the release of obligations), whereby itinerant priests would come to a town for a few days during the year, often during the patron saint's celebrations, to discharge the parishioners' spiritual duties, not only saying Mass and offering communion, confessions, and baptisms but also teaching the rudiments of the faith. He would keep a tally of the sacraments and other religious services provided, which allowed him to be paid by the colonial administrators. For the rest of the year, local communities relied on the pastoral services of *irmandades* and a variety of lay leaders, many of whom were women, such as *rezadeiras*, who, like Indigenous *pajés*, used a mixture of prayer and folk medicine to heal. In addition, *beatos(as)*,[17] holy ascetics who consecrated their lives to the church, often roamed the backcountry, praying, preaching, advising people on moral and spiritual matters, and taking care of shrines and cemeteries. The religious formation of these lay leaders came from a rich oral tradition of local beliefs and practices going back to Portugal that was reconstructed in

Brazil and passed on from generation to generation. As we will see later, Antônio Conselheiro, arguably one of the most prominent of these *beatos*, was at the center of one of the bloodiest and most tragic episodes of church-state conflicts in Brazilian history.

Also starting in the early seventeenth century but picking up momentum during the eighteenth century, as part of the *ciclo mineiro*, there were important expeditionary waves from São Paulo, which some scholars have termed the *ciclo paulista*, led by the *bandeirantes* (literally the "flag bearers"), settlers, prospectors, and frontiersmen who ventured out into the interior not only in search of precious metals and stones but also to "hunt" for runaway slaves and Indigenous people who could be enslaved, often raiding *quilombos* and the reductions set up by the Jesuits. These raids set the stage for later conflicts between the church and the state around the Jesuits.

As the Portuguese moved to the interior and struggled to settle it, they inscribed their Catholic vision upon the landscape, turning it into an arena for apparitions and other miraculous events.[18] I shall have more to say about this vision in the next chapter, but without a doubt, the most significant miracle associated with this period is the apparition of the Virgin Mary to three fishermen in the Paraíba River in the state of São Paulo in October 1717. Toiling in vain for many hours to catch fish to host a feast for the governor, who was passing through on his way to the mining town of Vila Rica in Minas Gerais, the fisherman prayed to Mary. When they cast their net, instead of fish, they pulled out an image of Our Lady of Conception, whose devotion was popular in Portugal, whereupon the fishermen caught so many fish that their canoe threatened to overturn. From a small chapel built to house the image, the devotion to Nossa Senhora Aparecida (literally, "Our Lady Who Appeared"), as she came to be known, spread until she became Brazil's patroness, signaling the country's foundational Catholic identity. Today, the image is revered at the second-largest Catholic basilica in the world. No wonder that a pastor of the rising Neo-Pentecostal Universal Church of the Kingdom of God challenged the devotion to Nossa Senhora Aparecida by kicking an image of her on TV (see the introduction).

Church-State Conflicts: From Colony to Independence

By the mid-1700s, the Jesuits, whose accumulated wealth had been exempted from royal control and taxation by the pope, had achieved significant power in Brazil and other Portuguese colonies, as well as in Portugal, where they controlled education, including the College of the Arts at the famed University of Coimbra. Charged by José I to administer the empire, the Marquis of Pombal (Sebastião José de Carvalho e Mello, 1699–1782) sought to strengthen Portugal's position vis-à-vis Spain and England and to centralize power in the crown, implementing a series of reforms and maneuvers to regulate and standardize commerce with the colonies as well as increase profitability. This meant challenging the power and influence of the Jesuits. While Pombal's main driving force was political and economic, he also had a deep mistrust of the Society of Jesus rooted in Enlightenment-based anti-organized-religion ideas that he encountered during his stays in Vienna and London. He saw the Jesuits as promoting scientific illiteracy and obscurantism, and thus, as an obstacle to a modern Portugal. The conflict between the Pombaline state and the Jesuits intensified as a result of the Treaty of Madrid (1750), which shifted the demarcation of land between Spanish and Portuguese South America, leaving seven Jesuit reductions in Portuguese territory. Although the Jesuits surrendered the reductions, agreeing to move to the Spanish side of the Uruguay River, the Natives refused to be relocated and rose up in arms, prompting an attack from a combined Spanish and Portuguese force, in the so-called Guaraní War (1753–6). More than a thousand Guaranís were killed in this war.[19]

Things came to a head when, in 1758, Pombal accused the Jesuits of participating in an attempt to murder the king in what became known as the Távora affair. This accusation triggered the society's expulsion from all Portuguese territories in 1759.[20] These conflicts were the harbingers of a re-accommodation of the church vis-à-vis the state during the national period when the nascent Brazilian republic, influenced by the anticlericalism of the Enlightenment, sought to curtail clerical influence over domestic affairs. Unlike many of the Spanish colonies, Brazil did not undergo major and lengthy wars of independence, becoming instead an independent monarchy. With Napoleon's invasion of Portugal in 1807, King João VI fled to Brazil, making Rio de Janeiro the capital of the empire. The defeat of the French in 1815 allowed the king to return to Portugal and proclaim Brazil a kingdom with equal status under the leadership of his son Dom Pedro I. In response to anti-monarchist movements in Portugal, Pedro I declared Brazil's independence in 1822 and named himself emperor with his father's acquiescence. Despite the mostly bloodless transition to an independent Brazil, there was significant unrest in the emerging country, stoked by revolutionaries who wanted a shaper break with the monarchy. Liberal forces in Brazil also agitated against Dom Pedro and his successor Pedro II. In 1889, the latter was deposed by a group of young military officers strongly influenced by positivism, a philosophy advocated by French intellectual Auguste Comte that argued for replacing myths and religious beliefs with facts and science. In fact, the motto in the Brazilian flag—*ordem e progresso* (order and progress)—was directly inspired by Comte's thought.

As the overthrow of Pedro II shows, the transition to a republic in Brazil was marked by anticlericalism and secularization. Secular elites inspired by the humanist ideals of the Enlightenment and the French Revolution sought a separation of church and state and a weakening of Catholicism's power and influence over society and culture. This weakening involved wresting the church's monopoly over education and the family, advancing instead public schools and universities, as well as civil marriage. Republican ideas also included a vigorous defense of religious toleration, opening the door for the growth of Protestantism via immigration as a way to break Catholic social and cultural hegemony. As I shall discuss in Chapter 5, leaders of the young Brazilian republic encouraged immigration from Protestant countries in Europe at the turn of the twentieth century, a time in which historic Protestant congregations were also beginning to engage in global missions.

Cultural and political transformations were also accompanied by dramatic economic changes, with the consolidation of industrial capitalism led by England and, eventually, the United States. Brazilian secular elites expanded the production of coffee as a way to integrate Brazil into the new world economy, albeit in a dependent position, still as an exporter of raw materials. Since the harvesting of coffee operates with itinerant salaried labor, the colonial relations of production based on slave and indentured labor began to crumble. I discussed above how in sugar-mill Christianity relations of production were deeply rooted in the *casa grande-senzala* nexus, which was buttressed by the corporate and hierarchical worldview of Luso-Brazilian Catholicism under the Padroado. These stable and predictable relations stand in sharp contrast to the mobility of industrial capitalism as exemplified by the railroad, whose introduction to Brazil both facilitated and triggered further internal population movements. As peasants were thrown out of their lands and as their livelihoods were threatened by new, volatile economic developments, they pushed back against the republic, giving rise to several millenarian and messianic movements in the late 1800s and early 1900s.

Millenarian movements draw from the expectation of the imminent second coming of Christ to advocate for the overturning of the current sinful status quo in the name of a return to a golden, mythical past or the founding of a new Jerusalem or kingdom of God. This return and founding are commonly led by

Christ-like messianic figures, often *beatos* and other lay religious leaders, who galvanize those oppressed by the wicked status quo through their charisma and denunciations of corruption. More specifically, Brazilian millenarian movements advocated the restoration of the monarchy, with the king as the only legitimate authority sanctioned by God, and the end of the republic and its secular ideals. During this period, millenarian movements in Brazil included Antônio Conselheiro's Canudos in Bahia (1893–7), the Muckers in Rio Grande do Sul (1872–98), Contestado in Santa Catarina (1912–16), Padre Cícero in Juazeiro (1872–1934), and Pedro Batista in Santa Brígida (in the 1930s). Most of these movements ended tragically. Except for Padre Cícero's, whose Juazeiro became one of Brazil's most important centers of pilgrimage, the other millenarian movements were violently crushed by the armed forces of the secular republic.[21] In Chapter 3, I will focus on Conselheiro and Padre Cícero to explore the conditions that led to the different outcomes.

Romanization: Scope, Limitations, and Paradoxes

Tensions between the Catholic Church and the secular state in Brazil dovetailed with the situation in Europe, where a variety of nationalist and liberal movements were active starting in the 1840s, including one that led to the unification of Italy and the loss of vast papal states. The Holy See reacted with a strong anti-modernist stand. In 1864, Pope Pius IX released his *Syllabus of Errors*, in which he condemned secularism, liberalism, rationalism, democracy, socialism, and civil marriage. This document was followed in 1870 by the dogma of papal infallibility (when the pope speaks ex-cathedra) in the wake of the First Vatican Council. For Brazilian Catholicism, the Vatican's assertion of papal power meant a re-orienting away from the collapsing institution of the Padroado, which as we have seen, had made the Brazilian Church dependent on a crown that was no longer in power. Brazilian Catholicism would become Europeanized, or rather "Romanized," shifting its point of reference toward the Holy See.

To carry out Romanization, Pius IX established pontifical colleges in Rome where Brazilian and other Latin American priests would come to be trained properly in accordance with the magisterium affirmed at the Council of Trent. By 1870, "fifty Brazilians were studying in the Eternal City, where they were groomed to become seminary rectors, theology professors, and bishops in their homeland. These profoundly Europeanized priests became the vanguard of Romanization" (Serbin 2006: 56). To this Brazilian vanguard were added many French, Italian, and Belgian priests who came to Brazil to take control of parishes, schools, and hospitals, all in order to missionize Brazilians properly. Nuns from orders such as the Franciscan Hospitaller Sisters, the Dominican Sisters of St. Catherine of Senna, and the Sisters of Jesus, Mary, and Joseph also came from Portugal at the beginning of the twentieth century to work in those institutions and to minister to the growing European immigrant population (Aquino 2014).[22]

Romanization's assertion of Tridentine orthodoxy, particularly of the centrality of the European and Europeanized clergy, collided head-on with Brazilian traditional popular Catholicism, which as we have seen, operated relatively autonomously through local lay leadership. It is thus not surprising that a key dimension of Romanization was the purification and outright elimination of local Catholic practices and organizations, like brotherhoods, deemed unorthodox, ignorant, superstitious, or even idolatrous by the newly trained clerical elites.[23] More specifically, this meant the undermining of local devotions, the destruction of popular shrines, or the dismissal of local miracles (as in the case of Padre Cícero's avowed conversion of the host into to blood),[24] as well as the introduction of new European-based saints and devotions, such as those of the Sacred Heart of Jesus, Christ the King, and Our Lady of Lourdes, which were seen as more "universal."

Romanization was only partially successful, disciplining local traditions but not eliminating them altogether. The end result was another layer of complexity and hybridization, as local traditions not only competed with those introduced by Romanization, but also many times blended with them, appropriating elements from them with a different meaning. To this day, brotherhoods, novenas, pilgrimages to local shrines, and festivals to local saints, *beatos*, and miracle workers continue to play a major part in the lives of Brazilian Catholics. Nevertheless, with the multiplication of dioceses, the creation of new seminaries, and the intensification of catechesis, Romanization did create a modernized Brazilian clerical elite, notwithstanding the fact that the movement had an anti-modernist thrust. This clerical elite eventually redirected the Brazilian church toward a new settlement with the secular elites, leading to what Pablo Richard (1987) has called a "New Christendom," a new tight interpenetration between a capitalist society deeply divided by class and a rigid Catholic hierarchy sanctioned by the Tridentine magisterium. As Pedro Ribeiro de Oliveira (1979: 326) puts it, with Romanization, "The Catholic religious apparatus constitutes itself . . . as a big organization, where the top has all the power of decision, and where a network of intermediaries assures the control of the lay base by

30   *Christianity in Brazil*

a relatively reduced clerical body," and such apparatus mirrors and tends to reinforce the relations of modern capitalist production, which concentrate key resources in the hands of a few. This re-accommodation of Brazilian Catholicism to the post-independence socioeconomic structure would, for the most part, continued up until the mid-1960s, when the imposition of a repressive military dictatorship and the church's opening to modernity with the Second Vatican Council (1962–5) reignited tensions with the state, bringing to the forefront progressive Catholic forces that had been overshadowed but were slowly gaining momentum amid the overall conservative tenor of national and global Catholicism.

Beyond Romanization? Brazilian Progressive Catholicism

Arguably, post-independence New Christendom reached its highest expression in Brazil during the regime of the Getúlio Vargas (1930–45, 1951–4), when the church established a "moral concordat"[25] with the state that, in many ways, echoed the unifying role that Catholicism played during colonial times (Beozzo 1986: 340). During this period, Catholicism became the de facto national religion, providing the moral cohesion and legitimation for an authoritarian social order that Vargas saw as the manifestation of his own leadership. The Constitution of 1934

> was prefaced with the phrase, "putting our confidence in God." Separation of church and state continues, but now the government could assist the Church financially "in the collective interest." Members of religious orders could now vote. Religious organizations were granted much more legal recognition. Spiritual assistance was permitted in the military and official establishments. Religious marriage was fully recognized in civil terms and divorce was prohibited. Probably most importantly, religious education was provided for within school hours and the state could provide subventions to Catholic Schools. (Bruneau 1974: 41)

The key Catholic actors during this period were Dom Sebastião Leme, archbishop of Olinda and Recife (1916–21), and later Cardinal of Rio de Janeiro (1930–42) (see Chapter 3 for a biographical take on him). A personal friend of Vargas, he oversaw the completion of the iconic *Cristo Redentor*, the Christ the Redeemer figure on the Corcovado Mountain overlooking Rio, as an all-embracing symbol of Brazil's Catholic identity. Leme and Vargas presided over the inauguration of the statue, underlining the intertwining of church and state interests in the New Christendom.

Yet, there is another side to Leme's work. He was also very supportive of the Dom Vital Center which, under the leadership of intellectuals Jackson de Figuereido and Alceu Amoroso Lima, became a seminal think-tank for the development of lay Catholic thought. More importantly, Dom Leme introduced Catholic Action to Brazil, a movement that initially aimed to bring back to the church the growing urban working classes, which were increasingly attracted by secular ideologies like socialism, communism, atheism, agnosticism, and fascism. The founder of Catholic Action, Belgian Joseph Cardijn, devised a "see-judge-act" (*ver–julgar–agir*) pastoral methodology to help priests understand the reality of workers in order to teach Catholicism more effectively. Working with small groups of lay people, priests were supposed to engage in a "*revisão de vida operária*" (a review of the worker's life) to examine the workers' everyday conditions and challenges (the "see" moment), draw from Catholic teaching to reflect on the religious and moral consequences and appropriateness of those conditions and challenges (the "judge" moment), and act accordingly to bring those conditions and challenges into line with Catholicism (the "act" moment).

A watershed moment for Catholic Action in Brazil was the election of Hélder Câmara as its national assistant in 1947. Câmara, who would eventually become archbishop of Olinda and Recife (1964–85) and a leading advocate for human rights and democracy, spearheaded a reorganization of Catholic Action into specialized sectors dealing with peasants, manual workers, and high school and university students. This reorganization enabled the movement to be present in more aspects of lay life and to deepen its experience of Brazilian social reality, with all its conflicts. As economic contradictions and political turmoil deepened in Brazil and the rest of Latin America during the 1960s, see-judge-act acquired a different valence, becoming a key source of progressive Catholic thinking.[26]

With its emphasis on using the church's teachings to reflect and act upon the challenges of the laity's daily life, Catholic Action dovetailed with other initiatives at the grassroots level such as the Movimento de Educação de Base (MEB—Popular Education Movement), a national literacy program that used the radio to reach remote areas in the country. At the heart of MEB was a "dialogical pedagogy" developed by educator Paulo Freire (Shor and Freire 1987: 11–31) that mirrored Catholic Action's see-judge-act methodology. Against traditional modes of instruction that emphasized rote memorization and regurgitation of materials deposited by teachers in the empty heads of their pupils—what Freire (1970: 72) called the "banking method"—he proposed a pedagogy which takes the experiences and worldviews of the students as its point of departure and involves an exchange of knowledge that edifies all participants. The goal of this pedagogy was *conscientização*, the emergence of a critical consciousness that empowers students "to name their reality" (86). Rather than passively accepting the ideas, symbols, and values of the ruling classes, which tend to obscure and perpetuate the arbitrary conditions of domination, peasants and workers would draw from their own cultural resources to grasp and transform reality according to their own needs, designs, and dreams. Conscientização anchors a "pedagogy of the oppressed" that is "forged *with*, not *for*, [them] (whether individuals or peoples) in the incessant struggle to regain their humanity. This pedagogy makes oppression and its causes objects of reflection by the oppressed, and from that reflection will come their necessary engagement in the struggle for their liberation. And in the struggle this pedagogy will be made and remade" (48).

Dialogical pedagogy and the task of awareness became essential ingredients in the vision and work of post–Vatican II progressive Catholicism among the poor in Brazil and elsewhere in Latin America, as we will see later in our discussion of liberation theology and base ecclesial communities.

After the Second World War, there was optimism in Latin America that capitalist development held all the answers, that it would eventually lead to social and personal well-being as developing countries followed the steps of the United States. This optimism began to fade in Brazil in 1964, when the military staged a coup, ushering in an authoritarian regime that would last twenty years. This military regime advanced an aggressive program of development based on the creation of industrial poles combined with severe repression of all dissidence. It was clear that the notion of capitalist development advocated by the United States did not lead automatically to democracy. Quite the contrary, in Brazil it seemed to go hand in hand not only with the violation of human rights, but also with more social dislocation, as masses of people moved from the countryside to the new industrial poles, which did not offer enough jobs and the infrastructural conditions to accommodate them. Development seemed to lead to disorderly urbanization, setting the conditions for growing inequality, social marginality, poverty, violence, and crime. I shall have more to say in Chapter 6 about how these social conditions accompanied the fragmentation of the religious field, more specifically of Christianity, in Brazil. Suffice it to say at this juncture that with the Catholic Church unable to respond adequately to the challenges of urban life for the growing working class and the poor, other expressions of Christianity, particularly Pentecostalism, came to fill in the gap with more flexible pastoral strategies and forms of organization.

The alternative to the view that capitalist development necessarily leads to the holistic promotion of the person began to take shape in the wake of the second meeting of the Latin American Episcopal Conference (CELAM) in Medellín, Colombia in 1968. At that meeting, the Latin American bishops took up the Second Vatican Council's call to bring the church up to date (*aggiornamento*) and be open to the outside world and read and respond to the "signs of the times." Reversing the dynamics generated by Trent and the First Vatican Council, Vatican II also decentralized the process of decision-making, giving regional bodies like CELAM and national churches the power to innovate in response to their specific contexts. At Medellín, the Latin American bishops confronted the reality of the region using Catholic Action's see-judge-act method. They saw a region in great turmoil, with repressive military dictatorships and revolutionary movements challenging them (since 1959, with the Cuban Revolution). They also saw a church that had historically sided with the dominant groups (up to Romanization and the moral concordat of the Vargas era) and had a weak presence among the growing sectors at the margins of society. They judged this alliance with dominant powers as contrary to the gospel, in which Jesus Christ chose to incarnate himself at the margins of the empire, among the poor to minister preferentially to them. As a transformative act, they recommended the creation of communities "where all of the peoples but more especially the lower classes have, by means of territorial and functional structures, an active and receptive, creative and decisive participation in the construction of a new society."[27] In order to diagnose the conditions in the region and offer viable solutions (the see and judge moments), the bishops drew from humanistic versions of Marxism, which provided an understanding of the dehumanizing effects of capitalism on the working class, as well as from dependency theory, which showed how the subordinate status of Latin American economies was the product of their unequal exchanges with dominant, core capitalist countries like the United States.[28]

There had already been important efforts to create grassroots Catholic communities before Medellín, including those in Barra do Piraí in the state of Rio de Janeiro and in Nísia Floresta in the archdiocese of Natal in the late 1950s and 1960s. However, Medellín encouraged the creation of *comunidades eclesiais de base* (CEBs—base ecclesial communities), small groups of workers, peasants, students, and neighbors who would gather with the encouragement of priests and nuns to reflect on their everyday life in light of the gospel and the church's social teaching, making them the principal pastoral tool to fulfill the hierarchy's "duty of solidarity with the poor, to which charity leads us. This solidarity means

34   *Christianity in Brazil*

that we make ours their problems and their struggles, that we know how to speak with them."[29] This shift in focus eventually came to be known as the "preferential option for the poor."[30] Despite opposition from significant conservative sectors of the episcopacy, no other church in the Americas would be as proactive as the Brazilian Catholic Church in promoting CEBs. Although there have been debates about the exact number of CEBs, most scholars agree that during their heyday in the late 1970s and early 1980s there were between 70,000 and 100,000 base communities of various kinds in Brazil.[31]

In CEBs, Catholic Action's see-judge-act and Freire's dialogical pedagogy cross-fertilized, spurring theological thinking around the notion of liberation as an alternative to that of capitalist development. While the birth of liberation theology could be traced to the publication of Peruvian theologian Gustavo Gutiérrez's *A Theology of Liberation* (originally published in Spanish in 1971, with its first outlines presented at a conference in Chimbote, Peru in 1968), Brazilian theologians, both Catholic and Protestant, were central to its development, refining and deepening it. Like other groups advocating for social justice during the military dictatorship, the Brazilian Catholic Church suffered persecution: Catholic lay leaders, priests, nuns, and bishops were harassed, tortured, and in some cases even killed. However, the church became the only institutional actor in civil society with enough clout and moral authority to denounce the military regime and offer relative protection to activists working for democratization. Thus, during the military dictatorship, progressive Catholicism, with liberation theology and CEBs as key pieces in a dense and dynamic network of grassroots organizations working on land tenure, Indigenous rights, legal aid, democratization, and social justice, became the most visible face of the church in Brazil.[32] These initiatives received crucial support from the National Conference of Brazilian Bishops (CNBB), which as part of the decentralization and engagement with the world called for by Vatican II, had been working actively to move Brazilian Catholicism beyond Romanization since 1952 (with Hélder Câmara as the conference's first secretary-general).

A few of the most significant progressive bishops are worth highlighting to give a sense of what Brazilian progressive Catholicism entailed. Paulo Evaristo Arns, Cardinal of São Paulo, not only denounced the military dictatorship outspokenly, but also, at personal risk, collaborated with Presbyterian minister Jaime Wright in photocopying and smuggling the military government's records on surveillance, detention, and torture, which eventually became the basis for *Brasil: Nunca Mais* (Brazil: Never Again), a book that played a fundamental role in the transition to democracy and civilian rule. Pedro Casaldáliga, bishop of

São Félix do Araguaia, became known for his strong advocacy for Indigenous peoples and small farmers through the Conselho Indigenista Missionário (CIMI—Indigenous Missionary Council) and the Comissão Pastoral da Terra (CPT—Pastoral Land Commission), as well as against US policy in Central America.

While not all CEBs and progressive grassroots organizations were explicitly involved in politics, whether advocating for clean water, paved roads, schools, and childcare centers in their neighborhoods or agitating for the transition to civilian rule (in 1985), the most important long-term legacy of Brazilian progressive Catholicism might be in the formation of grassroots leaders through the combination of the see-judge-act pastoral methodology and Freirian popular pedagogy. Many of the leaders who would form the Partido dos Trabalhadores (the Workers' Party), which would eventually become a dominant political force in the country, were deeply influenced by progressive Catholicism. They developed a voice, as well as critical thinking and organizing skills through their participation in CEBs, biblical circles, and other grassroots initiatives.[33] Certainly, this is the case of Luíz Inácio Lula da Silva, a press operator from the traditionally poor northeast who became president from 2003 to 2011.

Brazilian Christianity Unbound

With the transition to civil and democratic rule in the mid-1980s, many of the activists who had found protection and support in the church during the military dictatorship moved on to create and participate in their own secular organizations. This brain drain coincided with the election of Pope John Paul II in 1979. In light of his experience with the Soviets in Poland, John Paul II was very suspicious of the humanist Marxism that informed the social analyses of progressive Catholicism. He felt that the latter had become too influenced by secular modern ideologies like Marxism and socialism, which relativized the church's authority, undermining its ability to teach the truth of the gospel. To correct this imbalance, he proposed a "new evangelization," focusing primarily on the moral and spiritual conversion of the individual, particularly of Catholics who had moved away from the church, rather than on social action and political involvement. In practical terms in Brazil, John Paul II investigated, censured, and/ or silenced liberation theologians, such as Leonardo Boff, for avowed deviations from orthodoxy, and appointed conservative bishops to dioceses that had been led by progressives.[34] Without the vital support from bishops, many progressive

Catholic initiatives all but collapsed. For example, José Cardoso Sobrinho was named as the replacement for the retiring Hélder Câmara. Archbishop Sobrinho promptly closed down the Seminário Regional do Nordeste II (SERENE II) and the Theological Institute of Recife, both of which had been instrumental in training many priests and lay pastoral agents in liberationist thought.

To top it all off, the fall of the Berlin Wall in 1989 and the disintegration of the Soviet Union in 1991 pointed to the limitations of socialism, challenging progressive Catholicism's appeal to socialist ideals as an alternative to the contradictions of capitalism. The transition to democracy, the crisis of socialism, and John Paul II's conservative restoration also dovetailed with a recognition of the exponential growth of Evangelical Protestantism, particularly of Pentecostalism, in Brazil and throughout Latin America.

In Chapter 5, we will see that Pentecostalism has a long history in Brazil, coming to the country just a few years after the Azusa revivals in the early 1900s in California, one of the epicenters from which the movement radiated globally. Gunnar Vingren and Daniel Berg, two Swedish immigrants who had been baptized by the Holy Spirit in the United States, founded the Assemblies of God in Brazil in 1911 in the northeastern agricultural state of Pará, which was in the throes of a round of boom and bust as a result of the growth and collapse of the rubber industry (see their biographies in Chapter 3). Vingren's and Berg's story in the interior of Brazil shows that we should be careful not to overstate a linear history of Brazilian Christianity, expanding in progressive cycles from coastal cities to the countryside. Rather, Brazilian Christianity is polycentric, with multiple foci of creativity and innovation and, as we shall see in Chapter 4, with great regional diversity.[35] Still, even in the story of Pentecostalism, the cities on the eastern coast played an important role. In 1910, just the year before Vingren's and Berg's arrival in Brazil, Luigi Francescon, another immigrant to the United States—this time Italian—had come to the southern state of Paraná, moving eventually to São Paulo to found Congregação Cristã do Brasil (Christian Congregation of Brazil), the country's other major classical Pentecostal Church.

The growth of Pentecostalism was slow at the beginning, picking up momentum in the 1950s with the formation of Brazilian pastors who started to create their own movements and congregations. Amid the turmoil of the 1960s, Pentecostalism took off in Brazil. I will have more to say about this growth in the chapter focusing on denominations (Chapter 5), but just to offer a sense of the scope of the growth of Brazilian Protestantism, spearheaded by Pentecostalism, consider the fact that according to the 1960 census, Protestants accounted for less than 5 percent of the population. By the 2010 census, 22.2 percent of Brazil's population described themselves as Protestant, with two-thirds of them affiliated to various Pentecostal churches. Many of these Pentecostal churches like the Universal Church of the Kingdom of God, the Reborn in Christ Church, and the World Church of the Power of God are veritable transnational networks, with congregations in countries throughout the world, even in Europe and North America. The spectacular Pentecostal surge obscures the significant presence of other forms of Christianity, from the Church of Latter-Day Saints, also known as the Mormons, to Jehovah's Witnesses and Seventh-Day Adventists, alongside the so-called historical Protestant churches, that is, Lutherans, Baptists, Presbyterians, and Methodists.

The rapid growth of Evangelical Protestantism in Brazil is the most dramatic indicator of the diversification of Brazilian Christianity, and more broadly of the country's religious field. At 64.6 percent of the population, Catholicism continues to be numerically dominant, making Brazil the country with the largest Catholic population in the world. Nevertheless, Brazilian Catholicism shows great fragmentation, with the continued vitality of the traditional popular Catholicism of saints and Marian devotions introduced by the Portuguese and of progressive Catholicism, which is experiencing something of a renaissance with Pope Francis's emphasis on serving the poor and social justice. These two forms of Catholicism now compete, coexist, and cross-fertilize with Charismatic Catholicism. The latter represents a Catholic response to the success of Pentecostalism, focusing on the personal and deeply emotive experience of the divine through the gifts of the Holy Spirit, like speaking in tongues and divine healing, and using popular cultural and electronic media in the same way that many Pentecostal churches do.

Just like CEBs and liberation theology, Charismatic Catholicism emerged in the wake of Vatican II, as a laity-driven pastoral approach. The movement came to Brazil in 1968, introduced by Jesuits to the University of Campinas in the state of São Paulo. It started in the mid-1960s among Catholic students at Duquesne University, the University of Notre Dame, and Michigan State University in the United States.[36] As we shall see in Chapter 6, which addresses the social and political dimensions of Brazilian Christianity, this brand of Catholicism has a great deal in common with Pentecostalism, sharing the latter's concern for spiritual renewal and its focus on moral issues like the preservation of traditional marriage and the struggle against abortion. In that sense, Charismatic Catholicism is very much in line with the new evangelization advanced by John Paul II and his successor Benedict XVI. In fact, John Paul II in particular was enthusiastically supportive of the movement. Also, as with Pentecostalism, the networks associated with

Charismatic Catholicism, such as Canção Nova (New Song) and Shalom, have a prominent international presence, highlighting the central role that Brazilian Christians have come to play in the future of global Christianity through what some scholars have termed "reverse missionizing." Christianity was brought to Brazil through the trials and tribulations of colonialism and slavery, where, despite the persistent quest for orthodoxy, it interacted creatively, but always in the context of power asymmetries, with Indigenous and African-based religions, giving rise to novel rich and dynamic expressions. Now, it is Brazil that is taking these new vibrant forms of Christianity to Europe, flying in the face of the process of secularization.

With this bird's-eye view of the origins and trajectory of Christianity in Brazil, we can now turn to a more in-depth exploration of the various ways of being Christian to which this complex history has given rise.

2

Competing and Cross-Fertilizing Structures of Feeling and Experience

Ways of Being Christian in Brazil

We have seen how the widespread dynamics of tension, accommodation, and cross-fertilization among different elements, including Iberian Catholicism and Native and African-based religions, produced a variegated Christianity in Brazil. Thus, it is not surprising to find great diversity in terms of worldviews and ritual practices. Nevertheless, it is possible to identify some enduring theological-pastoral-praxical clusters in Brazilian Christianity. These clusters are internally varied and fluid, always in a reciprocal conversation with each other, as well as with the social, political, economic, and cultural contexts in which they operate. Still, they show enough relative stability and continuity to enable us to characterize them heuristically. These clusters include:

1. Traditional Luso-Catholicism (TLC).
2. Progressive Catholicism (PC).
3. Historic Protestantism (HP).
4. Alternative Christianity (AC).
5. Pentecostalism and Charismatic Christianity (PCC).

It is important to note that, while theology, that is, explicitly articulated beliefs and doctrines, is a key ingredient, these clusters are, borrowing from cultural studies scholar Raymond Williams (1977), more like dynamic, embodied "structures of feeling" and experience that shape and are shaped by forms of affective being-in-the-world, relationality, and belonging, linking humans with each other, with the natural world, and with various expressions of what they deem sacred.[1] Let us explore each of these Christian ways of life more in depth.

Traditional Luso-Catholicism (TLC) stems directly from the medieval Catholicism that came with the Portuguese during the conquest and colonization of Brazil. Its theological and ecclesiological bases were clarified, systematized, and affirmed at the Council of Trent (1545–63), which was called in response to the Protestant Reformation. TLC is strongly characterized by a dialectic between what, borrowing from sociologist Max Weber, we may call other-worldly and this-worldly mysticisms.[2] The mysticism label refers to the belief in the close intertwining of the supernatural and natural worlds, such that actions in one of the realms have direct effects on the other. In TLC, the visible world is the stage on which miraculous events unfold. In the previous chapter, we saw the pervasiveness of this logic in the history of Catholicism in Brazil from the discovery of the statue of Nossa Senhora Aparecida by fishermen in the Paraíba River in 1717 to the conversion of the Holy Host into blood that is alleged to have taken place when Padre Cícero Romão Batista (1844–1934) gave communion in Juazeiro, in the interior of Ceará, in 1889.[3]

Traditional Luso-Catholic mysticism also issues from Catholic nondualism, that is, from the tradition's emphasis on the belief in mediation and the close connection between body and soul, and between matter and spirit. Building on this tradition, in TLC, the souls of the departed go to various realms between heaven and earth, depending on the worthiness of their lives, sometimes even haunting the living. This belief in the tight link between the spiritual and material worlds explains the efficacy of prayers and special masses that are offered on behalf of the deceased: these are what sociologist Emile Durkheim (2001: 289) calls "piacular rites," meant not only as a remembrance and a collective way to express sorrow and to reweave the social fabric torn asunder by death but also to help the souls of the dead atone, receive more sanctification, and be allowed into heaven at the end of times. This notion that the spirits of the dead and the living are in ongoing close interaction has been shaped by Indigenous and African-based religions such as Candomblé and Umbanda, as well as Kardecist Spiritism, in the process of religious hybridization that is the hallmark of the Brazilian religious field.

The characterization of the other-worldly is helpful for understanding TLC's intense concern with the end of times. Such a concern, already implicit in early Christianity's eschatology, intensified in Iberia during the Middle Ages, a time of pervasive insecurity, marked by the vulnerability of rural populations to unpredictable natural phenomena such as droughts, floods, famines, and plagues, as well as wars and political instability. Given the challenging environment the Portuguese encountered during settlement in Brazil, this sense of fragility and dependence on protective supernatural forces and agents became further heightened. Furthermore, Indigenous religions and those brought by African slaves involve forms of "animism" that posit a non-dualistic reality, in which human and nonhumans, including animals, plants, and environmental forces, interact in tight "webs of life" (Ingold 2011).

Some words of clarification are needed regarding animism, for it is a term that comes heavily loaded with colonialist and orientalist baggage. E. B. Tylor (2010 [1871]), one of the founders of modern anthropology, used animism to theorize about the origins of religion. Operating mostly with accounts from missionaries, travelers, and imperial officials, he postulated that the latter originated as the mistaken—albeit logical at the level of mental development of "primitive" peoples—attempt to deal with the mysteries of death and dreaming by projecting souls and spirits (*animas*) onto the natural world. The notion that the complex myths and rituals of Indigenous peoples did not constitute fully evolved religion, but were, at best, the erroneous imaginings of primitive minds served missionaries to assert the superiority of Christianity and facilitate conversion of imperial subjects. Nevertheless, even with this serious pitfall, with the ontological turn in anthropology, the concept of animism has been "restored" and "reanimated" to relativize or "provincialize," in the words of Dipesh Chakrabarty (2000), European modernity as the only viable and normative way of being-in-the-world. Anthropologists like Philippe Descola (2013) and Tim Ingold (2011) argue that a retooled notion of animism helps to foreground vital and dynamic worldviews that have been denigrated and marginalized by Western modernity. For them, these worldviews are neither primitive nor naïve, rather they offer robust alternatives to European-derived dualism, reductionism, and instrumentalism (i.e., the means-ends use of nature, including fellow humans). I use animism in this latter sense. I would like to highlight how African-based and Amerindian structures of feeling and experience, which have a richness, robustness, and generativity of their own, have shaped and continue to shape Brazilian Christianity.[4]

The convergence of Catholic and Indigenous nondualisms was, however, not free of conflict. The Portuguese saw the Natives as practicing *feitiçaria* (sorcery/witchcraft), mistakenly imputing agency to human-made, profane objects (thus, the word derives from something *feito*, "made" in Portuguese).[5] In order to convert the Natives to Christianity, their idolatrous *feitiços* (magic charms) had to be destroyed. But Portuguese iconoclasm did not result in a disenchantment of the world, for they introduced their own forms of medieval "Christian materiality," their own sacred images, crosses, rosaries, and relics.[6] And as the miraculous appearance of Nossa Senhora shows, soon the Natives and enslaved people presented to the Portuguese secular and clerical authorities

42   *Christianity in Brazil*

autochthonous material expressions of the sacred that they had to recognize as efficacious and legitimate in light of the powerful popular devotions these expressions generated. We can, thus, conclude that Indigenous and African-derived animisms shaped the ways in which the Portuguese—with their own notions of interceding saints and atoning/wandering spirits of the dead—and their subjects translated and incorporated TLC.

We will see that controversies around *feitiçaria* would resurface as historic Protestants and especially Neo-Pentecostals challenged the hegemony of popular Brazilian Catholicism, which is grounded on the matrix of TLC. Recall the "chute da santa" episode in my introduction, in which a pastor of the Neo-Pentecostal Universal Church of the Kingdom of God (UCKG) kicked the image of Nossa Senhora on TV while declaring that it was just a worthless piece of wood. Paradoxically, as we shall see below, Pentecostalism, particularly in its more recent waves, also operates with a "pneumatic materialism," which posits the power of God through the Holy Spirit to heal bodies and bestow embodied gifts like glossolalia (Vásquez 2017). This pneumatic materialism also recognizes the agency in everyday life of demonic entities that cause illnesses, misfortune, and domestic strife. As churches like the UCKG establish transnational ministries in Africa, they have re-purposed the term *feitiçaria* to cast the process of conversion from Indigenous religions as a form of spiritual warfare (Van de Kamp 2016).

Returning to TLC, the vulnerability to random natural phenomena and the desire for the intervention of supernatural forces to control them explains why it carries a strongly millenarian dimension, a deeply felt sense that the present world is not only fleeting but also corrupt, unjust, and about to be overturned by the second coming of Jesus Christ, who will finally inaugurate a reign of harmony, abundance, and justice.[7] We saw in the previous chapter that in Portugal, this millenarianism often took the form of Sebastianism, the myth of the restoration of the empire by King Sebastião. This Sebastianism has appeared throughout Brazilian history, most dramatically in the case of Antônio Conselheiro (1830–1897, see Chapter 3). As Brazil became independent, many people in the countryside were dislocated, a process that in the northeastern *sertão* (backlands) was made worse by a persistent drought. Seeking to survive and rebuild their community, many poor peasants followed Conselheiro, who had been traveling from small village to small village, preaching the impending end of the wicked secular republic, which had instituted civil marriage, and the restoration of the Catholic monarchy. Conselheiro and his followers formed the settlement of Canudos in the interior of the state of Bahia. The rising federal government saw the settlement as a threat, sending several military expeditions to destroy it. The government eventually succeeded at the cost of more than 10,000 lives.[8]

In addition to his apocalyptic and millennial preaching, Conselheiro also called for repentance. This call demonstrates the this-worldly dimension of TLC. This world may be fleeting, but it is also a testing ground meant to prepare us for the beyond. Ergo, TLC is a penitential form of Christianity, one that stresses the need to engage in this-worldly acts of piety to expiate sins. However, maintaining a consistent ascetic style of living is only possible for the most pious, for saints and *beatos*. Most Catholics will engage in acts of piety, such as going on pilgrimage to the shrine of a particularly powerful saint at particularly trying times of our lives. Or alternatively, regular Catholics might participate in cycles of penance and celebration, which allow the faithful to satisfy the desires of the flesh and repent from expressing them; the interplay between festive and penitential dimensions of TLC is part and parcel of its this-worldliness, its embrace of the world and flesh, even with all its shortcomings. This interplay makes sense of the excesses of Carnival right before the austerity and solemnity of Lent.

Following the Council of Trent (1545–63), which affirmed Catholic doctrine in response to the Reformation, TLC is institutionally organized around the sacraments and the parish priest as their legitimate holder. Nevertheless, at the grassroots, the cult of the saints and Marian devotions take center stage.[9] As we saw in the previous chapter, in Brazil, as throughout Latin America, post-Trent traditional popular Catholicism evolved as a creative response at the grassroots to the institutional weakness of the church, which lacked enough priests to dispense the sacraments and, more generally, minister to the day-to-day religious needs of the population, especially in the vast countryside. This is why TLC developed a relatively autonomous cadre of local lay experts and a rich set of practices that the institutional church has not always found orthodoxic. In fact, the official church often sought to "purify" grassroots TLC in a process of "Romanization" that was not always successful.[10]

In TLC, the believer's relation with saints is personal, often very intimate and affective. Frequently, the devotee relates to saints as if they were members of his/her extended family. Just as in the physical world, a person in good standing has a powerful godfather and godmother to look after him/her, so too in the spiritual world, each one of us has an efficacious patron saint to protect and provide for us. We saw in the previous chapter how this hierarchical and corporatist worldview accompanied and buttressed the patriarchal colonial order anchored on the *casa grande-senzala* nexus. Arguably, despite the secularizing pressures of modernity, this "structure of feeling" has carried on to the present, with figures as diverse as Getúlio Vargas, Luiz Inácio Lula da Silva, and Jair Bolsonaro tapping into patrimonial politics.

Believers may have been committed to their patron saints by their parents upon birth or they may just come to the saint in search of a particular favor, which s/he is known to offer given his/her own hagiography. Particularly popular in Brazil is São João (St. John the Baptist), who is at the center of the *festas juninas*, a cycle of festivals in June, an especially critical time in the agricultural season when rain is crucial. Because of his association with water in Jesus Christ's baptism, the faithful celebrate São João for making the rains possible. I will have more to say about these festivals in Chapter 4 when I discuss regional variations in Brazilian Christianity. Another good example of the centrality of saints in Brazilian Catholicism is Santo Antônio (St. Anthony of Padua), a Portuguese Franciscan friar considered the saint of lost causes. Hagiographic accounts tell of how his powerful prayers moved one of his wayward students to return a book of psalms that he had stolen and return to the Franciscan Order himself. Many Brazilians pray to Santo Antônio when they are in dire straits, have lost a cherished item, or, for women, when they want to find a good husband.

While TLC recognizes Jesus Christ as the Son of God, at the grassroots, he functions almost like an especially powerful saint, associated with a particular miracle or image. Such is the case of Nosso Senhor de Bomfim (Our Lord of Good End), whose devotion was brought to Salvador, Bahia from Setubal, Portugal in the 1740s. The *festas de Bomfim*, which take place in early January, include masses, processions, and the ritual washing of the steps of the church that houses the original statue. In its focus on the crucified Jesus at the moment of His death, this devotion illustrates very clearly the penitential and celebratory dialectic behind TLC.

Devotees of a particular saint express their lifelong alliance in private by building elaborate home altars, before which they conduct daily prayers and rituals. In public, they may found or become members of *irmandades* (brotherhoods), groups of laypeople organized, often according to gender, ethnicity, and class, to serve a particular saint, planning and carrying out processions, pilgrimages, and festivals in his/her name. They may even build shrines dedicated to the saint's devotion through the collection of alms. *Irmandades* also engage in charitable works and build and maintain cemeteries for their members. As such, brotherhoods play a key role in the communal ritual life, addressing both the festive and penitential dimensions of TLC, sometimes even "throwing more weight around than the Pope."[11] As we will see when I explore regional variations,

Ways of Being Christian in Brazil 45

this was particularly the case in what scholars have called "Catolicismo Mineiro," (Minas Gerais Catholicism), which was shaped simultaneously by the lack of priests and by the fact that the laity had the financial resources to build exquisite baroque shrines. For Brazilians of African descent, *irmandades* served the vital role of preserving and affirming their ethnic, cultural, and religious identities. A good example is the *Irmandade da Boa Morte in Bahia*, which is actually a sisterhood founded by former slaves and their descendants that has been key in the development of Candomblé.[12]

The relationship between TLC and African-based religions is a complex and dynamic one. Some scholars have argued that Catholic saints only served as masks to hide the continued worship of African ancestors and deities from the censure of clerical and secular authorities. Others see a (gradual) mixing of traditions, such that various *orixás* and their Catholic correlates—for example, Xango, the god of thunder, fire, and justice, said to be the deified king of Obá of Oyo in Nigeria, and Moses/St. Jerome, lawgivers and scholars—become aspects of the same underlying vital force, that is, *axé*.[13] Here the monism of African-based religions resonates with and reinforces the non-dualistic worldview of TLC. In either case, it is clear that the religions brought by the slaves have shaped Brazilian Catholicism in dramatic ways, adding especially to its rich material and affective matrix, from rituals and symbols to music and foods associated with its penitential and celebratory cycles.

Whether it involves a lifelong alliance or a specific petition, the believer and the saint in TLC will engage in what sociologists term an "exchange of religious goods,"[14] in which the former makes a *promessa* (vow), pledging to undertake a significant (often public) act of piety, such as offering a blessed candle, praying the Holy Rosary a number of times, or even sponsoring celebrations of the saint's day. Believers could also carry the image of the saint during one of the processions in his/her honor.

In exchange, the saint is asked to intercede and work on behalf of the believer to bestow a favor, most of the time having to do with matters of health, love, and wealth. While each saint has his/her own specialty, Nossa Senhora Aparecida is seen as a universal intercessor. Her maternal love knows no boundaries and her position close to Jesus makes her particularly effective in responding to the needs of the faithful. Her unconditional maternal love also means that Mary is particularly attentive to the plight of the most vulnerable sectors of the Brazilian population. This preferential love for those at the margins of society is poignantly expressed in Mary's appearance: Nossa Senhora is dark-skinned. Whereas the Catholic Church does not always officially recognize figures that

46   *Christianity in Brazil*

are locally or even regionally seen as saints—a case in point here is Padre Cícero, who has not been canonized but is subject to a vibrant devotion in northeast Brazil—Marian piety plays a central role at both the grassroots and institutional levels. Today, the National Basilica of Our Lady Aparecida is the second-largest Marian shrine in the world, with capacity for at least 45,000 people. The Virgin Mary also occupies a central place in Brazilian progressive and Charismatic Catholicism, as I will discuss later.

We will see that modernist Catholic theologies, including post–Vatican II versions, have an ambivalent view of *promessas*, seeing them as part of an instrumentalization of the sacred and the result of a quietist attitude that leaves the solution of this-worldly problems to the supernatural rather than encouraging the believer to work with God in the building of his kingdom. Modernist Catholic theologies have also sought to make TLC more Christo-centric, teaching that miracles come ultimately from God, with saints simply as worthy ethical models and intercessors. Certainly, these theologies have, at the very least, sought to de-emphasize the widespread belief at the grassroots that it is the image itself that is miraculous.[15] This critique notwithstanding, the non-dualistic spirit-matter, supernatural-natural links in TLC offer an efficacious way to experience the potency of the sacred immanently in the material world, and to respond to the challenge of everyday life for many Brazilians, accounting for the enduring vitality of this strand of Catholicism. We will see that Pentecostalism, the fastest-growing strand of Christianity in Brazil, also posits a tight connection between spirituality and materiality.[16]

We can see that TLC's *Weltanschauung* stands in tension with other forms of Christianity and that, with industrialization and urbanization, this form of Catholicism has lost the hegemony it had when Brazil was more agrarian (more in Chapter 5). Nevertheless, TLC continues to be the main source for what Droogers (1987) has called a "Minimal Brazilian Religiosity." Certainly, it constitutes the rich generative theological and pastoral matrix in and against which other expressions of Christianity, and even other religions in Brazil, articulate themselves (Bittencourt Filho 2003). Central to this minimal Brazilian religiosity is the belief in the close entwinement of natural and supernatural realms, which enables spiritual entities of various sorts, from saints and Mary to the spirits of the ancestors and demons, to communicate with the living and shape the fate of humans, either to protect or harm, as well as to ritualize and sacralize "places, images and objects, as manifestation[s] or hierophan[ies] of this 'invisible upper world' in the earthly world" (Camurça 2009: 175).[17]

Theologically, *progressive Catholicism (PC)* shares many elements with TLC, beginning with nondualism, the entwining of spirit and matter and of human and divine histories. Thus, it would be wrong to claim that PC jettisons the sacramental view of the world affirmed at Trent. However, influenced by modernity's humanism—the recognition of human rationality as a legitimate source of truth along with divine revelation—PC sees the practice of faith not just as the performance of acts of devotion toward saints and Mary or of acts of penance in preparation for the end of time, but as an engagement in the present to contribute to the building of the reign of God. In that sense, PC advances more than simply a tight faith-life link, which in different forms is the hallmark of not only TLC but also Pentecostalism and Charismatic Christianities. Traditional Catholic theology moves downward, as it were, starting from the study of God's nature and the teachings he reveals to deduce the implications for everyday life. PC upturns this approach, moving upward from the challenges of everyday life. Rather than privileging orthodoxy, PC takes "orthopraxis" as its point of departure: the right kind of involvement and action in the world, asking what church teachings and God can say about a particular historical situation.

The sources of this upturning of traditional theology lie in the see-judge-act methodology of Catholic Action, which, as we saw in Chapter 1, started as a reformist movement that sought to preserve the relevance of Catholicism in response to changes brought about by modernity. The latter exposed growing numbers of people to industrialization and urbanization and, thus, to secular ideologies such as capitalism and socialism. As Brazil entered a period of repressive military dictatorship, Catholic Action became radicalized, giving rise to explicit critiques of the capitalist notion of development and to the advocacy of liberation as an alternative.

The result is what Clodovis Boff (2008) calls a *"teologia pé-no-chão"* (feet-on-the-ground theology) that, like Paulo Freire's pedagogy of the oppressed, starts from the concrete experiences of daily life among the poor and from their yearning to have a more humane existence, an existence that reflects what God wants for His children. Thus, as a key element of PC, liberation theology is a contextual theology that, starting from an awareness of the often desperate situation of poor and working-class Brazilians (the "see" moment), draws upon the Bible, Catholic social teaching, and the analytical tools of the social sciences to gain full consciousness of the actions, structures, and institutions that have led to this situation and assess whether these forces are just in light of the gospel (the "judge" moment). On the basis of that judgment, liberation theologians envision actions that would bring those forces more in line with God's salvific

48   *Christianity in Brazil*

plan (the "act" moment). Efficacious work, then, necessarily involves the reflection upon and transformation of the social and political structures that produce poverty and marginalization and undermine the dignity of the person, keeping him/her from having a close relationship with God. In that sense, PC stands in tension with TLC, often portraying the latter as passively reproducing social and political hierarchies. Despite TLC's strong reliance on lay leadership and the relative autonomy of this leadership, the exchange of religious goods at the heart of the cult of saints mirrors and sacralizes the patron-client power asymmetries that continue to characterize Brazilian society and politics from colonial times.[18] Rather than fighting to change the underlying conditions that generate "the pathologies of poverty," to draw from historian Andrew Chesnut (1997), the faithful rely on saints and other supernatural forces to address these hardships.

Because of its critique of TLC, some scholars argue that PC involves a "disenchantment" of the world, a process of rationalization on the part of vanguard Catholic elites that are not attuned to the enduring experience of the sacred in the now that the popular classes in Brazil continue to have.[19] These scholars see this disconnect as part and parcel of the crisis of PC, the rapid expansion of Pentecostalism, and the success of Charismatic Catholicism from the 1980s on. This diagnostic is only partly correct, however, since PC does strive to stay close to the ground through a variety of innovative pastoral initiatives such as *comunidades eclesiais de base* (base ecclesial communities) and *círculos bíblicos* (biblical circles), small groups of neighbors who come together to read the church's teachings and the Bible and draw from them to make sense of a member's personal problem or of a community concern. Powerful theological themes emerge during these reflections. The most common one is *a caminhada* (literally the walk or the long road), a theme that draws from the struggles to liberate the Hebrews from bondage in Egypt and to make it to the Promised Land. By referring to the story of Exodus, PC highlights some of its key theological themes: a God who intervenes in history on behalf of those who are in need and oppressed, a prophetic leadership that challenges injustice and points to an alternative, utopian way of life, and the hope and fidelity necessary to endure the long march to this utopian reality. The everyday struggles of present-day Brazilians to improve their communities, confront political corruption, and demand economic and political rights become cosmicized, embedded in a long but hopeful salvific history.

In terms of Christology, PC picks up key aspects of TLC, also emphasizing the suffering and crucified Christ rather than Christ "the winner" preached by

Neo-Pentecostalism's prosperity theology. In that sense, PC's preferential option for the poor is already prefigured by TLC. However, PC reads the Incarnation and Passion as signs of God's love for humanity, a love that brings Him to dwell among the poor at the edge of the empire and to liberate them from the sinful conditions that produce suffering and death. PC sees Jesus Christ as a liberator.[20] As Leonardo Boff writes: "The kingdom of God implies a revolution of the human world. The preaching of the kingdom of God concerns not only persons, demanding conversion of them. It also affects the world of persons in terms of liberation from legalism, from conventions without foundation, from authoritarianism and the forces and powers that subject people" (1978: 72). The same can be said of the Virgin Mary: Brazilian feminist liberation theologians, who are part of a newer wave of progressive Catholic thinking, see her not only expressing a preferential option for the poor but also, beyond TLC, healing the dualisms and exclusions caused by male-centrism through her maternal love.[21] The theme of healing dualisms will also be taken up by Leonardo Boff, arguably the leading Brazilian liberation theologian, whom we will encounter in the following chapter. In his more recent writings, he develops an eco-theology, which argues that the same socioeconomic structures that exploit the poor also instrumentalize and pillage nature, leading to a global ecological crisis. As an alternative, Boff calls for a "new covenant of the heart with all things" based on the holistic and inclusive spirituality of St. Francis of Assisi, showing once again the interconnection between PC and TLC.[22] Pope Francis picked up some of Boff's eco-theological themes in his landmark encyclical *Laudato Si*.

As part of the Reformation, which advanced many of aspects of the humanism that informed modernity, *historic Protestantism (HP)* echoes many of PC's theological themes, such as the valuing of individual conscience in the practice of the faith. As we saw in the previous chapter, historic Protestant churches embraced Enlightenment values at a time when the Vatican was engaged in a process of Romanization that was strongly anti-modernist. These values resonated with the young Brazilian republic's stress on order and progress. Moreover, Protestantism's notion of the "priesthood of all believers," that is, that all believers can have a meaningful and legitimate relationship with God from their own life-stations without the mediation of trained specialists (priests), produced forms of congregational organization that dovetailed with secular democratic ideals. Following its emphasis on *sola scriptura* (only the scriptures), HP invested heavily in education, since increased literacy would enable the faithful to read the Bible on their own and not require the mediation of clergy. This focus on education, together with strong advocacy of a social

50   *Christianity in Brazil*

gospel that was characteristic of mainline Protestantism at the turn of the twentieth century, has given HP a consistently progressive tenor. Like PC, HP holds a basically optimistic view of the inherent capacity of humans for spiritual progress and for building societies that reflect this progress. And because HP wanted to curtail the power of the clergy, a power that led to abuses in the sale of indulgences, it reduced and redefined the sacraments, presenting them as collective acts of remembrance, celebration, or recognition rather than actions performed by the priest to transform the natural world (as in the Catholic notion of transubstantiation—the actual change of the substances of the wine and bread into the blood and flesh of Christ during the Eucharist). As such, just like PC, HP disenchants the "magical" cosmos of TLC, with its saints, miracles, spirits, and apparitions, and rationalizes the practice of Christianity, bringing it more in line with secular modernity's rational world.

The military dictatorship's repressive actions in the 1960s and 1970s radicalized HP's progressive tendencies in ways that mirrored the increasing prophetic role of PC. In fact, one can argue that the work of Protestant theologians such as Richard Shaull and Rubem Alves at the Presbyterian Seminary in Campinas played a seminal role in the emergence of liberation theology in Brazil.[23] Years before Catholic theologian Gustavo Gutiérrez wrote *A Theology of Liberation* (1971), considered the founding document of the movement, Shaull, influenced by the thought of Dietrich Bonhoeffer, had collaborated with other young Protestant theologians like Jether Ramalho, Waldo César, and Júlio de Santa Ana in the Social Responsibility Sector of the Evangelical Confederation of Brazil and in *Iglesia y Sociedad en America Latina* (ISAL—Church and Society in Latin America) to generate a contextual theology of revolution that defended a historically informed and biblically grounded ethical imperative to radically transform oppressive secular structures in the struggle to create more just societies.[24] Shaull was also instrumental in the publication in English of Paulo Freire's *Pedagogy of the Oppressed,* a book that, as we have seen, profoundly influenced pastoral work at the grassroots.

ISAL's work illustrates another important element of historic Protestant theologies—ecumenism, which stands in contrast with the more sectarian tendencies of some forms of Pentecostalism that construe the Brazilian religious arena in primarily competitive terms.

Alternative Christianity (AC) is a heterogeneous cluster that includes a variety of Christianities, including the Church of Latter-Day Saints (LDS), also known as the Mormons, Jehovah's Witnesses, and Seventh-Day Adventists, which trace their origins to the Second Great Awakening in the US between the 1830s and 1870s. As in the case of Mormons, they may have additional authoritative teachings and writings beyond the Hebrew Bible and what mainstream Christians understand as the New Testament, which are the product of ongoing divine revelation to their founders or elders. Thus, AC churches tend to stress the prophetic dimensions of Christianity. These revelations may be in sharp tension with traditional Christian doctrine: for example, Mormons generally do not accept the Trinitarian view of God developed at the Council of Nicaea (325 CE). Nevertheless, alternative Christians do see Jesus Christ as their personal savior. AC shares HP's evangelicalism, that is, the emphasis on missions and spreading the gospel. However, the missionary strategies of alternative Christian churches are more similar to those employed by many Pentecostal churches, emphasizing door-to-door proselytism. Also, in contrast to HP's low tension vis-à-vis the larger Brazilian society, AC churches evince a more sectarian approach. From their foundation, these AC churches have advocated a form of millenarianism, the imminent coming to an end of human history and the inauguration of God's true reign, that in Brazil parallels the Sebastianism of TLC. This theological parallel has facilitated conversion, at least at the level of worldview, from TLC to AC. We saw in the previous chapter that millenarianism runs deep in Brazilian history. In terms of worldview, the LDS Church, which is one of the most dynamic alternative Christian churches in Brazil, stresses kinship, the eternal nature of marriage, and the baptism and salvation of one's living and deceased relatives in a manner that bears a strong affinity with the importance of the family, in its extended form, in TLC. As a counterbalance, doctrinally based (up until 1978) Mormon negative attitudes toward Blacks have adversely affected the reception of the LDS Church in a country where half of the population can trace their ancestry to Africa (Grover 1984).

Pentecostalism and Charismatic Christianity (PCC) is built around the immediate and powerfully corporeal experience of the Holy Spirit. In Brazil, the term Charismatic is primarily applied to Catholics who, like Pentecostals, place the experience of the Holy Spirit front and center. However, unlike Pentecostals, Catholic Charismatics remain faithful to the sacraments, the Virgin Mary, and, to some extent, the community of saints. In PCC, the natural and supernatural worlds interpenetrate, allowing for the manifestation of wondrous events in the midst of everyday life. In that sense, Pentecostal and Charismatic Christianity has more in common with TLC than with HP, which as we saw earlier, disenchanted faith in its effort to take away the sacramental power of the priest.

Chief among the wondrous phenomena that PCC sees as heralding Christ's imminent second coming (just as for alternative Christianities) are embodied "gifts" (charismas) of the Spirit. Classical Pentecostal churches such as the Assemblies of God traditionally elevated glossolalia, the ability to speak in tongues, as the first and definitive sign of baptism in the Holy Spirit. The recent Neo-Pentecostal wave has shifted focus toward exorcism and divine healing (*cura divina*), advancing a gospel of health and wealth that does not see a contradiction between other-worldly salvation and this-worldly rewards (Mariano 2004). PCC sees the experience of the Holy Spirit as fully transformative, totally reconstituting the sinner, not just spiritually and morally, but also in terms of physical well-being and success in his/her daily life. This is because working through the Holy Spirit, Jesus liberates the individual from bondage by the Devil and his minions, who are engaged in a cosmic spiritual war with God in preparation for the end of times. For those churches in the Neo-Pentecostal wave of PCC, these possessing demons are the cause of all the misfortunes, ills, and suffering that afflict large sectors of the Brazilian population. Exorcizing and "chaining" them, then, offers the possibility of a new life in the here and now, even as the faithful prepare for the second coming of Jesus Christ.

PCC proselytizes aggressively against TLC, attacking it for its presumed superstition and idolatry. Moreover, particular Neo-Pentecostal churches, such as the Igreja Universal do Reino de Deus and the Igreja do Poder de Deus, often go as far as linking TLC with what they see as "witchcraft" (pejoratively *macumba*) in African-based religions. Such an attitude helps us make sense of the "chute na santa" affair, the kicking of an image of the Nossa Senhora Aparecida (Our Lady Aparecida) by a UCKG pastor on TV that I mentioned earlier and in the introduction.

Prima facie, PCC would seem to be Christo-centric when compared to the central place that saints and Mary occupy in TLC. Indeed, those practicing this theological-pastoral cluster of Christianity often speak of "having a personal encounter with Jesus Christ" or of "accepting Jesus as their savior." Nevertheless, for all its aggressive proselytism and iconoclasm, just as in TLC, PCC are all about mediation, the vital mediation of the Holy Spirit in this case. More generally, PCC shares with TLC the sense that supernatural forces act in the material world, affecting the fate of believers. And just as the spiritual world can affect the material world, actions in the latter, such as powerful prayers, the laying of hands, or tithing, have the potential to mobilize the spiritual forces to exorcize and heal. For example, the rapidly expanding Igreja Mundial do Poder de Deus (IMPD), founded by Valdemiro Santiago, a dissident from the UCKG, has adopted the motto: "*Vem ca Brasil! O Milagre esta aqui!*" (Come here Brasil! The Miracle is here!). Capitalizing on the Holy Spirit's power to work miracles through Santiago's prayers and body and, once again, illustrating the power of Christian materiality in the midst of late modernity, the IMPD has been very successful in selling towels soaked with his sweat as he preaches to large multitudes. These towels are reputed to have healing powers. In fact, some of the faithful report eating bits of the towel and getting healed from stubborn tumors. In perhaps the most extreme version of this tight link between materiality and spirituality, a pastor of the Assemblies of God's Cathedral of Awakening has been captured on video telling his congregation during tithing in the middle of the service: "It's the last time I say it, [the name of a specific person] donated the card, but not the password. Then, it doesn't work. Then you're going to ask for a miracle from God and God will not give it and you'll say God is bad [*ruim*]."[25] Cases like this which involve a direct exchange of symbolic and material goods have led some Evangelical Protestants to criticize Neo-Pentecostalism for not being faithful to the founding principles of the Reformation, adhering to the same enchanted worldview that led to abuses in the Catholic Church, such as the commerce with indulgences.[26]

Given the shared pneumatic materialism that characterizes both Pentecostal and Charismatic Christianities and TLC, it is helpful to designate Pentecostalism as a "virgophobic" religion of the Spirit and Charismatic Catholicism as "virgophilic."[27] That is, while Pentecostals reject the supernatural power of Mary, Catholic Charismatics make her a central figure in prayers and ritual life, marking a clear distinction from Pentecostalism.

There is also some tension between progressive Catholicism and PCC. Progressive Catholics have been particularly vocal against Neo-Pentecostal churches, seeing their theology as having a strong elective affinity with the individualist, speculative, get-rich-quick ideology of present-day capitalism. At best, Pentecostalism represents an attempt to "reach through divine power that which society has refused to give" to (poor) Brazilians (Rolim 1985: 90). Certainly, this would make good sense of the prominence of exorcism and divine healing in fulfilling the Universal Church's motto: "*Pare de sofrer!*" (Stop suffering!). Nevertheless, this reading of the expansion and function of Neo-Pentecostalism is too simplistic, dismissing the popularity of this movement as nothing more than the product of a false consciousness emerging from unresolved social pathologies. We need instead multicausal analyses that take into account not just socioeconomic factors but also cultural and religious variables (Mariano 2011). I will have more to say about the growth of Brazilian Neo-Pentecostalism in Chapters 5 and 6 when I address denominational and sociopolitical dynamics.

54   *Christianity in Brazil*

Neo-Pentecostals have re-interpreted theologically the notion of liberation, which for Brazilian progressive Catholics means "*a luta*," the struggles to achieve a more just and inclusive society, as a sign of the coming reign of God. For Neo-Pentecostals, liberation means the breaking of demonic bonds through the redemptive gifts of the Holy Spirit. Jesus is a liberator, not from dehumanizing sociopolitical structures, but from demonic possession in the context of a planetary politics of the spirit, a cosmic spiritual warfare between God and the Devil. For Brazilian Neo-Pentecostals, as for Neo-Pentecostals in Nigeria, Sweden, and the United States, the trope of war carries the image of a muscular Jesus, a conquering Jesus who defeats demons, granting success to those who follow Him. This victorious Jesus stands in stark contrast to the suffering, crucified Jesus of TLC and PC.

Despite clear Christological differences, we can see TLC, progressive Catholics and Neo-Pentecostals as spiritual and moral responses to the difficult conditions faced by poor Brazilians. These three theological-pastoral clusters are interested in the this-worldly well-being of their followers, even as they prepare for the end of times. Marjo De Theije has rightly argued that we should not overdraw differences between, on the one hand, PC as a modernist, elitist, disenchanting religion and, on the other hand, Charismatic Catholicism as a re-enchanting and mass movement that represents a conservative backlash against the contradictions of modernity. According to De Theije, on the ground in Brazil, "[b]oth groups have the reading and interpretation of the Scriptures as an important element in their practice," connecting the word of God with everyday life. Moreover, they both create opportunities for ordinary men and women for voice and leadership in the process of giving "meaning and form to their own religious lives" at the local level so that, from "the perspective of the parishioners . . . the differences between CEBs and CCR groups are more a matter of style than content. The idea that the two movements are fundamentally opposed to each other finds little support at the local level."[28]

The cross-fertilization between progressive and Charismatic strands within Catholicism is evident in many of the *novas comunidades de vida consagrada* (new communities of consecrated life), such as Toca de Assis and Canção Nova, which gather "men and women, married or single, young people, families around devotional, sacramental and, to some extent, doctrinal experiences and projects of evangelization" (Carranza 2009). These communities are characterized "by the small number of their members. [Because] they are more socially controlled groups, that is, [because] they are under the authority of a leader, who can be the founder or guru [*formador*], coexist more intensively, sometimes under the same roof, and share not only their evangelizing and conversion ideals but their economic resources" (Carranza 2009). Theologically, the new communities combine a deeply affective and performative (i.e., involving music, popular culture, and electronic media) religious experience driven by the gifts of the Holy Spirit with many of the pastoral-pedagogical strategies developed by base communities. As in the base communities, in the *novas comunidades* there is a concerted effort to link life and faith tightly, to live one's faith in the day-to-day, to translate one's beliefs and spirituality into a transformative way of life inside and outside the church. The *novas comunidades* also draw from TLC, reworking monastic practices, popular devotions (to the Sacred Heart, the Eucharist, or the Virgin Mary), and the medieval spirituality of Franciscans, Salesians, and Carmelites and their accompanying tertiary orders.[29] This blend of Tridentine and post–Vatican II ways of being Catholic is particularly appealing to young, urban middle-class Brazilians who are facing the challenges of a rapidly paced and globally networked postmodernity because these communities allow for vigorous involvement in larger society, but in a moral and spiritual key, stressing the renewal of self, family, and community. The *novas comunidades* might be augmenting Catholic Action's pastoral methodology, turning it into a see-judge-actcelebrate spiral, where the emphasis falls not on the task of *conscientização*, the rational analysis and critique of injustices that contradict Catholic social teaching, but on the ludic, affective, and aesthetic dimensions of living out one's faith. A good example is Toca de Assis, which was founded in 1994 in the city of Campinas, São Paulo, also the birthplace of the Brazilian Catholic Charismatic movement (Fernandes and Souza 2014). It is now spread throughout Brazil and has a mission in Quito, Ecuador. Inspired by the life of Francis of Assisi, the group has as its "charisma the adoration to the Blessed Sacrament [the Eucharist], and love for the abandoned poor in the street." As such, the "fraternity" "provide[s] a service of relief to the needs of the poor (baths, clothes, food) seeking the restoration of their dignity through spirituality and a better social promotion . . . . The most important being the presence of the love of God to them and through our company to manifest that the Holy Church has its eyes turned towards them."[30] This stress on charity and love for the poor differs from PC's critique of the structures that produce poverty.

In that sense, the theology and praxis of the *novas comunidades* have many parallels to Pope Francis's denunciation of capitalism's "unfettered pursuit of money"[31] that leads to social inequalities and environmental destruction, his renewed stress on serving the poor, and his call to take "the Church to the streets,"[32] but without the direct and explicit political involvement that was often part of the modus operandi of base communities and liberation theology during the 1970s and 1980s. Both Francis and the *novas comunidades* may signal the new direction that Catholicism is taking in Brazil, and in the rest of Latin America, in response to an increasingly diversified religious field, marked by the dramatic growth of competing forms of Christianity.[33]

This chapter has explored the multiple ways of being Christian in Brazil from a theological-pastoral-experiential point of view. I now turn to how these worldviews and ways of life are illustrated by some of the key figures in the history and contemporary practice of Brazilian Christianity. We will see that these multiple and dynamic structures of feeling and experience have been produced and reproduced—created, tweaked, contested, consolidated, circulated, and/or cross-fertilized—by the practices of religious innovators and entrepreneurs embedded in them.

3

Religious Innovators and Entrepreneurs

Brazilian Christianity from a Micro Perspective

As we have seen in the previous chapters, many men and women have been involved in implanting Christianity in Brazil and turning it into a Brazilian Christianity. I use the term "implantation" here not to echo the imperial-orientalist-patriarchal discourse of clearing a savage, empty, and virgin land and planting the spiritual seeds to harvest souls. Rather, I borrow the term from Foucault's idea of sexuality as a "perverse implantation," as the deployment on and internalization by individuals and populations as a whole of a cluster of power-inflected discursive and non-discursive devices that give rise to particular forms of subjectivity.[1] In a similar fashion, domination and resistance are inextricably tied to the "cultivation" of "authentic" Brazilian Christians in a process in which religious motivations and institutions have been closely intertwined with political and economic interests in different historical periods.

In hearing the voices of some of the protagonists in the implantation, there is always the danger of taking their worldviews and justifications at face value. Russell McCutcheon (2001) has helpfully warned scholars of religion to be "critics," not caretakers. Still, inspired by the "lived religion" school, I believe there is great epistemological value—a rich vein of relevant empirical evidence, for one thing—in paying attention to how individuals experience the efficacy of what they deem religious.[2] We can see Brazilian Christianity's structures of feelings in action, as specific men and women operate through them to navigate the challenges, predicaments, and contradictions of everyday life. My hope is that these "micro-views" of what it means to be a Christian in Brazil will be adequately contextualized and interrogated as they intersect with the scales and points of entry that I offer in the other chapters.

Given the diversity, complexity, and dynamism of Brazilian Christianity, it is impossible to offer a comprehensive treatment of all its shapers. Thus, in this chapter, I focus on those figures who have had the most significant and lasting

58   *Christianity in Brazil*

impact on the current configuration of and trends within Christianity in the country.

The Foundational Period

The Jesuits

We saw in Chapter 1 that the activity of the priests of the Society of Jesus was crucial to the process of Christianization in Brazil and the establishment of Catholicism as the country's hegemonic religion.[3] In many ways, the Jesuits have become a symbol of national identity, known not only for literary works that would shape Luso-Brazilian culture but also for their interaction with Indigenous Brazilians, an interaction which forced them to learn native languages and forge a Christianity adapted to the local conditions. This interaction was not free of domination, exploitation, and exclusion. And while the Jesuits tended to protect the Indians from the slavery imposed by the European settlers, if in a paternalistic way, they did not offer the same degree of protection to enslaved Africans and their descendants. Nevertheless, the Jesuits' pastoral work did involve an important dimension of transculturation that was seminal to the hybridity that pervades Brazilian Christianity. The key figures here are Manuel da Nóbrega, José de Anchieta, and António Vieira. They characterize the order's combination of proselytizing zeal, monastic discipline, rigorous education, and preaching eloquence.

Manuel da Nóbrega (1517–1570)

Manuel da Nóbrega was born in Sanfins do Douro, Portugal, and graduated in Canon Law and Philosophy from the Universities of Salamanca and Coimbra in the year 1541. He joined the Society of Jesus in 1544 and entered the pages of Brazilian history for celebrating the first Mass recorded in the country in 1549 in the Bay of All Saints in Salvador. In addition, he was at the head of the first Jesuit mission in the Americas, developing an Indigenous catechetical methodology that served as a model for the whole order. The premises of his evangelizing praxis involved extending the category of "gentile," which was central in Apostle Paul's letters, to the unconverted peoples in the Americas. We know about his pastoral methods through the many letters that he wrote to Portuguese bishops and to the Spanish founder of the Society of Jesus, Ignatius of Loyola, reporting on the living conditions of the Indians, recounting the difficulties of building and maintaining Christian spaces, and requesting more missionaries to cover the vast and hostile territory.

Nóbrega's letters acutely reflect European prejudices and concerns. According to religious studies scholar Sylvester Johnson (2012), the colonizers took enormous interest in the bodies of the natives, including their sexuality, while denying their own corporality. Indeed, Nóbrega repeatedly stressed the urgent need to dress Indigenous children, whose nudity was shocking. João Capistrano de Abreu, a respected Brazilian historian, accurately describes the Jesuit worldview in relation to the colonization of the Indians when he states that the Jesuits considered them peoples with "wild souls" and "infantile intelligences," who could be "imprinted" with the good, but who were prone to "drunkenness," sexual licentiousness, and cannibalism (Abreu 2000: 78). Moreover, Nóbrega detailed how he took it upon himself to evangelize and take care of *"curumins"* (Indigenous children in the Tupi language), spelling out in many of his letters some of the activities in support of this cause. He understood that children internalized Christian teachings and the order's spiritual exercises more easily than adults, who were more resistant to the new culture:

> In this house, the boys have their exercises well ordered. They learn to read and write and go very far; others [learn] to sing and play flutes; and others, the *mamelucos* [the sons and daughters of the Portuguese and indigenous women], more clever, learn grammar, and [even] teach to a grammarian youth of Coimbra, who came here banished. (Leite 1940: 45)

In several of his letters, Nóbrega denounced the practice of anthropophagy of the Indians against the Christians. For the Jesuit, the habit of eating human flesh was not justified and, in his reports, he underlines that the act was practiced indiscriminately against the Christians, even when most of them had not wronged the so-called gentiles.

> After Brazil is discovered and settled, the gentiles have killed and eaten a large number of Christians and taken many ships and a lot of farm . . . . And if they say that Christians rip them off and treated them badly—some did so—and others would pay for the damage they did. But there are others to whom Christians have never done wrong, and the Gentiles took and ate them, depopulating many places and big farms. And they are so cruel and bestial as to kill those who never wronged them, clerics, monks, women of appearance, that the brute animals would enjoy them and would not hurt them. (Leite 1940: 76)

Nóbrega's denunciations, however, must be properly contextualized. According to Langfur (2014: 5), almost no one well versed in the sixteenth-century sources doubts that the coastal Tupi-speakers ritually consumed enemies they captured in battle. But dubious conclusions developed from these realities. Conversion provided the ultimate confirmation for colonists that their mission was just, that the natives, given the right conditions, might be guileless lambs, willing—even eager—to submit themselves to church. Alternatively, cannibalism was only the most disturbing of behaviors invoked to condemn them as savages, to legitimate their slaughter, to justify their enslavement and the seizure of territory.

As I wrote in Chapter 1, in their writings the Jesuits engaged in a Catholic orientalism that exoticized for European audiences the lands and people they encountered and helped justify their missionary work toward them. Indeed, Nóbrega's letters caused admiration among Europeans, captivating them with "things of the New World" (Leite 1940: 21). They are also the first work of Brazilian ethnology and offer important insights into the formation of Brazilian Christianity, and more generally of Brazilian culture. Nóbrega's letters reveal the tensions inherent in the process of implantation and consolidation of Catholicism in the country. They show the moral and theological contradictions and ironies of trying to eradicate a behavior the colonizers found abhorrent while teaching the natives about a savior whose real—not symbolic—flesh and blood are ingested in the Eucharist. The letters also expose conflicts among the Portuguese Crown, the governors in Brazil, and the Society of Jesus, who, while collaborating in the conquest and colonization, often did not see eye to eye, especially regarding the living conditions of the first inhabitants in the newly occupied territories.

José de Anchieta (1534-1597)

The second member of the Jesuit triad at the roots of Brazilian Catholicism, José de Anchieta, was born in the Canary Islands. Like Nóbrega, he received a solid humanistic formation, coming from the College of the Arts in Coimbra. His parents—John Lopes de Anchieta and Mencia Days Clavijo y Lerena—who knew Ignatius of Loyola's family, taught him how to read at an early age. Deeply influenced by the Renaissance, Anchieta eventually mastered Latin, Greek, and Hebrew under the tutelage of the Dominicans (Navarro 2006). He entered the Society of Jesus in 1551, arriving as a young novice in Brazil in 1553 in Salvador, alongside other Jesuits in the fleet of the second governor-general of the country, Duarte da Costa (Navarro 1997). The young Anchieta suffered from scoliosis and doctors in Portugal recommended that he seek tropical air. The need to take care of his health thus coincided felicitously with Nóbrega's requests for help in carrying out the work of evangelization in Brazil.

Religious Innovators and Entrepreneurs

After a few months in Salvador, Anchieta moved to the captaincy of São Vicente, where on January 25, 1554—on the day the Catholic Church celebrates Apostle Paul—he said a Mass inaugurating the first Jesuit college, in effect laying the foundations for São Paulo, now the most populous city in South America. Around 1570, he headed back north, becoming the director of the Jesuit college in Rio de Janeiro. During his administration, Anchieta actively encouraged missionary work among the Indians, including the creation of new villages to concentrate and catechize them, and the organization of expeditions throughout the territory in order to bring Indigenous groups in the interior to settlements in the coastal region (Barbosa 2006: 41). Anchieta also worked with Nóbrega in crafting a peace treaty with the Tamoios Indians (also called Tupinambás), ensuring the stability of the European settlement in Rio de Janeiro.

Jesuit reports highlight Anchieta's eloquence and charisma, which were critical in successful negotiation with the natives (Franco 1898). On several occasions, the priest was threatened with death, as the Tamoios had a deep distrust of the Portuguese settlers and were disgusted by their slavery practices. For this reason, they tended to ally themselves with French Calvinist Nicholas de Villegagnon, whose brief biography I will present later on. The disputes between Portuguese and French in the "French Antarctic"[4] commanded by Villegagnon lasted approximately seven years. Anchieta collaborated with Governor Mem de Sá (1500–1572), sent by the Portuguese Crown to put an end to Villegagnon's expeditionary experience, playing an instrumental role in the eventual expulsion of the French Calvinists (see Chapters 1 and 5). In fact, Anchieta was present at the execution of Jacques Le Balleur, a Huguenot missionary who came with Villegagnon, at the hands of Mem de Sá. More importantly, Anchieta contributed decisively to the success of the peace treaty with the Tamoios: he approached the Indians skillfully using religious symbols and experimenting with inculturated ways of translating the Christian gospel. Anchieta drew from Christian notions of heaven and hell, punishment, grace, healing, and God's promise of salvation at the end of times, notions which not only resonated with the symbolic universe of the Tamoios but also re-signified them in Christian terms.

A priest of the Society wrote the following regarding the conflicts between the Tamoios and the Portuguese and Anchieta's modus operandi:

> Great was the hatred that the Tamoyos of Rio de Janeiro had to these [attempts to secure] peace. So, they set their minds to stop them. Eight canoes full of Indians came to kill him [Anchieta], jumping on land full of wrath, with the arches made, they sought him. Arriving before him, the Father spoke to them. His words had such a force that the Indians, tamed and amazed, left, saying

62 *Christianity in Brazil*

rightly that what was said of him (that he tied the hands of men), without doing him any harm. (Franco 1898: 33)

After the establishment of the peace treaty, Anchieta continued his work of catechization, maintaining a cordial relationship with the Indians, despite the fact that they perished in large numbers because of the diseases introduced by the Europeans. Franco (1898: 35) writes that "He had so much love for the Indians and they for him, that there were many tears from both sides: they wept at becoming separated from their elder father, who divined their future successes, taught them holy things, and healed them and consoled in their disease."

In one of his letters, Anchieta criticized the conduct of the Portuguese colonizers with the Indians, who in his view were tricked by the Portuguese as part of a strategy to divide and enslave them.

the Portuguese go to the hinterland and deceive these people, telling them to come with them to the sea and that they will be in their villages as they are in their land and would be their neighbors. The Indians, believing that it is true, come with them and the Portuguese, in case the Indians change their minds, very quickly dismantle their fields and thus they bring them, and when the Indians reach the sea they [the Portuguese] divide them among themselves, some take the women, others the husbands, others the children and sell them. (Anchieta 1933: 381–2)

Beyond his letters, Anchieta is recognized for his excellent grasp of the Tupi language, for which he composed grammatical guides that were crucial to the missionary work of the Society of Jesus and the implantation of Christianity in Brazil. Of particular note are *Diálogos de Fé* (Faith Dialogues) and *Arte de gramática da língua mais usada na costa do Brasil* (Arts of the Grammar of the Most Used Language in the Coast of Brazil), the latter of which circulated widely in the territories and Portugal.

As Christianity gained a firmer foothold in Brazil, Anchieta traveled throughout the country as a Jesuit provincial, leaving his mark at every step. When he died in the state of Espírito Santo in 1597, Bartolomeu Simões Pereira, prelate of Rio de Janeiro, proclaimed him "Apostle of Brazil." Today, in a city called Anchieta, which the Jesuit founded in 1569 during his many travels, there is a prominent national shrine consecrated in his honor, part of a large collection of buildings owned by the Jesuits throughout Espírito Santo.[5] Although a Spanish national, Anchieta is considered the third Brazilian Catholic saint, having been canonized by Pope Francis in April 2014. In 2015, the National Conference of

Bishops of Brazil declared him the country's co-patron. All of these titles attest to Anchieta's profound influence on Brazilian Christianity.

Antônio Vieira (1608–1697)

Antônio Vieira was, in effect, the first Jesuit trained in Brazil. He arrived from Lisbon at the age of six, with his family. His father, Cristóvão Vieira Ravasco, was the son of a mulatto woman, reflecting the mixture of races and cultures that was already taking place in Iberia. Antônio studied the arts at the Jesuit college located in Salvador, Bahia, becoming a novitiate in 1625.[6] His great oratory skills soon gained him wide recognition and he became known especially for his work entitled *The Sermons*, a series of moving letters and homilies that reveal both his deep erudition and excellent training in rhetoric, as well as his clear political voice and diplomatic skills. *The Sermons* can be divided into two groups: the purely religious texts and those addressing political and social issues of the day, taking biblical texts as a starting point.

Vieira first preached in Bahia in the year 1633 and, reflecting the competition among colonial powers for the Americas, his early sermons were marked by a strong concern about the presence of the Dutch in the state of Pernambuco from 1630 to 1654. For instance, during his second year of novitiate, he struggled to come to terms with God's providence in allowing for the Dutch invasion:

> But You, Lord, want it and order it this way. Do what serves You: deliver Brazil to the Dutch, deliver the Indies to them, deliver to them [. . .] all that have and possess (as you have already given them so much). Put the world in their hands, and us, the Portuguese and the Spaniards, leave us, repudiate us, undo us, finish us! (Sermon XIV: 311–12, cited in Besselaar 1981: 14)

Although colonialism was driven by economic and geopolitical considerations, Vieira's impassioned conversation with God shows the centrality of Christianity in the enterprise. After all, as Calvinists, the Dutch were heretics to the Portuguese. For Vieira and other Catholics, this was a war between Christians and heretics, one that called for the unequivocal affirmation of the sacredness of the Portuguese Army (Silva 2006: 42–3).

While he did his share of pastoral work in Brazil, proselytizing intensely along the Tocantins River, Vieira is best known for his transnational activities, especially for his diplomatic trips to England, France, and Holland and his engagement with the crown and the Inquisition on behalf of the Natives and "new Christians." In a sermon delivered in the city of Maranhão during Lent in 1653, Vieira asked his fellow settlers:

> Do you know what God wants of you during Lent? That you break the chains of injustice and let free those whom you have captive and oppressed . . . . You, your wives, your sons, all of us are able to sustain ourselves with our own labor. It is better to live from your own sweat than from the blood of others. (Vieira 1966: 83, 86)

A year later, in June 1654, he sailed for Lisbon, where he successfully argued before King João IV in defense of the Natives, securing laws that forbade their enslavement and gave the Jesuit administrative control over the missions. As we have seen in Chapter 1, despite contradictions and limitations, these missions gave Indigenous people a measure of protection against the excesses of a colonial economy that was increasingly driven by slavery and big plantations.

Vieira also spoke eloquently against the discrimination suffered by Muslim and Jewish converts, the so-called new Christians, also derogatorily called *conversos* and *marranos*, following the end of the Reconquest. In particular, he criticized their unfair treatment by the Inquisition, calling for a reform of this institution. In turn, this call brought him to the Inquisition's attention, before which he was accused of heresy for advocating messianic and millenarian views in connection with the Portuguese Crown. Vieira defended Sebastianism, the belief in the return of Sebastião I of Portugal to rebuild the crumbling Portuguese empire.

Despite his oratory dexterity and attempts to ground his messianic vision on biblical sources, Vieira was sent to prison from 1665 to 1667 and was forbidden to teach, preach, and write. With the rise of Pedro II of Portugal in 1683, he regained his freedom and began a campaign to clear his name, a campaign that took him to the Vatican. Eventually, he returned to Bahia, exempted from the Inquisition's oversight, becoming the Jesuit provincial and dedicating himself to the publication of his sermons.

Vieira's biography demonstrates not only the role of the Jesuits in the formation of Brazilian Christianity but also how Brazilian Christians, from the outset, entered the larger, international conversations about the future of the religion, contributing to theological, pastoral, and institutional innovation.

The Protestants

Chapter 1 showed how Protestantism was present in Brazil from the country's inception, contributing to the richness and vitality of Brazilian Christianity. Now, I highlight one of the figures who were instrumental in its introduction to the country.

Nicolas Durand de Villegagnon (1510–1571)

The French Admiral Nicolas de Villegagnon, a commander of the Order of Malta, also known as the Order of Saint John of Jerusalem (a Catholic international organization of a military nature), came from a family of Catholics who lived in Provins, known as the city of ramparts in France. His father, Louis Durand, acquired property in a nearby village and was knighted in 1513 by King Francisco I. Villegagnon's mother, Jeanne de Fresnoy, gave birth to thirteen children and was widowed when Nicholas was only eleven years old (Mariz and Provençal 2015).

Although trained in Catholic theology, Villegagnon studied at the College de La Marche et de Montaigu in Paris alongside John Calvin, building a long-standing relationship with him. This relationship eventually led Villegagnon to be named as commander of a fleet assembled by French king Henry II, at the behest of Vice-Admiral Gaspar de Coligny who had sympathy for the Reformation, to form a Protestant colony in Brazil. Henry II had previously persecuted, tortured, and imprisoned French Protestants—the Calvinist Huguenots—whose numbers were growing in his domain. The expedition to Brazil thus not only achieved the goal of removing the Huguenots but also gave Henry the chance to compete with the Portuguese Crown for the riches of the New World.

There is much controversy over Villegagnon's intentions in leading the expedition to Brazil. Some scholars suggest that his interest was economic, that he used a religious conflict as a vehicle to enrich Henry II and himself.[7] In other words, his primary goal was to establish a trading post to extract commodities like brazilwood and precious metal and stones. Others argue that because of his friendship with Calvin, Villegagnon was truly interested in the Christianization of the Americas and the creation of a religiously free space, where dissenting Christians would not be persecuted by the Inquisition. The fact that conflicts over the meaning of the Eucharist quickly erupted in the colonies, with Villegagnon rejecting the Calvinist view that it represented simply an act of remembrance rather than the actual transubstantiation of the elements, may attest to the fact that he did not really assimilate all aspects of Protestant theology and liturgy. In fact, after his return to France in 1559, following the failure to consolidate the French colony and having been handsomely compensated by the Portuguese for giving up his land claims in Brazil, Villegagnon challenged Calvin to a debate on the Eucharist, which the latter declined. He also persecuted Huguenots, helping to put down the plot known as the "Amboise Conspiracy" (1560), in which the Protestants sought to abduct Francis II, son of Henry II, and his adviser the Cardinal of Lorraine, in order to take power over France. However, despite these demonstrations of his ultimate allegiance to the Catholic order, many Catholics of his time regarded Villegagnon with suspicion. In that sense, he reflects the fluidity and contested nature of Christian identities and practices during the Reformation.

Like the Jesuits, Villegagnon befriended the Tamoios Indians who endearingly called him Pay Colas (as in Father [Ni]Colas) (Abreu 2000: 76). However, the French Protestants seemed to have had a lower opinion of the intellectual and spiritual capacities of the Natives than the Jesuits. The Huguenots did not see the natives as "blank slates" or children in need of education, but as "brutal and stupid savages" to whom the "path of salvation" should be opened (Léry 1961: 41). Expeditions were expected to bring not just Protestant pastors, but people well-trained in the new religion so that the process of transmitting true Christianity would have the expected effect. This goal appears to have never been fulfilled and many of the French colonists blamed Villegagnon. In the words of Jean de Léry, who had to live among the Tupinambá for a time after his conflict with Villegagnon forced him out of the French settlement,

> Just as you should not attribute to the apostles the destruction of the churches they built, or the ruin of the Roman Empire to the brave warriors who conquered for it so many beautiful provinces, those who laid the first foundations of the things that I refer to in relation to America only deserve to be lauded. The error and discontinuity must be assigned to Villegagnon and those with him who (contrary to what they did at the beginning and what they promised), instead of continuing the work, abandoned the fortress that we had built, and the country that we called Antarctic France to the Portuguese, to which they adapted very well. (Léry 1961: 22)

According to Léry, Villegagnon betrayed his avowed loyalty to the Reformation. What's more, he may never have taken the ideals of Calvinist Geneva to heart:

> We soon found out, despite the rightful concept of an old writer who claimed that it is hard to simulate virtue for a long time, we perceived that in him [Villegagnon] there was only ostentation. For although he had, along with João Cointa,[8] publicly abjured Popery, they were both more willing to debate than to learn and make good use [of the ideas of the Reformation], and they did not take long to promote disputes regarding the doctrine and especially concerning the Holy Supper. (Léry 1961: 75)

Villegagnon's life highlights the religious and political conflicts within Christianity as the religion comes to the New World. His biography demonstrates the centrality of Christianity, particularly of theological disputes, and its entwinement in the economic and political dynamics behind colonization. He was a man of his times, not only driven to take advantages of the economic opportunities opened by the European discovery of the Americas, but also buffeted by the enduring force of tradition and the gathering winds of religious change, which brought to the fore new ideas, practices, and forms of organization.

Grappling with Modernity: Popular Prophets, Messiahs, and Saints

As modernity began to challenge the old Catholic order that was closely connected with the plantation economy through processes such as industrialization, urbanization, and a new phase of capitalist globalization, as well as through independence and revolutionary movements and the dissemination of Enlightenment ideas, Brazilian Christians sought creative ways to respond to the dramatic changes. We saw in Chapter 1 that among these responses were millenarian movements that offered powerful visions of an enduring Catholic Brazil, standing up to the gathering forces of secularization and religious diversification. I focus here on two figures at the core of the most significant millenarian movements and whose example and life stimulated popular Catholic devotions: Antônio Conselheiro, who was associated with the Canudos War (1896–7), and Father Cícero Romão Batista, known for the "miracle at Juazeiro" in 1889. Both figures were deeply imbued in the structures of feeling and experience of traditional Luso-Catholicism, demonstrating its enduring capacity to inspire sociopolitical action, even in the face of the secularizing pressures of modernity. I also introduce Dom Sebastião Leme, the archbishop of Rio de Janeiro, to show, that despite the overall conservative tenor of institutional Brazilian Catholicism, there were important reformers and innovators in the hierarchy at the turn of the twentieth century who set the stage for the emergence of progressive Catholicism after the Second Vatican Council.

Antônio Conselheiro (1830–1897)[9]

Antônio Vicente Mendes Maciel, better known as Antônio Conselheiro for his practice of traveling across the poor and parched lands of northeast Brazil, dispensing moral and spiritual advice (*conselhos*), and taking care of crumbling chapels and cemeteries, was one of the most prominent religious lay leaders of nineteenth-century Brazil. Born in Quixeramobim in the state of Ceará, he grew up in an intensely Catholic household, with his parents wanting him to become a priest. At the time, this was one of the few occupations that guaranteed financial stability and status, especially for a family of small merchants. Unfortunately, at a very young age, Antônio's mother died and his father remarried, changing the family dynamics. There is evidence that Antônio suffered physical abuse from his stepmother and his by-then-alcoholic father. The death of his father when he was twenty-five years old forced him to abandon altogether his studies and any dreams of becoming a priest and become responsible for the family business, a task at which he failed, falling into debt and running into trouble with the law. With the collapse of his own marriage—he learned that his wife was having an affair—Antônio withdrew to the *sertão* (the arid hinterlands), long a place populated by wondering *penitentes* (ascetics who would often mortify themselves, seeking absolution for their sins) and characterized by popular pilgrimages. By the mid-1870s, he had become a well-known religious figure, filling the void left by the severe scarcity of priests that made it difficult for poor communities in the interior to fulfill their basic religious duties. Antônio took it upon himself to preach to and advise the communities and care for sacred places, especially cemeteries, which given the ever-present possibility of death in the region had enormous importance.

In 1877, the northeast suffered a devastating drought that left many starving, and tales of Antônio performing miracles, healing, and feeding people began to circulate. Soon, people started seeing him as a holy man, a spiritual father, and a prophet sent to help and protect them. Here, as we saw in the previous chapter, Antônio's work and mission fit the worldview of the traditional Luso-Catholicism that dominated the Brazilian countryside, particularly in the northeast, a Catholicism in which the political authority of the local boss (*o coronel*) was deeply entwined with the moral authority of the *padrinho* (the godfather) and the spiritual power of the priest and the patron saint. Demonstrating the close entwinement between the supernatural and natural worlds, between the sacred and the profane, at the heart of traditional Luso-Catholicism, Antônio eventually came to be identified with Jesus Christ; people, in fact, called him "Bom Jesus."

The abolition of slavery in 1888 further dislocated people, throwing many former enslaved people out of the plantations. While deeply exploitative, the plantation structure at least enabled those under it to survive, as landowners had to provide a minimum of sustenance to their slaves in order for them to work effectively. With abolition, formerly enslaved people were left to their own devices, subject to a capitalist economy that required a vulnerable and flexible voluntary workforce. Under these conditions, many of the dislocated people began to gather around Antônio. Tired of wandering about and being pursued

Religious Innovators and Entrepreneurs 69

by the law under false accusations that he had murdered his wife and mother, Antônio had decided to settle in the banks of the river called Vaza Barris, which cuts the states of Bahia and Sergipe, in the Valley of Canudos (named after a drought-resistant reed), forming a "New Jerusalem" he called Belo Monte (Beautiful Hill).

At Belo Monte, Antônio oversaw a subsistence economy based on communal ownership of the land, where formerly enslaved persons and those displaced by the drought did not have to contend with greedy *fazendeiros* (big ranchers). Conselheiro's teachings condemned injustices and social inequalities, calling for a return to traditional moral values overturned by the coming of the secular republic in 1899. Among other things, the nascent republic instituted civil marriage and took public education out of the hands of the Catholic Church. Conselheiro saw these political transformations as part of the same injustices that oppressed the residents of Canudos. Drawing from the Sebastianismo that, as we saw, was at the roots of Brazilian Catholicism, he strongly advocated for the return of the deposed monarchy:

> The republic wants to end religion, God's masterpiece which has existed for nineteen centuries and will remain until the end of the world, because God protects his work. [Religion] has suffered persecution, but it has always triumphed over impiety . . . human power is impotent to end religion. The president of the republic, however, moved by unbelief, which generates all sorts of illusions, thinks that he can govern Brazil as if he were the monarch legitimately sanctioned by God. . . . we can see that civil marriage annuls marriage as it is demanded by holy mother Church of Rome, against its most explicit teachings. . . . Civil marriage is indisputable null, it leads to the sin of scandal . . . Without the legitimate and natural affection that your families should have . . . corruption is invading, [producing] the terrible effect of incredulity. It is in this crisis that your responsibilities grow as guardians of your families, as if at this moment a voice tells you: fathers, defend the morality of your families. (Conselheiro 2008: 149–50)

Once again, religious and moral concerns interacted with economic motives, for Conselheiro's challenges against the legitimacy of the secular republic intermingled with the fact that Canudos's communal model contradicted the economic interests of the new nation-state and of the local colonels, triggering a strong reaction from the new national elites in Rio de Janeiro and São Paulo, which sent the army to crush Belo Monte. Conselheiro's religiously inflected cries against the injustices inflicted upon the poorest of the poor in the northeast and dreams of the restoration of an imagined golden era, when the local bosses were truly fathers to their people and protected them from the harshest aspects of natural disaster, economic uncertainty, and exploitation, can be read in a Marxist key: "as the sigh of the oppressed creature, the heart of a heartless world, and the soul of soulless conditions" (Marx in Tucker 1978: 54).[10]

Conselheiro's followers put up stiff resistance to several military expeditions. However, in 1897, Canudos finally succumbed to a massive operation by the Brazilian army, which then proceeded to obliterate the city, killing most of its inhabitants. Conselheiro died of dysentery during the long siege of his city. Journalist Euclides da Cunha accompanied some of the expeditions, producing a vivid account of the Canudos War in *Os Sertões*, now considered a classic of Brazilian literature.[11] Although not unsympathetic to the plight of Conselheiro and his followers, Cunha is heavily influenced by the modern ideologies of positivism and pseudoscientific social Darwinism, portraying Conselheiro one-dimensionally as a mad and dangerous fanatic, an "uncivilized" rabble-rouser who gathered around him the most violent, "racially degenerate" *jagunços* (gunmen) and the "scum of the earth."[12] Here, Cunha was simply expressing the strong prejudices that the republic's rising secular urban elites had against rural Catholicism. Conselheiro's words of farewell tell a different story. They are words of an ardent Christian struggling to make sense of overwhelming sociopolitical and religious forces, a humble man caught between the tectonic plates of changing church and state relations and the coming of modernity. They stand as testimony to the tragedy involved in the tearing asunder of the social, religious, and moral fabric of everyday and family life for poor Brazilians in the northeast:

> I ask your forgiveness if in my advice I have offended you. Although on some occasions I proffered excessively rigid words combating the damned republic, reprimanding vices, and moving hearts to the fear and love of God, do not think that I nurtured the least desire to stain your reputation. Yes, the desire for you to be saved (which speaks louder than anything . . .) forced me to act in this manner. . . . Good-bye people, good-bye birds, good-bye trees, good-bye fields; accept my farewell. (Conselheiro 2008: 152)

Conselheiro's example of autonomous lay leadership in tension with established religious and secular authorities, who either ignore the voices of poor Brazilians or contribute to their oppression, highlights the transformative potential of Christianity. Amid his deep longing for a lost and romanticized past, Conselheiro tapped into prophetic and utopian images and visions which we also see expressed in progressive Catholicism and liberation theology. In addition, his movement allows us to read Brazilian Pentecostalism in a different light. While

Pentecostalism often sets itself against the enchanted world of Conselheiro's traditional popular Catholicism, both are expressions of a Christianity built around charismatic lay leaders who articulate a powerful critique of the corrupt status quo and draw from an intense eschatological desire. Both of these aspects resonate with popular beliefs and with the needs and hopes of vast sectors of Brazil's population.

Padre Cícero (1872–1934)[13]

Although a contemporary of Antônio Conselheiro and, just like him, the charismatic leader of a powerful movement within traditional popular Catholicism in the northeast, Cícero Romão Batista, affectionately known by the people as *Padre* (Father) Cícero, became the "saint of Juazeiro," the focus of one of the strongest national devotions. The factors leading to the different legacies of these two similar leaders are a combination of varying life experiences and politics within the church and between the church and the rising secular republic. Born in Crato, a town in the southern part of the state of Ceará, Cícero, like Conselheiro, showed from childhood a great inclination toward the priestly life, devouring the inexpensive hagiographies that circulated widely in the region. In particular, he was touched by the biography of St. Francis de Sales, a sixteenth-century French saint who was bishop of Geneva and wrote about the ideal of devoting oneself to a life of penance, abnegation, and charity. In his will, Father Cícero wrote about how reading this biography made him commit to a life of chastity at the age of twelve. Like Conselheiro, Cícero lost his father at an early age and had to take care of his family's small business, facing many financial difficulties. Thus, in many ways, their lives mirror each other. However, unlike Conselheiro, who was never ordained, Father Cícero became a priest in 1870, after concluding his studies at the Seminary of Prainha in Fortaleza. This difference proved critical to the success of his movement, affording him a measure of institutional protection at a time when the Brazilian Catholic Church was defining itself vis-à-vis the secular state and the Vatican and its Romanizing efforts (see Chapter 1).

In 1872, shortly after his ordination, he was transferred to Juazeiro, where he quickly became very popular due to his tireless pastoral work, which included home visits, counseling, and all kinds of religious and social care for a population castigated by the harsh economic conditions of the time and the barrenness of the region. In 1889, as he was saying Mass in the Chapel of Our Lady of Sorrows, the wafer consecrated by Father Cícero and received by Maria de Araújo, a deeply pious local woman, turned into blood, which was said to be the blood of Jesus Christ. Although the "miracle at Juazeiro" repeated itself in front of various witnesses over the next few months, the bishop of Ceará, Joaquim José Vieira, refused to sanction the event as legitimate, even after a commission of inquiry formed by clergy and medical experts had determined that there were no natural explanations for the phenomenon. Dom Joaquim sided with a second commission that concluded that it was all a ruse, stripping Padre Cícero of the power to perform the sacraments and ordering that Maria de Araújo be moved to a cloister. In spite of the bishop's actions, Cícero's reputation continued to grow, not only among the laity, with larger numbers going on pilgrimage to Juazeiro to partake in the miracle, but also among the local clergy. Eventually, there were appeals to Rome to recognize the miracle, which Pope Leo XIII rejected, siding with the Brazilian hierarchy. For the Brazilian bishops and the Holy See, the miracle at Juazeiro flew in the face of the effort to Romanize the Catholic Church, to centralize doctrine and ritual in papal orthodoxy. In ratifying Padre Cícero's suspension from the holy orders, the Vatican accused him of manipulating popular beliefs contrary to church dogma. These efforts of Romanization in general, and in particular in the dismissal of Father Cícero's miracle, did not sit well with the expanding Brazilian clergy, who, as historian Ralph Della Cava notes, felt that the Europeans were condescending, that they were sure that "Our Lord does not leave France to work miracles in Brazil" (1970: 48).[14] In fact, word of Padre Cícero's miraculous deeds spread through a network of local priests, who felt these miracles were an excellent, locally grown antidote to the rising threat of Protestantism, Freemasonry, and secularism.

Despite the great fervor that Padre Cícero generated and the fact that he even traveled to the Vatican to make his case personally before the pope, the Holy See refused to recognize the miracles and upheld the bishop of Ceara's prohibition. Nevertheless, Cícero continued to say Mass and perform his pastoral duties. Given his enormous popularity, it is not surprising that he eventually got involved in politics, reluctantly becoming the first mayor of Juazeiro in 1911, when it was elevated from a town to a city. To a great extent, this transformation was the result of the growing number of pilgrims coming to Juazeiro, who required infrastructure and economic activity to sustain them. Padre Cícero had been overseeing all the facilities and felt that he needed to enter politics to serve these pilgrims and the larger cause of Catholicism. As mayor of a growing city, he forged alliances with other local and regional bosses to advance common projects and support state governors friendly to their interests. Thus, in contrast to Conselheiro, whose "power base" was people dislocated by drought and economic and political changes, Padre Cícero had the support of the local and regional clerical and civil elites, support that enabled him to operate within the structures of *coronelismo* and escape the fate of Canudos, despite disagreeing openly with the federal government and advocating a traditional, devotional Catholicism and a moral outlook very similar to Conselheiro's. In his testament, he took pains to insist "in good conscience [*sem nenhum peso de consciencia*] that I never made revolutions. I never took part in them. I never sought them" (Batista 2008: 155).

Padre Cícero remained mayor of Juazeiro for fifteen years, only losing some of his political influence with the Revolution of 1930 that put an end to the old republic. He died in 1934, still unreconciled with the Vatican. Throughout the years, Padre Cícero's religious prestige only continued to grow, nurtured by other charismatic leaders in his mold, such as Capuchin Frei Damião (1889–1997), who is in the process of beatification himself. In 1970, Ave de Jesus, a movement of penitents making strict vows of celibacy and poverty in preparation for the impending end of time in 2000 (the end of the second millennium) emerged in Juazeiro do Norte, led by the charismatic "Mestre José," a *beato* who migrated from Pernambuco following a vision of Padre Cícero. Emulating Antônio Conselheiro, the penitents wander the streets of the city in their coarse tunics, fervently praying and performing works of penance. They believe that Padre Cícero is Jesus himself, part of the Holy Trinity, along with the Father and Our Lady of Sorrows. Anthropologist Roberta Campos (2000) sees Ave de Jesus as keen evidence of traditional Luso-Catholicism's resilience and capacity for individual and collective meaning-giving and renewal, despite the strong tendencies toward fragmentation in Brazilian Christianity. I shall have more to say about this in the conclusion when I reflect on the future of Christianity in Brazil.

Today, the Shrine of Our Lady of Sorrows, where the miracle in Juazeiro took place, is a major basilica and one of the main pilgrimage centers in Brazil, receiving hundreds of thousands of pilgrims annually.[15] A 27-meter-high statue of Cícero's likeness was erected in 1969 in Serra do Catolé, at the location where Padre Cícero used to carry out his spiritual retreats. He was eventually canonized by the dissident Brazilian Apostolic Catholic Church. In 2006, Bishop Fernando Panico petitioned the Vatican to formally forgive Padre Cícero. Nine years later, writing on behalf of Pope Francis, the Secretary of State of the Holy See, Pietro Parolin, sent a letter to the Diocese of Crato, rehabilitating Padre Cícero:

Your Excellency, it is not the intent of this message to rule on historical, canonical, or ethical questions of the past. Due to the distance of time and complexity of the material available, they continue to be the subject of studies and analysis, as evidenced by the multitude of publications on [the subject], with the most varied and diverse interpretations. But it is always possible with the distance of time and the evolution of various circumstances, *to re-evaluate and appreciate the various dimensions that marked the action of Father Cícero as a priest* and, leaving aside the most controversial points, highlight the positive aspects of his life and character, as currently perceived by the faithful. . . . It is undeniable that Father Cícero Romão Batista, in the arc of his existence, *lived a simple faith, in sync with his people*, and for this [reason], he was, from the beginning, understood and love by these very same people. . . . [His] *intense devotion to the Virgin Mary* marked profoundly the people of the Northeast.[16]

This letter of reconciliation opens the possibility that Padre Cícero, already considered in Brazil as the *santo do sertão*, could eventually become canonized by the Vatican. The letter also throws into relief the enduring power of traditional popular Catholicism and its paradoxical relationship with the institutional church. Even when the latter seeks to discipline and repress it, with the right leadership and under certain conditions this grassroots Catholicism may persist and eventually force the hierarchy to recognize its legitimacy, offering a way for the institution to reconnect with the ways in which Christianity is lived on the ground.

Sebastião da Silveira Cintra Leme—Cardinal Leme (1882–1942)

Following the First Vatican Council (1869–1870), the Catholic Church engaged in a process of centralization in reaction to the perceived threats of modernity. In Chapter 1, we saw how in Latin America, and in Brazil specifically, this entailed Romanization—the attempt to establish and affirm an overarching orthodoxy anchored in the Holy See and the figure of the pope. This process of Romanization often meant the delegitimation of local beliefs and practices, as well as lay leaders and organizations. Nevertheless, there were significant countervailing forces seeking to open the church to the world, and in the process, to strengthen the role of lay leadership in Brazilian Catholicism. Cardinal Leme offers a prime example of these forces. He was born to a petit-bourgeois family—his father was a professor—in the interior of the state of São Paulo, in the small city of Espírito Santo do Pinhal. His parents placed great emphasis on faith and learning: Leme took his first communion in 1894 and studied at home with his mother before joining Avila College. With the encouragement of the local vicar, he entered the seminary and his dedication and hard work quickly caught the attention of

Joaquim Arcoverde de Albuquerque Cavalcanti, who was then the bishop in São Paulo and would eventually become the first Latin American cardinal. In 1896, Leme was sent to Rome, to the Pontifício Colegio Pio Latino-Americano, which had been created as part of the process of Romanization to ensure a rigorous, uniform training for clerical leaders from the region. He studied humanities and went on to obtain a doctorate in philosophy and theology from the Pontifical Gregorian University.

Upon his ordination in 1904, Leme returned to Brazil. His aptitude for letters and humanities made him director of the *Ecclesiastical Bulletin*, a diocesan newspaper that addressed theological and pastoral issues. In addition, he founded the newspaper *Gazeta do Povo* and became a professor of philosophy of the Episcopal Seminary of São Paulo. In all these endeavors, Leme was guided by the strong belief that the people lacked training and information about their own religion. Thus, he sought to expand vehicles and resources that could defend Catholicism from the intense anticlericalism that accompanied the formation of the republic. It is in this context that Leme became the president of the Confederation of Catholic Associations in 1907, a position that gave him special access to lay movements and their leaders, making it possible for him to nurture Catholic Action. This movement was crucial in developing autochthonous lay Catholic intellectuals and in setting the bases for Brazilian progressive Catholicism.

In 1911, Leme became the auxiliary bishop of Rio de Janeiro. His tenure was marked by differences with Cardinal Arcovede over the direction that the Brazilian Church should adopt, particularly in relation to its role in modern society. These conflicts intensified when Leme, in effect, became the archdiocese's administrator, as Cardinal Arcoverde had to travel to Rome for an extended period. Eventually, Leme was transferred to the diocese of Olinda and Recife, where he served from 1916 to 1921. In Olinda, he continued to expand religious instruction for the laity. In 1916, the year he was named archbishop of Recife, he signed an agreement with the government of the state of Pernambuco for the implementation of religious education in public schools. Agreements such as this signaled a re-accommodation of church-state relations that have been temporarily disrupted by the independence period. In 1916, Leme also penned a pastoral letter which was a veritable call to arms, pointing to the church's political fragility and the poor training of the faithful, as well as emphasizing the need to produce intellectuals, strengthen Catholic education, and combat disbelief and other religions such as Spiritism and Protestantism that were attracting increasing numbers of Brazilian Catholics. According to the archbishop,

76   *Christianity in Brazil*

> We [Catholics] are the absolute majority of the nation. Uncontested rights assist us with regard to civil society and politics, of which we are the majority. To defend [these rights], to claim them, to obey them, is an inalienable duty. And we have not fulfilled it. In fact, Catholics, we are the majority of Brazil, and yet, the principles and organs of our political life are not Catholic. The law that governs us is not Catholic. The holders of authority dispense with our faith. (Ferraz 2009)

This letter circulated widely, consolidating Leme's status as a leader within the Brazilian Catholic hierarchy. Leme's growing standing within the church was matched by his increasing political clout. For example, during the First World War, he anticipated that as Brazil declared war on Germany in 1917, the conflict would affect German priests in the country. So, he arranged for the police to provide protection to foreign priests. In addition, Leme proposed amendments to the 1925 Constitution to make Catholicism the official religion of Brazil. The so-called Plínio Marques amendments—named after the congressman who formulated them—met with strong criticism from Protestants, Freemasons, and other religious groups. At first, the amendments were rejected. Subsequently, however, the 1934 Constitution incorporated many of the Catholic demands, although it did not establish outright Catholicism as the official religion.

Leme's stature was further enhanced when Pope Pius XI elevated him to cardinal in 1931. The year before he had succeeded Cardinal Arcovede as the archbishop of Rio de Janeiro. The early 1930s were a very turbulent period in Brazil. In October 1930, the old republic had come to an end with a revolution that brought the Estado Novo (New State) under Getúlio Vargas. On the one hand, the Estado Novo's stress on a centralizing, bureaucratic-authoritarian state drawing support from the emerging urban, industrial working class posed a strong challenge to the Catholic Church's place as the preeminent institution in Brazilian life. On the other hand, Estado Novo's anti-communism and stress on unity and order resonated with Catholicism's organic view of society. According to Thomas Bruneau (1974: 84), "the revolution of 1930 provided the Church, under the leadership of skilled and cunning, Cardinal Leme, the opportunity to return to the public domain: to regain the state structures in order to create and influence." The cardinal saw the statue of *Cristo Redentor* (Christ the Redeemer) on the Corcovado Hill as the quintessential symbol of the return of the Catholic Church to a preeminent place in Brazilian society. Towering over Rio de Janeiro with His arms outstretched, the Christ seemed to be literally embracing and encompassing the heart of Brazil. The statue was dedicated on October 12, 1931, by Leme, with Vargas in attendance, marking the establishment of a new "moral concordat" (see Chapter 1) between the church and state relations under the Estado Novo.

As I discussed in Chapter 1, arguably Leme's longest-lasting contribution to Brazilian Christianity was laying the foundations of an institutional infrastructure that encouraged the development of an articulate and influential Catholic lay intelligentsia. He actively supported Jackson Figueiredo in the formation of the Dom Vital Center, named after Vital Maria Gonçalves de Oliveira (1844–1878), a Capuchin friar who, as the archbishop of Olinda, entered into a dispute with the emperor over the lifting of prohibitions against Freemasons, a dispute for which he was imprisoned. Up until 1941, the center was the largest and most important Catholic think-tank in Brazil, gathering lay luminaries such as Heráclito Sobral Pinto, Hamilton Nogueira, and Alceu Amoroso Lima. The center published the magazine *A Ordem* to disseminate Catholic doctrine and thinking. In 1940, Leme also collaborated with Lima, Jesuit Leonel Franca, and other Catholic intellectuals in the foundation of the Catholic Institute of Higher Studies—later renamed Pontifical Catholic University of Rio de Janeiro (PUC)—which remains one of the most distinguished private universities in Brazil. Finally, the cardinal was instrumental in the introduction and growth of Catholic Action, a movement that called industrial workers, peasants, and university and high school students to draw from their faith to make sense of the challenges of everyday life.

Although Cardinal Leme left an indelible mark as a modernizer, encouraging the church's, and particularly the laity's, engagement with Brazilian society, thus laying the groundwork for the dramatic transformations that would follow the Second Vatican Council's call for *aggiornamento*, he was motivated above all by a drive to *a restauração católica*, to restore the hegemony of Catholicism in Brazil and to fight Protestantism, Spiritism, and popular piety.

Modern Protestantism and Pentecostalism

We have seen how, following the expulsion of the French and Dutch in the sixteenth century, it took two centuries for Protestantism to return to Brazil. In Chapter 1, I also discussed how this return was propelled by the interplay of immigration and missionary work. Given the denominational diversity within Protestantism, there were many, many actors involved. I have chosen to focus on three: one who was responsible for the introduction of a mainline denomination, congregationalism, to Brazil and who also worked to bring back

78   *Christianity in Brazil*

the Reform tradition after the collapse of Villegagnon's Antarctic France, and a pair who brought Pentecostalism, the most dynamic version of Protestantism, to the country.

Robert Reid Kalley (1809–1888)

Robert Reid Kalley was born in a suburb of Glasgow, Scotland. Although born to a long-standing Presbyterian household and baptized within the tradition, young Kalley became an agnostic during his years at the University of Glasgow, where he studied medicine rather than pursuing the career of a church minister as had his grandfather, a prominent parson. In particular, Kalley was impressed by the writings of Thomas Paine (1737–1809), an Anglo-American political thinker and activist known for his involvement in the American and French revolutions and for his *Age of Reason*, in which he advocated a type of deism built on the primacy of reason over revelation and on the principle of freedom of thought and the rejection of institutionalized religious dogmas. In that sense, Kalley offers a good example of the worldview, deeply influenced by Enlightenment notions of the value of rationality and individual rights, that animated many of the missionaries that re-introduced Protestantism to Brazil.

Following the completion of his studies, Kalley became a ship doctor, an occupation that allowed him to travel extensively and witness first-hand the suffering and needs of people abroad. During one of those trips, he cared for a woman with terminal cancer whose strength and faith in the face of illness made him reconsider his Christian upbringing and his own faith (Matos n.d.). Upon his renewed commitment to faith, Kalley became a member of the church of Scotland and married Margaret Crawford. He also enrolled in the London Missionary Society, studying at the Glasgow Theological Academy, known for a moderate brand of Calvinism. Plans to go to China had to be scrapped due to Margaret's illness. Instead, the couple headed to the Island of Madeira, off the coast of Morocco, in search of a favorable climate. This decision marked the start of their long engagement with Luso-Brazilian cultures. In Madeira, Kalley began to study Portuguese and honed his skills as a minister and teacher, setting up schools to teach people how to read the Bible, all the while continuing to practice medicine.

Protestant presence on the island soon triggered persecution by Catholics. In 1843, Kalley was forbidden to treat any patients, then incarcerated for six months, and, with his house and library in flames, forced to flee Madeira with 200 of his followers. This forced departure inaugurated a period of intense traveling, which took Kalley to places as diverse as Trinidad, Ireland, Malta, and Palestine. Margaret died in Palestine in 1851, just six months after having been baptized by Kalley himself. The following year, he met and married Sara Poulton, a Sunday school teacher who was the daughter of wealthy and prominent congregationalists. Poulton had a broad artistic training that included music, painting, poetry, and the ability to master languages, skills that would prove crucial in the couple's missionary work in Brazil (Every-Clayton 2002).

After a two-year stint in the United States, where they met some of the key congregational leaders, including Henry Ward Beecher, the brother of Harriet Beecher Stowe, and facilitated the settlement in Illinois of the Madeirans who had fled with him to Trinidad, the Kalleys headed to Brazil. The book *Sketches of Residence and Travel in Brazil* (1845) by American Methodist Daniel Parrish Kidder inspired them to choose Brazil as their next missionary field. The Kalleys arrived in Rio de Janeiro on May 10, 1855, and quickly picked up the work of distributing Bibles and evangelical pamphlets initiated by James Cooley Fletcher in the early 1850s. Eventually, the couple set up their base of operation in Petropolis, a city in the mountainous outskirts of Rio de Janeiro where Emperor Pedro II had his retreat palace. The Kalleys rented the house of the US ambassador, which was next to Dom Pedro's, a fact that allowed them to develop a friendship with the emperor. In fact, it is said that the emperor had a habit of visiting the Scottish doctor to hear his travel stories (Léonard 2002: 50). The house also served as a school for English and German children. At the same time, Robert Kalley began to publish a series of articles in the local press on religious and public health issues.

Despite the emperor's sympathy, the Kalleys were strongly vilified. As we have seen in Chapter 1 and will see in Chapter 5, which deals with denominational diversity, although the constitution of 1824 proclaimed the freedom of religion, it restricted Protestants' access to various aspects of public life, such as civil marriage, education, and even the use of cemeteries. The Kalleys' residence was attacked many times by local Catholics, who threw rocks and excrement on the stairs, prompting Robert to threaten, despite his usual prudence, to denounce publicly the failure to live up to the letter and spirit of the constitution. Catholic animosity toward the Kalleys intensified with the Protestant baptism of Gabriela Augusta Carneiro Leão and D. Henriette, two ladies in the imperial court, and with the establishment in 1858 of the Fluminense Evangelical Church, which started with fourteen members, counting some Americans and Portuguese, in addition to the Kalleys (Léonard 2002: 51, 105–25).

Their missionary work picked up in pace when, at the suggestion of James Cooley Fletcher, the Kalleys invited the Madeirans they had settled in the United States to come to Brazil. Working now in Portuguese, the Kalleys expanded their mission to the Province of Pernambuco, where they founded the Evangelical Church Pernambuco in Recife in 1873. The following notes from Robert's trip to Recife show the church's humble beginnings and his pastoral methods in getting it started:

> Small house in poor dirty street . . . . Meeting in room at the back about 12 feet square. Pretty well filled. Not expecting to be more than two weeks among them, I proposed to follow a short course in preaching and life with God. The certainty of His being-the glory of His nature-the excellence of His character. His right to govern. Man . . . Sin . . . The Substitute . . . . The everlasting results for believers . . . During the first week we had four meetings besides that of the church, . . . the members present being only 4. On other evenings between 20 and 30. Besides these I had made a list of those desirous to be baptized and I took occasion to meet and converse with them on the Lord's Day morning. . . . During 2nd week 5 general meetings, besides conversations, enquiries about register for marriages-and a large room for a lecture about Jerusalem . . . . During that week we had 7 meetings, one being that of church at which it was unanimously agreed that 12 should be received as members. (Cited in Every-Clayton 2002: 126)

Robert Kalley's ministry in Brazil was multi-dimensional. Alongside his pastoral work, he made important contributions in public health, to which most Brazilians had very limited access. In one of his articles in the "Jornal do Comercio," the doctor advised the public about preventive measures against yellow fever and cholera, diseases that were widespread in Brazil at the time. The local media often carried items about the availability of an "English Protestant pastor" to assist the Sanitary Commission in favor of the health of the poorest (Alcântara 2012: 48).

Susan Kalley's work was equally innovative. In addition to founding a music school, she produced the first book of Protestant hymns in Portuguese, a crucial tool in the reception of the Kalleys' message. Moreover, she instituted the first women's fellowship, introducing the values of literacy, education, and leadership to a group that has been central to the propagation of Catholicism, but which has not traditionally had access to power both within the Catholic Church and Brazilian society at large. Today, women play a significant role in Brazilian Protestantism, particularly in Pentecostalism, often converting their husbands/partners and the rest of their families.

Robert and Susan Kalley epitomize the charismatic, cosmopolitan, and educated leaders that were involved in bringing Protestantism back to Brazil at the outset of modernity. They "considered themselves as global actors working for the benefit of common humanity," often circulating along dense transnational missionary networks (Neilssen et al. 2011), carrying Bibles and, arguably more importantly, Enlightenment values that challenged the hegemony of Catholicism at a critical time when church-state relations in Brazil, and more widely in the Americas, were being reconfigured.

Gunnar Vingren (1879–1933) and Daniel Berg (1884–1963)

The story of the founding Assembly of God in Brazil is well known, documented by numerous sources, many of them produced by the church's publishing house, CPAD (Campos 2005; Mafra 2007). At the heart of this story are two Swedish immigrants/missionaries. Gunnar Vingren was born in Östra Husby in the northern part of Sweden. He was a gardener, just like his father. Vingren was baptized in a Baptist Church in Wraka, Sweden, in 1897, and soon after, at the age of nineteen, he succeeded his father in Sunday school. In his diary—organized by his son Ivar Vingren—he writes about catching "the fever of the United States." With Sweden experiencing a deep economic crisis and the danger of widespread famine as a result of an uneven process of industrialization, many Swedes went to the United States in search of new employment and economic opportunities. It is estimated that more than a million Swedes migrated to the United States from the 1840s to 1920s. In Vingren's words, "the greatest country in the North attracted [him] tremendously" and he emigrated to the United States in 1903 (Vingren 1985: 23).

Vingren arrived in Boston, but, like many other Scandinavians coming to the United States, he soon headed to the Midwest, settling in his uncle Carl's house in Kansas City, Missouri. There he worked as a stoker before moving to St. Louis to work in the botanical gardens. Feeling strongly called be a missionary, he joined the Baptist Theological Seminary in Chicago, completing his studies in 1909. In Chicago, he also attended the Baptist General Convention, where he met the young Daniel Berg, a blacksmith born in Vargön, a small province located in southern Sweden, who had migrated to the United States in 1902. Berg was raised as a Baptist, but in a visit back to Sweden, he heard about the Pentecostal revival that had been ignited in Azusa, California, and Topeka, Kansas, and had radiated throughout the United States. He became deeply involved in the movement upon his return to Chicago. Eventually, he received a call from the Holy Spirit to quit his job at a market in Chicago and move to South Bend, Indiana, where Vingren had moved to be minister to a Baptist Church. Vingren, who had also been baptized by the Holy Spirit, had transformed the church in South Bend into a Pentecostal congregation.

The story is told with variations, but Vingren and Berg began to study the Bible and to pray intensely for a sign. It came from Adolf Ulldin, a member of their church who told them that he had a vision that they should go to do missionary work in a place called Pará. Having never heard of such a place, they went to the public library, where they discovered that it was a state in northern Brazil at the mouth of the Amazon River. They then decided to head to the Belém, the state's capital and largest city, which at the time was undergoing a dizzying boom-bust cycle connected to the production of rubber to supply the growing auto industry in the United States.

When they came to Brazil in 1910, Vingren and Berg were hosted by Belém's Baptist Church, which was, at the time, undergoing an internal crisis. They stayed at the house of Raimundo Nobre, who was in charge of the Baptist congregation. He was initially very supportive, allowing the young Swedes to preach to the congregation. Eventually, he broke from them and wrote a twenty-seven-page tract against Vingren's and Berg's stress on baptism in the Holy Spirit and glossolalia. Upon the break, the Swedes set up the Apostolic Faith Mission (Missão da Fé Apostólica—MFA), adopting the same name given by William Seymour to his church in Azusa, with eighteen members from Nobre's church. The MFA would be renamed Assemblies of God in 1918 (Araújo 2016).

In Belém, the young Swedes experienced the usual trials and tribulations of missionary work, getting by on meager resources and struggling to learn Portuguese. Berg even had to secure a job at a local smelting plant in order to purchase Bibles and New Testaments from the United States and support Vingren while he studied the language during the day. At night, Vingren would, in turn, teach Berg Portuguese. They also faced the diseases endemic to the region and the open hostility of Brazilian Catholics. In his diary, Vingren describes Brazil in primitivist terms, echoing colonialist discourse, but also providing a good picture of the challenges he and Berg encountered:

> In truth, we arrived to a romantic world, where there were enormous jungles with huge orchids and *cipó* [a vine] all around. We had to travel all the time on the river; there was no open place where we could walk. Even the houses were built on stilts at the muddy edge of the river. We saw several wild animals in the forest . . . . On March 22, 1911, I made a first trip to a place called Soure . . . . On that same day, Catholics had prepared an act of witchcraft [*um feitiço*] against us and they wrote on a lamppost: "This Vingren is a Protestant Pope." On the following day, the Catholic priest publicly tore up a copy of the New Testament . . . . The

Religious Innovators and Entrepreneurs

work continued to expand more and more in that region [crisscrossed by] the Bragança railroad, so that many new churches were constituted, but always under persecution. It was also following that railroad—a distance of 400 kilometers—that Daniel Berg traveled on foot, carrying his suitcases full of Bible packages [*porções bíblicas*]. Many times, his feet were so wounded and full of blisters that he had to walk barefoot. Suffering hunger and needs of all kind, he walked from door to door, evangelizing people and distributing New Testaments. (Vingren 2008: 175)

It is worth noting in the quote above that Vingren and Berg understood the process of conversion to Pentecostalism as requiring, first and foremost, breaking the connection between Christianity and paganism that they saw Brazilian popular Catholicism establishing. Just as they experienced hostility from Catholics, they also assumed an explicitly anti-Catholic posture.

The work of evangelization was slow at first: in 1911, Vingren registered only thirteen people baptized in water and four with the Holy Spirit. However, by 1914, 190 had been baptized in water and 136 with the Holy Spirit. In fueling this growth, Vingren and Berg focused on divine healing.

The work of God continued and the word was confirmed everyday by miracles and wonders. A brother was cured from a very serious sickness in his leg. A sister was cured from an incurable illness in her lips. Another who had headaches for ten years was cured. A paralyzed man who was on his deathbed and could not talk was cured and later came to our services. (Vingren 2008: 177)

At a time when tropical diseases were rampant, and many Brazilians contracted malaria and yellow fever, especially in Pará, a religion that promised the cure for the ills of the body found very fertile ground, particularly among the socially deprived.

The biographical material on Vingren and Berg is not as detailed for the years beyond those heady days of the Assemblies of God's foundation. Nevertheless, both remained very active. In 1917, Vingren married Frida Strandberg, a nurse who had also received a call to go to Brazil and was sent by her church in Stockholm. They traveled tirelessly throughout Brazil, from Alagoas and Pernambuco to the Brazilian South, living in São Paulo, Santa Catarina, and Rio de Janeiro, planting congregations at each step. He also created and edited for many years the Pentecostal newspaper *Mensageiro de Paz* (Peace Messenger) and was instrumental in the organization of the General Convention of the Assemblies of God in Brazil in 1930, which represented a coming of age for the AG's Brazilian leadership. After living in Rio de Janeiro for several years, he returned to Sweden in 1932 due to advancing stomach cancer, where he died a year later.

84   *Christianity in Brazil*

Younger and more energetic than Vingren, Berg continued his intense missionary work in Belém, not only following the railroad but also navigating the waterways, going from island to island. With the financial help of the AG, he managed to get a sailboat which he named *The Good News* (Barros n.d.). In the 1920s, just like Vingren, he married another Swede and moved to São Paulo, where Pentecostalism was gathering momentum.

It is difficult to overstate the role of Gunnar Vingren and Daniel Berg in the formation of the largest and most dynamic sector within Brazilian Protestantism. They stand as towering, almost mythical figures demonstrating the missionary zeal and resourcefulness that have characterized the movement since its origins.

The Contemporary Religious Scene

We have seen in Chapter 2 that, in the highly pluralistic contemporary religious arena in Brazil, the strongest voices within Christianity come from progressive Catholicism and Charismatic Christianity, in both its Neo-Pentecostal and Catholic versions. To bring these voices to life, I focus on four prominent figures within these Christian structures of feeling and experience.

Edir Macedo (1945–): Brazilian Neo-Pentecostalism

Known for its bold character—with an emphasis on public and visceral exorcisms of demonic spirits that cause illness, suffering, and misfortune—its high-capacity investments in media and infrastructure, and its rapid internationalization into more than 180 countries, including the United States, the Universal Church of the Kingdom of God (UCKG) is without a doubt one of the most dynamic Pentecostal churches in Brazil. Its health and wealth gospel, focus on spiritual warfare, and success can be better understood by delving into the biography of its founder: Edir Macedo Bezerra.[17] He was born in Rio das Flores, a city located in the southern state of Rio de Janeiro, which, according to the 2010 census, has a population of 8,500 inhabitants. His parents, Francisco Bezerra and Eugenie de Macedo Bezerra, were Catholics and had five children, including Edir. Macedo repeatedly interrupted his studies because of family financial difficulties. His father was a merchant who did not achieve much success in business, forcing the family to move frequently. They lived in Petrópolis (state of Rio de Janeiro) and Simão Pereira (Minas Gerais) before moving to Abolição, a suburb in the city of Rio de Janeiro. Macedo began to study mathematics and statistics in several universities, but the always-pressing need to work and help the family made it impossible for him to complete his studies. (Note here the similarities with Antônio Conselheiro and Padre Cícero.) At one point, he had two jobs, his long-term job as a lottery agent—later chief treasurer—for the state of Rio de Janeiro, and as a researcher at the Brazilian Institute of Geography and Statistics in the 1970 census. The financial instability, the strong-yet-unfulfilled quest for upward mobility, which Macedo shared with large numbers of Brazilians in the working and lower-middle classes, and his experience with the commodification of desire at the state lottery shaped his adoption of prosperity theology.

Macedo grew up Catholic, but like for many Brazilians, his family's religious history was marked by religious experimentation. Before encountering Evangelical Christianity, he had contact with Umbanda, an experience that made him thoroughly familiar with the African-based spirits that the UCKG would explicitly battle. The turning point came when he was eighteen years old. His sister Elcy, who had been suffering from acute asthma, was cured during a service at the New Life Christian Church, founded in 1960 by Robert McAlister, a Canadian Pentecostal missionary who had one of the first and most successful religious radio programs in Brazil. This miraculous healing influenced Macedo's decision to abandon Catholicism and critique particularly the cult of the saints as ritualistic and ineffective instead of enabling a genuine encounter with a saving God. He joined New Life and learned from McAlister the importance of the media in spreading the Christian message.

In 1971, after a whirlwind romance of eight months, Macedo married Eunice Rangel, also a member of New Life. He decided to branch out on his own in 1975, preaching at first to small groups on Saturdays in Kiosk (*Coreto*) of Méier, a plaza in a northern suburb of Rio de Janeiro known for its intense commercial activity. Armed only with his Bible, a microphone, a keyboard, and a portable speaker, he honed the oratory skills that he would later deploy from the pulpit of the UCKG. While there are echoes of the hardships faced by Vingren and Berg in Macedo's humble beginnings as a pastor, the financial success the latter eventually achieved would be unimaginable to the Swedish missionaries who introduced Pentecostalism to Brazil.

Seeking a more stable setting, he joined forces with his brother-in-law Romildo Ribeiro Soares to found A Cruzada do Caminho Eterno (the Eternal Way Crusade). Eventually, they rented a former funerary house with a capacity for 400 people, and on July 7, 1977, they held the first UCKG service. By 1980, disputes over authority and visibility led Soares to break the partnership and found his own church—the International Church of the Grace of God—which

86   *Christianity in Brazil*

has become one of the UCKG's fiercest competitors. In the meantime, following McAlister's model, Macedo purchased time slots in several radio stations to preach to and counsel his followers, acquiring in 1984 Radio Copacabana, the station which transmitted McAlister's popular program. Aware that TV was beginning to displace radio as the medium with greater impact in the country, Macedo purchased the Rede Record in 1989. Founded in 1953, the network achieved notoriety in the 1960s for its musical programs, but its fortunes had declined by the 1980s due to fierce competition TV Globo, the largest media network in Brazil (Mariano 2003). By 2007, Macedo had turned Rede Record into the second-largest media conglomerate in Brazil through programming inspired by TV Globo. Like Globo, Rede Record produced *telenovelas* (Brazilian soap operas), which are widely popular across class and race lines, often adding explicit religious themes and combining them with TV series successful in the United States, such as *The X-Files* and *CSI*. Rede Record now has a global reach, beaming its signal not only to Lusophone countries like Portugal, Angola, and Mozambique but also to the United States. This is part and parcel of Macedo's project to make the UCKG truly universal.

The purchase of Rede Record generated much speculation regarding the source of the money that allowed a transaction of such scale. Competitor TV Globo was happy to stoke this speculation. Certainly, Macedo saw the hand of Rede Globo in the wide circulation of a number of allegations of embezzlement, as well as the charges of charlatanism, quackery, and swindling, which led to his arrest in 1992. He spent eleven days in prison, which in his speeches and writings he likened to the persecution suffered by the early Christian Church, particularly the time that the Apostles Peter and Paul spent in jail. This reading of his troubles with the law strengthened solidarity among his followers, generating a sectarian us-versus-them attitude toward Brazilian society. His days in prison also had a profound impact on Macedo, deepening his crisis thinking—his view that life is characterized by a series of obstacles and affronts—and his conviction that the gifts of the Holy Spirit offer the best way to overcome tribulations. Being arrested and put in jail was "like a heart attack. Suddenly terror. I began to experience a bit of hell . . . it was a great lesson in life, [I learned] to transform adversities . . . as they say, 'if you have lemons, make lemonade'" (Lemos and Tavolaro 2007: 20, 24).

Beyond the charges of exploitation of the faithful through the promise of cures and economic success in exchange for generous financial contributions to the church, Macedo has been accused by his critics of introducing a *"teatralização do culto"* (theatricalization of worship) (Campos 1997), a market logic that has turned religious services into massive and lavish entertainment events, such as crusades at packed stadiums and concert halls. This logic has come to dominate the Brazilian Pentecostal scene. As the leading expression of the theatricalization of faith, the UCKG has purchased and restored many old movie theaters and built large structures from which it offers a variety of religious goods, from exorcisms to prayers for economic success targeted to businesspeople. The sheer monumentality of these buildings and the spectacularity of practices have become the trademark sign of the UCKG's spiritual power and efficacy, and key vehicles for proselytization (Coleman and Vásquez 2017). A good example of these monumental structures is the Catedral Mundial da Fé (World Faith Cathedral) in Del Castilho, a northern suburb in Rio de Janeiro. Completed in 1999 and covering an area of 72,000 square meters, the temple is ten stories high and has a capacity for about 12,000 people. It includes libraries, bookstores, classrooms, cyber cafes, and a TV and radio studio, as well as gardens and even a helipad. The cathedral was the UCKG's headquarters until the completion in 2014 of an even more colossal structure—Solomon's Temple. You may recall that I began the book offering this temple as a window into the key dynamics that are defining Christianity in Brazil today. Built at the cost of $300 million and standing eighteen stories high, Solomon's Temple is meant to be a replica of the original temple in Jerusalem, as Macedo imagines it (Romero 2014). Making reference to Joseph's dream in the Hebrew Bible that foretold how his brothers would eventually bow before him after having sold him as a slave, Macedo declared that he foresaw "all religions and nations of the world bowing down [*estarão se curvando*] before Solomon's Temple." Envisioning São Paulo as an alternative global, spiritual city, Macedo also stated that he would like Solomon's Temple to eclipse Dom Leme's *Cristo Redentor* at Corcovado in Rio de Janeiro as the image the world has of Brazil. Indeed, just as Getúlio Vargas attended the unveiling of the Cristo, the inauguration of Solomon's Temple was a dazzling event attended by top political, financial, and media leaders in the country, signaling that a church that saw itself as persecuted by the larger society is now part of the Brazilian elites.[18] In fact, *Forbes* estimated Macedo's net worth at $1.24 billion, making him the richest pastor in Brazil and placing him among the country's 150 richest people (at 64th place) (Antunes 2013, 2014).

Politically, as we will see in Chapter 6, the UCKG has come to play a leading role in *bancada evangélica* (the Evangelical caucus) in the Brazilian Congress. In the municipal elections of 2016, Bishop Marcelo Crivella, a nephew of Macedo and a member of the UCKG, became the mayor of Rio de Janeiro amid a deep

88 *Christianity in Brazil*

financial crisis in the wake of the Olympics and a failing national economy marred by widespread corruption.

For all the trappings of success, between 2000 and 2010, the Universal Church lost 228,000 members or about 10 percent of its followers. In a highly pluralistic environment, the UCKG is facing dilemmas similar to those encountered by Catholicism, that is, new Neo-Pentecostal churches with a fresher appeal and more experimental techniques pose a stiff challenge (Fernandes 2012). I will have more to say about the reasons for this decline in numbers in Chapters 5 and 6. Amid these challenges, Macedo continues to demonstrate his religious creativity, business acumen, and sense of drama: for the inauguration of Solomon's Temple, he let his gray beard grow long and he wore a yarmulke and tallit, intending to appear as if he were a high priest of the original temple. During the ceremony, a gilded replica of the Ark of the Covenant which had been processing through the streets of São Paulo entered the temple to the call of shofars. With all these symbols and rituals, Macedo is seeking to distinguish the UCKG from its competitors by appropriating powerful symbols from Judaism, particularly from its messianic tradition, as a way to prove that his church is more foundational, authentic, and universal, going back to the roots of Christianity. In Macedo's own words:

> biblical faith is one . . . . It is impossible to separate Christianity from its Jewish roots. Jesus and his Twelve Apostles were Jewish, and he didn't ignore the principles of the Jewish faith. On the contrary, he enhanced and completed what Abraham, Isaac and Jacob had started. Solomon's Temple is a way to reconstruct the Biblical principles of faith as God himself meant . . . . This is not a temple of the Universal Church, but a universal temple—for all humanity, of every race and faith, for anyone who wishes to know the God of the Bible.[19]

Marcelo Rossi (1967–): Charismatic Catholicism[20]

Although American-Brazilian Jesuits Harold Joseph Rahm and Edward Dougherty introduced the Catholic Charismatic Renewal to Brazil through their work in Campinas in the late 1960s, Father Marcelo Mendonça Rossi has become the face of the movement. Born to a middle-class practicing Catholic household in São Paulo in 1967, Rossi participated in meetings and masses of the CCR in childhood and adolescence. However, he did not identify explicitly with the movement until the age of nineteen, when one of his close cousins died in a car accident and he discovered that an aunt had a cancerous tumor. Once again, we see how personal and family crises, often involving health issues and life-and-death matters, spurred creative transformations for a key religious figure. Prior to his conversion, during his teen years, Rossi was known as a very disciplined bodybuilder, exercising and lifting weights every day. In fact, he majored in physical education at the Santo André Integrated Faculty.

Shaken by the two tragedies and moved by Pope John Paul II's call to engage in a new evangelization, Rossi decided to become a priest, changing his major from physical education to philosophy and theology. What most impressed Rossi was John Paul II's athleticism, which allowed him to travel widely and frequently to proclaim the faith vigorously (Clark 1999). Instead of an old, irrelevant church, the pope offered the image of a strong, thin, youthful, go-getter Catholic. Taking advantage of his training in physical education, Rossi began to develop a style of worship that would make the Catholic body an important instrument of direct communication with God through the transformative power of the Holy Spirit. Although there had already been *padres cantores* (singing priests) in the preceding decades, he constructed a new model of priest that stands out not only for heavy use of media, but also for its up-tempo style and the content of the message. Rossi privileged above all rhythm and the capacity to move people emotionally, making religious adherence primarily a matter of emotion without great doctrinal elaboration (Fernandes 2005a). Many of his songs, TV programs, and masses involve dynamic choreographies meant to make people jump, dance, scream, cry, laugh, clap, and run in a demonstration of devotion, redemption, vitality, and health. As he is fond of saying at his events: "God will transform your sadness into happiness."

This kinetic style gained notoriety in the mid-1990s. In 1997, Rossi gathered more than 70,000 people at the Morumbi Stadium in São Paulo for an event called *Sou Feliz por ser Católico* (I am happy to be Catholic), which sought to affirm Catholic identity over and against the growing presence of Pentecostalism. That same year, he recorded the first of his nine Christian records, which to date have sold more than eleven million CDs. In Rossi's view, music is an excellent vehicle to reach young Brazilian Catholics who have moved away from the church:

> St. Augustine said that "those who love, sing, and those who sing, pray twice." All kinds of music bring people closer, so we cannot have prejudice [against it], provided it is used well. A knife in the hand of a surgeon can save a life, but in the hand of a murderer . . . . So what's important is to bring the young person to know Christ and, certainly, music is a great instrument for that.[21]

Rossi's daily programs on Rede Vida (Life TV Network), which has a national reach, and Radio América AM also draw large and loyal audiences. In light of his success in multiple media platforms, many in the Catholic hierarchy began to think of Rossi's model of the young, attractive singing priest leading large, charismatic worships as an alternative and more effective vehicle than the progressive base ecclesial communities to engage the laity and stanch the ongoing hemorrhage of Catholics to Pentecostalism. As we saw in the case of Edir Macedo and his UCKG, the most successful Pentecostal churches adopted a highly performative and affective gospel of health and wealth. Indeed, mirroring these churches, Padre Marcelo, as Rossi is affectionately known by the Brazilian public, also heavily stresses themes of healing, deliverance, prayer, and self-help in his music, sermons, speeches, and TV appearances.

While there is no denying the role of Padre Marcelo as an innovator in matters of liturgy and the image and function of the Catholic priest, it is important to note the institutional support that nurtured his innovation. Rossi received support from Fernando Antônio Figueiredo, bishop of the diocese of Santo Amaro in the greater metropolitan area of São Paulo, who asked him to say Mass in the parishes of Perpétuo Socorro and Santa Rosalia and appointed him as rector of the Byzantine Rosary Shrine in 2002. The bishop also supported the launch of the "Padre Marcelo Portal," an internet site that provides links to his various projects, in 2003. For five consecutive years, the portal won the iBest Award,[22] a recognition given to the best Brazilian websites. In that same year, Rossi starred in his first film, *Maria, mãe do filho de Deus* (Mary, Mother of God's Son), produced by Columbia Pictures, Sony Videos, and Globo Filmes. Here, it is important to underline the role of Rede Globo, the largest media network in Brazil, in the crafting of Marcelo's global image and the dissemination of his Charismatic brand of Catholicism. The network provides a vehicle for Rossi to compete nationally and globally with Edir Macedo's Rede Record.

Although consistently attracting crowds as large as 20,000 people, the Byzantine Rosary Shrine soon proved insufficient to host the many faithful who wanted to attend Father Marcelo's events. In 2012, Rossi inaugurated the Mother of God (Theotokos) Sanctuary. With its 30,000-square-meter space and capacity for 100,000 spectators, Mother of God is the largest Catholic temple in Latin America and rivals the monumentality of UCKG's Solomon's Temple (Campanha 2012). From there, Rossi holds a variety of Masses and events, including an early Sunday morning service transmitted by Rede Globo TV and the daily *Momento da fé* (Moment of Faith]), a one-hour program carried by Radio Globo with an estimated audience of three million listeners (Arêas 2007).

Despite his enormous success and uplifting message, Rossi has suffered some setbacks. While John Paul II was enthusiastic about the place of the Catholic Charismatic Renewal in his new evangelization initiative, his successor, Benedict

XVI, was more cautious about its potential, seeing the danger of the movement becoming a goal unto itself and undermining the parish structure built around the sacraments (and the priest as their legitimate holder). Thus, when Benedict XVI visited Brazil in 2007, Rossi was not invited to participate in the ceremonies. Soon after, he suffered a deep depression that brought about a dramatic weight loss. In a TV interview, he declared that he foolishly followed a radical diet of only lettuce, onions, and hamburgers.[23] From then on, Father Marcelo began to take an interest in food issues to the point of writing a widely popular book disputing the notion that obesity is a purely physical illness and exploring spiritual ways to overcome it and attain well-being. In 2010, he fell from a treadmill and injured his knee. Wheelchair-bound for a number of months, he took the time to write and publish two books, including *Agape*, published by Rede Globo, which has sold more than ten million copies.

All these setbacks point to the challenges that electronic media pose for a Christianity built around a charismatic religious figure. In a recent interview, Rossi reflected on the cost of "excessive exposure" and the relentless focus on innovation and image that privileges fresh faces and young, perfect bodies:

> I lost all necessary freedoms. For example, anything I do wrong today, everyone has a cell phone. So, a picture will be on the internet, it will be somewhere . . . . Wow, how I feel it! Going out on the streets, shopping by myself, going to a restaurant that I want, as I want. But at the same time, everything has its price. I paid that price. What frightens me most is the fanaticism. This is the greatest danger anywhere, in any religion. They often put us on a pedestal, even in idolatry. I am a human being. That's what I explain to people. Every human being, I go through pain. I never hid [it] from anyone.[24]

Father Marcelo's struggles with depression, body weight, and physical injury might be a sign that his influence has peaked unless he is able to reconfigure his message to continue to appeal to his followers. Nevertheless, his model of the celebrity priest lives on, inspiring a younger generation, such as Padre Fábio de Melo and Padre Alessandro Campos, who, among other things, have incorporated the *estilo sertanejo* (the country style of music), which is currently very popular in Brazil.[25]

Leonardo Boff (1938–): Progressive Catholicism

There are many Brazilians who have played a seminal role in progressive Catholicism. Just to mention a few: Hélder Câmara, Pedro Casaldáliga, Paulo Evaristo Arns, Clodovis Boff, José Comblin, Frei Betto, and Carlos Mesters.

92   *Christianity in Brazil*

To close the chapter, I have chosen to highlight two figures: Leonardo Boff, arguably the most globally prominent Brazilian liberation theologian, and Ivone Gebara, who represents a new generation of liberation theologians, expanding the traditional concern for economic justice to include a deep awareness of gender and environmental concerns. Gebara is also a powerful symbol of the incalculable and, sadly, frequently unrecognized contributions of women to Brazilian Catholicism and, more generally, Christianity.

Born in Concórdia, in the southern state of Santa Catarina, Genézio Darci Boff, popularly known as Leonardo, gained widespread fame for his foundational contributions to liberation theology, particularly in the areas of Christology and ecclesiology, and for the punishment he received from the Vatican in 1985 as the Holy See took a more conservative turn with the election of Pope John Paul II. Leonardo is the child of two Italian immigrants: Mansueto Boff and Regina Fontana Boff. While the father was a deeply religious scholar and teacher, his mother died unschooled. Leonardo's vocation, as well as those of his brother Clodovis, also a prominent theologian, and his sister Lina, who belongs to the Congregation of the Servants of Mary of Reparation and is professor emeritus in the field of Mariology at the Catholic University of Rio de Janeiro, was strongly shaped by Mansueto Boff's religious fervor.

In 1959, Boff joined the Order of the Friars Minor. The Franciscans gave Genézio Darci the religious name of Leonardo, in honor of Franciscan Leonardo de Porto Maurício (1676–1751), who had been declared the patron saint of missionaries by Pope Pius XI. Boff was ordained in 1964, the year in which the military overthrew the democratically elected government of João Goulart, installing a repressive regime that would last until 1985. From 1962 to 1965, Boff studied theology at the Franciscan Theological Institute (ITF) in Petropólis. The ITF was founded in 1896 by the German Brothers with the approval of Emperor Dom Pedro II. Since then, it has become one of the most important centers for theological studies in Brazil, drawing from the Franciscan stress on humility and care for the poor and the environment. In addition to Boff, the ITF counts Cardinal Paulo Arns among its distinguished alumni. Dom Paulo was one of the leading progressive voices in the CNBB (the Brazilian Bishops National Conference) during the military dictatorship and the transition to democratic rule. Boff would eventually become faculty at ITF, teaching topics such as systematic theology, ecumenics, and ethics for more than twenty years. He also became editor of the *Revista Eclesiástica Brasileira*, the top theological journal in Brazil, and was part of the editorial board of *Vozes*, the publishing house of the Franciscan Order and one of the most dynamic progressive Catholic presses in Latin America.

In 1968 and 1969, Boff did postgraduate work at Würzburg University (Germany) and Oxford University (England), focusing on the areas of linguistics and anthropology. He then completed his doctorate in philosophy and theology in 1970 at the Ludwig Maximilian University of Munich, Germany, under fellow Franciscan Boaventura Kloppenburg, a close associate of Cardinal Joseph Ratzinger, who would later become the Prefect of the Congregation for the Doctrine of the Faith and Pope Benedict XVI. Kloppenburg would go on to become the bishop of Nova Hamburgo, in the state of Rio de Janeiro, and one of the most vocal critics of liberation theology. Boff's thesis, entitled *Die Kirche als Sakrament im Horizont der Welterfahrung. Versuch einer Legitimation und einer struktur-funktionalistischen Gründlegung der Kirche im Anschluss an das II. Vatikanische Konzil* (*The Church as a Sacrament in the Horizon of the Experience of the World. An Attempt to Offer a Structural-Functional Foundation to Ecclesiology in Light of the Vatican II Council*), became the basis of his book *Church: Charism and Power*, published in Portuguese in 1980, for which he would be silenced by the Vatican.[26]

Boff's main concern in this book is a search for a "healthy" ecclesiology which "depends on the right relationship between [*sic*] Kingdom-world-church, in such a way that the Church is always seen as a concrete and historical sign (of the Kingdom and of salvation) and as its instrument (mediation) in salvific service to the world" (Boff 1985: 2). Given this concern, Boff worries that the dominant hierarchical model of the Catholic Church, with its emphasis on orthodoxy, is not up to the task. This hierarchical model either conflates the church with the kingdom, absolutizing the institution and "creat[ing] an abstract and idealistic image of the Church that is spiritualized and wholly indifferent to the traumas of history," or fuses the church with the world, mirroring and justifying the latter's power dynamics and its dominant economic and political interests (which tend to be interests of the elites), and erasing the relative autonomy of the secular realm. In particular, Boff is troubled by the prospect of the Catholic Church becoming a thoroughly mundane, overly bureaucratized, impersonal, and static church, based on a taken-for-granted distinction between a clergy with total sacramental authority and a passive laity. Against these "pathologies," Boff proposes a new ecclesiological experience that borrows heavily from the early Christian communities, with a fuller and more egalitarian engagement of the laity in the various charisms of the church. Boff sees the genesis of this new church in the base ecclesial communities (CEBs—see Chapters 2 and 5):

Many functions, genuinely new ministries, appear in [CEBs]—ministry of community coordination, of catechesis, of organizing liturgy, of caring for the sick, of teaching people to read and write, of looking after the poor, and the like. All this is done in a deep spirit of communion, with a sense of joint responsibility and with an awareness of building and living actual church. . . . The church is beginning to be born at the grassroots, beginning to the born at the heart of God's people. (Boff 1986: 23)

On March 11, 1985, the Congregation for the Doctrine of the Faith sent a notification, signed by Cardinal Ratzinger, "regarding the errors in [Boff's] book." The letter charged Boff with "ecclesiological relativism," with reducing the church to its historical manifestations, and ignoring "the universal church," whose "great task, which is aimed at interpreting, developing, and applying under the guidance of the Holy Spirit the common inheritance of the unique gospel, entrusted once and for all by the Lord to our fidelity." Ratzinger continues: "prophetic denunciation in the church must always remain at the service of the church itself. Not only must it accept the hierarchy and the institutions, but it must also cooperate positively in the consolidation of the church's internal communion; furthermore, the supreme criterion for judging not only its ordinary exercise but also its genuineness pertains to the hierarchy." In light of these errors, the notification concludes that Boff's views on the structure and function of the church "endanger the sound doctrine of the faith."[27]

Boff had already been called to the Vatican to answer to these charges in a closed-door, four-hour meeting. He had also penned an extended response in which, even recognizing "that the church is and continues to be holy with the holiness of Christ, with grace, with the sanctity of its saints and of its divine institutions," he affirmed that "the church is *sempre reformanda* (always in need of reform)" (Boff 1990: 431). Referencing Vatican II's vision of the church as the "pilgrim people of God," Boff argued that "[c]ertain institutional, doctrinal, and liturgical rigidities hamper the creativity demanded by the church in the face of today's enormous social and pastoral challenges. Theology must address these obstacles and show that they can be overcome within the church by balancing institutional elements (power) with pneumatic ones (charisms)" (432). He also rejected the charge of relativism, contending that the historicization of the church—placing it in its proper historical context through the use of social scientific tools, such as Marxism—does not undermine the doctrine of the faith and lead to division, but rather facilitates living out the gospel and achieving greater communion between the hierarchy and the laity. Boff concludes that "[the] option for the poor has led our bishops to return to a simple way of living, gospel-centered and closer to the struggles of the people" (434).

Boff felt that his defense had been effective and had put the matter to rest. However, he was ordered to observe one year of "obsequious silence," during which time he could not publish or teach the magisterium and had to surrender all his editorial duties. He accepted the penalty, and even though he resumed his duties in 1986, by 1992, he was facing a new threat of punishment by the Vatican. He then resolved to resign from his teaching post at the seminary and Catholic University and leave the priesthood. At the time, he declared:

> In practice, separation from the Church does not prevent me from doing many things. I participate in a grassroots church, which does not need a parish. We celebrate life, not mere rituals. Christianity is much more complex than a hierarchical issue. I have not stopped being faithful to Christianity; I continue participating in the celebrations.[28]

Boff married theologian, educator, and human and environmental rights activist Márcia Maria Monteiro de Miranda. He also intensified his involvement with base ecclesial communities, serving as a valued adviser. Since the mid-1990s, Boff's thinking and writing have increasingly addressed ecological issues and focused on spirituality and mysticism, linking them with his earlier concerns for economic justice and political empowerment. Drawing from Franciscan spirituality, he has argued that the same voracious global capitalism that excludes and impoverishes vast sectors of the world's population is also threatening to destroy nature. According to Boff, the unfettered drive "for maximum profit with minimum investment in the shortest possible period of time" has placed human beings "*above things*, making use of them for their own enjoyment, never . . . *alongside things*, as members of a larger planetary and cosmic community" (Boff 1997: 2, emphasis in the original). As an alternative, he advocates simplicity and greater respect for, and sense of embeddedness in, the whole of creation.

Boff considers this shift to ecological concerns as a natural outgrowth of his earlier work. In fact, he traces this shift to his conflicts with the Vatican in the mid-1980s. "When the Vatican sent me a letter through Cardinal Casaroli, Secretary of State, saying that I should study, to devote myself to the diocese, change my theology. Then I realized [that] I already had the idea to follow up on my first theological work, which was on the cosmic Christology. And then I started to read heavily on [ecology]." Boff identifies a particular text as a watershed in his intellectual evolution.

> For me, the text that marks my change was a tribute to Burle Max in 1979, which dealt with the theme of St. Francis and non-modernity. It is the first work that assumes that perspective: "O São Francisco que mora em cada um de nós" [The

96   *Christianity in Brazil*

Saint Francis who lives in each of us]. In this article, I analyze the two paradigms: modernity's mode of being [which is] "be above things" and the archaic way of "being with things," eros's marriage with agape.[29]

The guiding thread in this evolution is the theme of redemption: the restoration of full life. "Invoking ecology . . . expresses a yearning for a way of redemption. How are we, human beings and environment, with our common destiny, to survive together. How are we to safeguard creation, in justice, participation, wholeness, and peace" (Boff 1997: 5).

With Gustavo Gutiérrez, Boff has become one of the foremost exponents of Latin American progressive Catholic thinking. Following his entry to lay life, he became a professor of ethics, philosophy of religion, and ecology at Rio de Janeiro's State University. He also has lectured in many high-profile universities throughout the world, such as the University of Salamanca (Spain), the Catholic University of Lisbon, the University of Basel (Switzerland), the University of San Carlos (Guatemala), and Harvard University. In 2001, he received honoris causa doctorates from the University of Turin (Italy) and the University of Lund (Sweden), as well as the Right Livelihood Award in Stockholm, considered an alternative to the Nobel Prize.

As I wrote in Chapter 1 and as we shall see in Chapter 6, with the election of Pope Francis in 2013, the Vatican's hostility toward Latin American progressive Catholicism has all but disappeared. In fact, Francis has made care for the poor and the critique of the excesses of capitalism central themes in his papacy, echoing the concerns that have animated Boff and other liberation theologians. Moreover, the timeliness and germaneness of Boff's thought—Ivone Gebara's as well—are evident in Francis's recent encyclical on the environment, *Laudato Si.*

Ivone Gebara (1944–): Progressive Popular Catholicism

The child of Syrian and Lebanese parents, Gebara was born in 1944 in São Paulo, a city known for its enormous diversity and, more specifically, for its large community of immigrants from the Middle East. She studied philosophy at the Pontifical University of São Paulo (PUC-São Paulo) under José Comblin (1923–2011), a Belgian priest who was a prominent liberation theologian. During those years, Gebara remembers meeting

> some Catholic nuns who were very political and extremely involved with the struggle for liberation and against poverty. I began seeing that as an alternative lifestyle for me. It was not very clear, but it seemed a better life, with more

freedom than having a husband and a traditional family life. (Cited in Nogueira-Godsey 2013: 91)

She thus decided to enter the order of the Augustinian Order of the Sisters of Our Lady in 1967. She also traveled to the Catholic University of Louvain, Comblin's alma mater, to pursue advanced studies in philosophy and theology. While the whole church was brimming with experimentation following the Second Vatican Council (1962–5), Louvain was at the forefront of progressive Catholic thinking.[30] Many of those who became the leading voices of liberation theology in Latin America, including Gustavo Gutiérrez and Clodovis Boff, studied at Louvain. In 1973, Gebara's studies were interrupted by a call to take Comblin's place at the Theological Institute of Recife (ITER). The institute was founded by Bishop Hélder Câmara and was considered one of the most innovative centers of liberationist thinking. In the midst of the most repressive years of the military dictatorship, Comblin had been expelled from Brazil due to his radical thinking, leaving his post at ITER empty. During the years Gebara taught at ITER, she combined pastoral work in Camaragibe, a poor neighborhood in Recife, with advanced studies in philosophy and theology, eventually earning a PhD at PUC-São Paulo with a thesis on French philosopher Paul Ricoeur.

Following Câmara's retirement, John Paul II appointed conservative José Cardoso Sobrinho, who proceeded to dismantle systematically all the institutional infrastructure that Câmara created to support progressive initiatives, including ITER. The closure of ITER in 1989 had a profound impact on Gebara, leading her to a sustained reflection on the question of power, particularly patriarchy within the church and in society at large, economic oppression, and the exploitation and destruction of nature. This is already evident in her first book, *Trindade, palavra sobre coisas velhas e novas. Uma perspectiva ecofeminista* (*The Trinity, a Word about Old and New Things: An Ecofeminist Perspective*), published in 1994. In this book, Gebara uses the creative and dynamic tension between unity and difference enshrined in the notion of the Trinity to articulate an alternative vision of creation, one that stresses interdependence and reciprocal care. Her criticism of current power structures and her articulation of alternative ways of thinking and living only sharpened and deepened in subsequent works, such as *Teologia ecofeminista. Ensaio para repensar o conhecimento e a religião* (1997) (Ecofeminist Theology: Essay Rethinking Knowledge and Religion) and *Vulnerabilidade, justiça e feminismos—antologia de textos* (2010) (Vulnerability, Justice and Feminisms—Anthology). In total, Gebara has written more than thirty books, which have been translated into multiple languages.

98 *Christianity in Brazil*

As we saw in Chapter 1, the 1990s were a period of acute conflict between the Vatican and Latin American liberation theology. Along with other liberationist thinkers, such as Leonardo Boff and Jon Sobrino, Gebara was investigated, censured, and silenced by the Holy See. In Gebara's case, the Vatican objected to an interview she gave in 1993 to the Brazilian magazine *Veja*, in which she called for the decriminalization and legalization of abortion. She went on to affirm that the position that abortion is a sin is not grounded in the Christian scriptures but "fabricated throughout the centuries" by "priests, celibate men enclosed in their world" (Gebara 1993: 7–8).

Gebara's controversial position that "abortion is not a sin" came as a response to the harsh social reality faced by poor women in Recife, among whom she lives and conducts her pastoral work. In particular, she was frustrated that the difficult and painful everyday dilemmas in the areas of sexuality and reproduction that Brazilian women confront are not fully understood by the church. Gebara thus wanted to advocate a new theology that was attentive to gender inequalities and that elevated women, recognizing and honoring them as true historical subjects with transformative power in the same way that classical liberation theology elevated the poor and the politically oppressed. Her discourse on the decriminalization and legalization of abortion, a subject that in later decades was central to secular feminist political efforts, prompted the Vatican to silence her. In 1995, the Vatican forbade her to express herself in speech and writing for two years. She used that time to obtain a second doctorate, this time on religious studies at Louvain.

During her silence, Gebara wrote a book entitled *Rompendo o silêncio. Uma fenomenologia feminista do Mal* (2000) (Breaking the Silence: A Feminist Phenomenology of Evil). The title of the book not only marks the regaining of her voice but an attempt to confront "evil as lived in the feminine." Here, in addition to drawing from Ricoeur's hermeneutics, she engages feminist thinkers such as Simone de Beauvoir and Julia Kristeva to go beyond dualistic thinking about evil, which she argues is associated with a masculine, hierarchical, retributive worldview, and to understand evil in a more nuanced, inclusive, and redemptive way.

In an interview given in 2017, more than twenty years after the *Veja* article, Gebara nuanced her position.[31] She acknowledged that at the time of the interview she was "still a very young [*novata*] activist in feminism, and even newer in feminist theology" and cautioned against "some radicalisms that maybe are not constructive." Her remarks about abortion, which were meant to be off the record, were not "a principle from above . . . but coming more from a compassionate attitude when one sees a 14 years-old [*sic*] girl pregnant or a woman who was raped." Under those conditions, the contribution of feminist theology is "to open the discussion" and "to invite people to reflect on their beliefs." A key aspect of this reflection is the question of class because although "abortion in Brazil is very connected to the questions of social class, this discussion does not appear." In her emphasis on class, Gebara's thinking shows continuity with the themes that animated the first wave of liberation theologians.

Gebara has continued to publish and lecture widely, both in Brazil and abroad. Her efforts to bring liberation theology into conversation with feminism and ecological thinking have been truly pioneering. Even though Brazilian Catholic feminism is diverse and not all those who would consider themselves as feminist within the church would come to Gebara's conclusions,[32] she has influenced a new generation of Brazilian and Latin American Catholic theologians like Maria Clara Bingemer, Ana Maria Tepedino, and Margarida Brandão. Moreover, the original cohort of liberationists, including Leonardo Boff, has embraced some of her themes and arguments. Her plea for a more flexible approach to Catholic morality, particularly around issues of sexuality, the body, and the role of women in the church, anticipated by many years Pope Francis's tentative yet significant calls for a more inclusive, compassionate, and less judgmental and punitive church. In that sense, Gebara represents the leading edge of a Catholicism in productive flux and a Christianity built by a growing number of diverse and articulate voices from the Global South.

I hope these brief biographies of the makers of Christianity in Brazil show its creativity, richness, and diversity and bring to life the different ways of being Christian that I characterized in the previous chapter. I now would like to explore this bountifulness from a geographic perspective.

4

Regional, Urban, and Rural Diversity

With an area of more than three million square miles, Brazil is the largest country in South America and the fifth largest in the world. It is thus not surprising that the country encompasses enormous geographic diversity, from the vast Amazonian lowlands to the southeastern highlands, from the populous cities in the Atlantic coast to the arid and sparsely inhabited areas of the interior in the northeast. Combined with a substantial demographic diversity, the product of successive waves of immigration and racial/ethnic mixing, the variegated geography contains great cultural and religious diversity, often mapped out regionally. The country is divided into five regions, comprising 26 states (plus the Federal District of Brasilia) and 5,570 municipalities. In addition to geographic and demographic specificities, each region is also characterized by different economies and different forms and levels of social inequality. All these variables shape—and are shaped by—how Brazilians experience and practice their religions, particularly their Christianity as the religion of the majority.

The Regions in Broad Strokes

The northern region is the largest in territory, formed by the states of Acre, Amapá, Amazonas, Pará, Rondônia, Roraima, and Tocantins. Containing the Amazon River Basin, the region is sparsely populated, although it has relatively large cities like Belém and Manaus, which were the base of operation for rubber barons who fed the US automobile industry at the turn of the twentieth century. These cities now anchor free trade zones. The north is still very much a frontier region, undergoing extremely rapid transformations and experiencing often violent conflicts over land tenure.[1] Between 2000 and 2010, the population of this region grew at almost double the rate of growth for the country as a whole (12.38 percent vs. 22.98 percent—see Table 2). As we saw in Chapter 1, Swedish missionaries (Vingren and Berg—see also the previous chapter) introduced Pentecostalism to Brazil in this region. According to the 2010 census, this region concentrates the largest percentage of Evangelical Christians in the country: 28.5 percent. Moreover, in several states of this region, the percentage of the population who declare themselves Catholic falls below the national average, which now stands at 64.6 percent. Conversely, many of the states in this region have proportions of Protestants significantly above the national average (22.2 percent). For example, the percentages of the population declaring themselves Protestant in the states of Acre and Rondônia are 32.7 and 33.8, respectively. In light of these data and history, one could hypothesize that the combination of intense social upheaval, particularly migration, which challenges established traditions and community ties, with the presence of long-standing Pentecostal networks proffers conditions that are conducive to the growth of Evangelical Protestantism and the erosion of Catholicism. More on this later.

The Brazilian northeast, popularly known as *o Nordeste*, is constituted by the states of Maranhão, Piauí, Ceará, Rio Grande do Norte, Paraíba, Pernambuco, Alagoas, Sergipe, and Bahia. The region contains many coastal cities that promote development around tourism. This region has the highest percentage of Catholics in the country (72.2 percent), well above the national average. The six Brazilian states with the highest percentage of Catholics are in this region (with Piauí at 87.9 percent, followed by Ceará, Padre Cícero's state, at 81 percent). *Nordestino* Catholicism has a very strong popular component, characterized by practices and beliefs that are not necessarily in line with official Catholicism, but are preserved at the grassroots level and transmitted, often orally, from generation to generation. There are several reasons for the relative strength of Catholicism in the northeast. The first is the length of exposure, as Portuguese colonization of Brazil started in this region. More importantly, as we saw in the first chapter, this colonization proceeded through the imposition of a plantation system built around patriarchal relations buttressed by the hierarchical Tridentine Catholic worldview. In other words, this system depended on the penetration of traditional Luso-Catholicism in the domestic sphere—in the separation and organization of everyday life in *casa grande e senzala*, the masters' and slaves' quarters. This deep seepage has allowed Catholicism to remain the dominant religion in the region. While the corporate fabric of agrarian life was challenged during the independence period and by modernization, particularly by urbanization and industrialization, in comparison to the southeast, the region still remains strongly rural. Even so, the percentage of Catholics is higher than the national average, not only for the northeast as a whole, but also for large cities within the region. The top two state capitals with the highest percentages of Catholics—Teresina (80.6 percent) and Fortaleza (74.5 percent)—are in the *Nordeste* region.

The most densely populated part of the country is the southeastern region, which includes the states of Rio de Janeiro, São Paulo, Minas Gerais, and Espírito Santo. This region is dominated by large cities like Rio de Janeiro, Belo Horizonte, and São Paulo, the chief financial center and most populous metropolis in South America. We will see in Chapter 6 that the conditions associated with urban life in Brazil, particularly the uncertainties and perils posed by unemployment, precarious housing, lack of access to adequate health care, crime, and violence, set up a context in which Pentecostalism's practices, worldviews, and forms of organization resonate with the everyday needs and expectations of vast sectors of the population. Indeed, this region has the second-largest proportion of Evangelical Protestants in Brazil and, within the region, the state of Rio de Janeiro has the distinction of being the state with the lowest percentage of Catholics (49.8 percent) in the country, while having a healthy proportion of Evangelicals (29.3 percent) and a significant number of practitioners of Umbanda and Candomblé.[2] In this region, Catholicism and Protestantism are also challenged by secularization, with growing numbers of urban Brazilians declaring themselves as having "no religion."

Southern Brazil is formed by the states of Santa Catarina, Paraná, and Rio Grande do Sul. It is the smallest region in terms of territorial extension, but it has a relatively high population density. While cities in the southeast like Rio de Janeiro and São Paulo are highly diverse, with large numbers of immigrants and their descendants, the Brazilian south has been particularly marked by immigration from Europe, particularly Germany and Italy. These immigrants have not only settled in large cities but also in small towns in the countryside, forming tightly knit communities that preserve their ancestral traditions and languages. As we will see in the next chapter focusing on denominational diversity, Lutheranism and other mainline Protestant churches were introduced to Brazil through this region. Nevertheless, as with the northeast, the southeastern region is one of the strongholds of Brazilian Catholicism.

Finally, the Midwest, also known as the west-central region, encompasses only three states plus the Federal District: Mato Grosso, Mato Grosso do Sul, and Goiás. This is the second-largest region in terms of territory, but, like the north, it is not heavily populated. Also like the north, it is very much a frontier region with a population growth well above the national average (see Table 2). Here, it is interesting to note that both the Midwest and the north have high percentages of Evangelicals, a fact that, as we will explore below, calls for further investigation into the correlation between the expansion of Evangelical Protestantism and rapid population growth. Moreover, a good part of the region's population is concentrated in the state of Goiás, which is characterized by a large number of new religious movements, such as *O Vale do Amanhecer* (the Valley of Dawn) and *Cidade Eclética* (Eclectic City), located in the highlands surrounding Brasília, the country's new capital since 1960 and a city that symbolizes Brazil's role as the country of the future and the leader of humanity's new era (Vásquez and Souza Alves 2013). So, the correlation here might be more accurately between rapid population growth, urbanization, and religious differentiation.

Table 1 summarizes the population totals, population density, and the proportions of Christians by region in 2010.

The Human Development Index (HDI), which takes into account variables such as income, educational levels, and life expectancy, offers a good summary of the different life conditions that Brazilians face by region and which they try to address by drawing from, among other things, the symbolic and material resources afforded by their religions. Generally, on a scale of 0 to 1, countries/ regions with an HDI above 0.8 are considered to have "very high human development." Those between 0.70 and 0.79 have "high human development," and those between 0.55 and 0.69 have "medium human development."

With HDIs of 0.766 and 0.754, respectively, the southeastern and southern regions of Brazil are considerably "more developed" than the north (0.667) and northeast (0.664).[4] However, thanks to social policies implemented when the Workers' Party was in power, the northeast region has seen a significant

Table 1 Population and Religious Affiliation by Region of Brazil

Region	Population	Population density: number of inhabitants per km^2	Catholic % of the population in 2010	Protestant % of the population in 2010
Brazil	190,755,799	22.43	64.6	22.2
The southeast	80,364,410	86.92	59.5	24.6
The northeast	53,081,950	34.15	72.2	16.4
The south	27,386,891	48.56	70.1	20.2
The north	15,864,454	4.12	60.6	28.5
The Midwest	14,058,094	8.75	59.6	26.8

Source: IBGE Census 2010.[3]

increase in its HDI from 2000 to 2010, an increase that reflects the rapid changes occurring in the region. Nevertheless, we will see below that the more challenging socioeconomic and geographic conditions faced by Brazilians in the northeast and the north resonate with penitential and celebratory expressions of Catholicism, as well as with Pentecostalism and its spirit-filled worship and apocalyptic theology.

Regional Religious Diversity in Brazil

While each of Brazil's regions is internally diverse, there are shared cultural and religious dynamics that not only give each region its own distinct character but also give Brazilian Christianity its own identity A good way to recognize these dynamics is by focusing on popular festivals, which often originated from the religious traditions of whoever first settled a given region and have been reinterpreted by their Brazilian descendants. Traditional Luso-Catholicism has been particularly influential, providing elements like the cult of the saints, Marian devotions, processions, prayers, brotherhoods, religious architecture, and sacred rituals, objects, and music as the raw materials with which to craft local and regional celebrations and identities. These elements have blended creatively with the cultures and religions of indigenous Brazilians and those of African descent.[5]

Anthropologist Rita Amaral (2003) argues that Brazil has a cultural ecumenism that enables a type of cultural hybridity powerfully expressed in popular festivals. Despite enduring segregation, exploitation, and social inequality, since colonial times this ecumenism has facilitated the translation and implantation of European cultural and religious patterns. The religious aesthetics and materiality—the icons, music, foods, dances, and landscapes that accompanied Christianity in its encounter with other religious traditions—have enabled the formation of both relatively stable regional identities and a shared sense of *brasilidade* (Brazilianness). Furthermore, this religious materiality interacts closely with secular institutions and practices, such as capitalism and tourism, leading to the constant conversion of sacred goods into art, commodities, and/or money, and vice versa. According to the Ministry of Tourism, in the year 2014, approximately eighteen million people traveled throughout Brazil motivated by faith. The calendar of tourist events organized by the Ministry showed that in 2016 approximately 17 percent of events were related to popular religious festivals and sites of pilgrimage.[6]

106   *Christianity in Brazil*

The best example of shared Brazilianness is the Shrine of Aparecida do Norte in the interior of the state of São Paulo, which brings together some twelve million visitors a year, especially to celebrate the feast of the patroness of Brazil on October 12, a day that is also a national holiday. Another set of religiously inflected festivals that are widely celebrated throughout Brazil are the *festas juninas* (the June festivals) in honor of St. John the Baptist, though they also involve homages to St. Anthony and St. Peter, who are recognized in the Catholic liturgical calendar during that month (Rangel 2008). Like many Catholic festivals, the *festas juninas* are strongly associated with agriculture and the cycles of nature. They also blend, at turns seamlessly and at other times uncomfortably, the religious and the secular. Originally, the festivals marked the middle of the summer in Portugal, but in Brazil, they signal the beginning of winter and the gathering of the harvest. In fact, the festivals can be seen as a celebration of rural life, with people dressing up as *matutas* (hillbillies). Each region celebrates these festivals with its own idiosyncrasies down to the food. For instance, in the south and southeast, where temperatures can drop significantly during winter, it is common to drink *quentão* (mulled wine), build and dance around bonfires, and gather to watch elaborate firework displays. In the northeast, *festas juninas* coincide with the end of the rainy season and, in addition to thanking St. John for bringing life-giving rains, they celebrate abundance, with corn and sugar cane at the center of the celebrations. This is the time to enjoy *canjica de milho* or *munguzá doce* (sweet corn-coconut pudding). The northeast is also particularly known for colorful and elaborate square dances, where large synchronized *quadrilhas* (dance troupes) dance to country tunes, all dressed up in stylized peasant attire.

In addition to these nationally shared expressions of Brazilian Christianity, each region of the country inflects Christianity in its own way. I noted above how the northeast is the most Catholic region of Brazil. Central to this Catholicism is the widespread practice of pilgrimages (*romarias*) to sacred places that populate the landscape. In Chapter 2, we discussed how the indigenization of traditional Luso-Catholicism took place in the vacuum left by the scarcity of priests to perform the sacraments for communities scattered throughout the interior. We also saw how this Catholicism tends to oscillate between celebration and penance, reflecting the unpredictability and harshness of the climate and terrain and the capacity of its inhabitants to endure. So, it is not surprising to encounter many miracles in this region—rains that come out of nowhere, bread that multiplies and feeds many, Holy Hosts who transform into blood—amid the ever-present danger of drought or famine, nor to see people gravitating to

Regional, Urban, and Rural Diversity   107

figures and places associated with these miracles. In the previous chapter, we highlighted the figure of Padre Cícero as one of the forgers of grassroots popular Catholic devotions. Indeed, Juazeiro do Norte, which he oversaw as mayor for a couple of decades, is a major center of pilgrimage in the region. For more than 120 years now, pilgrims have been traveling, often traversing long distances by foot, every March to celebrate Padre Cícero's miracle. Very often, the pilgrims fast during the trip, or walk on their knees or carry heavy stones on their backs for part of the journey as a way to atone for their sins, ask for intercession from Padre Cícero, or fulfill a *promessa* (a vow) to him. These days, it is estimated that close to 2.5 million people come to the city during the celebrations. Padre Cícero also encouraged other pilgrimages to Juazeiro, including the Romaria dos Finados, paying tribute to the dead and to Nossa Senhora das Dores (Our Lady of Sorrows) in November, and the Romaria da Nossa Senhora das Candeias (Our Lady of the Candles) in February, in which thousands of people process through the streets of Juazeiro, candles in hand.

In the *Nordeste*, this penitential Catholicism is dynamically complemented by the celebratory Catholicism of festivals like the *folia dos reis* (literally, the revelry of the kings) which takes place on January 6, commemorating the Three Magi's visitation of the newly born Messiah. At the heart of the *folia* is the exchange of symbolic and material gifts between God and the believers and between performers and participants in the festival. The exchanges are consummated performatively, through music (with local instruments like accordions, *sanfonas* [concertinas], and *violas caipiras* [country guitars]), dance, and parading all decked in colorful attire (dressed as clowns and royalty). The *folia dos reis* is celebrated with variations throughout Brazil, but arguably the most nationally prominent version is the *Reisado* of Garanhuns, a city in the northeastern state of Pernambuco, which is in the process of being officially declared part of the national cultural heritage.[7]

As the sentence above implies, this is not to say that festivals, pilgrimages, and processions only take place in the northeast. In fact, each region has its pilgrimage centers and traditional religious celebrations. For example, the penitential dimension of Brazilian traditional popular Catholicism is arguably best illustrated by the *procissão do fogaréu* (the procession of the torches), a more than two-centuries-old march in the midwestern city of Goiás, in which the faithful, traditionally men, re-enact Christ's arrest on Holy Thursday. The so-called *farricocos*, hooded figures standing for Roman soldiers and Jesus Christ's accusers, set out at midnight in procession toward the Garden of Olives, represented by the St. Francis of Paula Church. The procession alternates among periods of intense

108   *Christianity in Brazil*

expiatory prayer, solemn silence, and the sounding of the *matraca* (rattle), the latter meant to ward off the Devil, who is thought to be loose on the streets. The precise date of the first procession of torches is unknown, but there is consensus among scholars that the tradition was introduced in the eighteenth century by the Spanish priest João Perestrello Vasconcelos Spindola who founded the *Irmandade do Senhor dos Passos* (the Brotherhood of the Lord of the Steps) as a way to rebuild his church. This brotherhood established and spread the procession.[8]

In the north, the most well-known Catholic festival is Círio de Nazaré (in Belém), which attracts more than a million pilgrims. The massive celebrations revolve around the wooden image of Nossa Senhora de Nazaré (a dark-skinned Mary seated and nursing baby Jesus), which was found by a lowly *caboclo* (descendant of Portuguese and Indigenous parents) in 1700, after mysteriously traveling from Nazareth to Portugal, where it performed miracles before re-appearing in Brazil. Included in the celebrations is a river procession of hundreds of boats (after all, Nossa Senhora de Nazaré is not only the patroness of Pará but also of sailors). The island-hopping missionary work of Daniel Berg, one of the founders of Brazilian Pentecostalism (see Chapter 3), mirrors the fluvial travels of Our Lady of Nazareth. In both cases, the extension and topography of the region impose certain demands on religious practice, affording a network of rivers as a way for Christianity to move.

While pilgrimage, processions, and festivals are part and parcel of various regional expressions of popular Catholicism, particularly in the northeast, they are very often influenced by elements of Afro-Brazilian culture and religion. This is especially the case near the Atlantic coast in the states of Bahia and Pernambuco. For instance, the Feast do Nosso Senhor de Bonfim (the Lord of Good End) in Salvador, Bahia, a city that received close to two million of the estimated four million slaves who were brought to Brazil, combines elements of traditional popular Catholicism and Candomblé.[9] In early January, in preparation for the feast, Candomblé practitioners, dressed in all white, wash the steps of the church of Nosso Senhor de Bonfim with perfumed water, ritually reenacting through song and dance what their enslaved ancestors did, commanded by the members of the fraternity in charge of the celebrations. The Lord of Good End (i.e., the crucified-risen Jesus Christ) is associated with Oxalá, the father of all *orixás* (ancestor spirits or divinities in West African Yoruba religion) and the creator of humans, who represents, among other things, purity (ergo white is his color).

Catholic festivals in the northeast not only blend with Afro-Brazilian cultural and religious aspects, but also popular culture, entertainment, and media, as tourists come to the region to enjoy its tropical climate, beautiful beaches, and enticing cuisine, and along the way participate in the religious celebrations. Sometimes the religious celebrations blend into the Carnival, which, after all, had a religious origin, marking the start of Lent (thus following once again the oscillation between celebration, abundance, and excess on the one hand, and on the other hand, penance, scarcity, and restraint that characterizes popular traditional Catholicism). In Pernambuco, for example, the Carnival is known because it features *frevo*, a style of music and dance that combines ballet with *capoeira* (an Afro-Brazilian martial art) to the tune of martial music, echoing the marches that the Brazilian military used to play at traditional religious processions.

Christianity presents specificities in other regions of Brazil. As we saw in Chapters 1 and 3, particularly in the sections that discussed the early Jesuit missions and the Protestant experiments in the França Antártica, indigenous groups played a central role in the formation of Brazilian Christianity. However, these coastal populations were quickly decimated by the conquest and colonization. In the interior of Brazil, especially in Amazonia in the country's northern region and other borderlands at the "edge of the empire," indigenous communities were able to subsist, and even thrive, establishing dense fluvial networks of trade and mobility that brought different groups together in a process of ethnogenesis (Prado 2015; Roller 2014). These groups have continued to contribute to the Brazilian religious field, and more specifically to Brazilian Christianity, in significant ways. A good case in point is ayahuasca religions, such as *Santo Daime, União do Vegetal* (Union of the Vegetable), and *Barquinha* (Little Ship).[10] These religions are built around the ritual production and consumption of a psychoactive brew out of the leaves and roots of Amazonian plants, a brew that has been part of the healing and prophetic work of indigenous shamans and that was passed on to *caboclos* and other Brazilians as they ventured into the forest to collect rubber, mine, build roads and large dams, or, more recently, as they have come as religious tourists to fulfill a nostalgia for Brazil unspoiled by European modernity.[11] To various degrees, these religions mix what anthropologist Eduardo Viveiros de Castro (1992) has termed indigenous "multinaturalism," the notion that humans, nonhuman animals, and plants in the forest share a common spiritual substrate that can allow for the passage from one physical form to another, with Catholic beliefs about the sacred power and mediating role of saints.[12] In Santo Daime, for example, ayahuasca is equated with Jesus in its power to heal and to provide enlightenment, a deep connection with all the universe. Marijuana, which is also used in Daime rituals, is often associated with the Virgin Mary (called *Santa Maria*). Moreover, the prayers recited during the preparation of ayahuasca very prominently include Hail Marys, Our Fathers, and a novena called "*cerco de Jericó*" (literally, the siege of Jericho), a weeklong prayer very common among Charismatic Catholics engaged in spiritual warfare (seeking to break "the walls" of sin and vice that affect family and professional life). The ingestion of ayahuasca is also construed in a sacramental way similar to taking Communion. While many indigenous people who have converted to Evangelical Protestantism would reject these sorts of syncretic practices, their Christianity also contains strong elements of indigenous traditions, including transposing the figure of the shaman onto the pastor baptized by the Holy Spirit, healing, chanting halleluiah, and prophesizing (Vilaça and Wright 2016).

The 2010 census found that of the 817,963 people who declared themselves indigenous, 51 percent are Catholics (down from 58.9 percent in 2000) and 25 percent are Evangelical Protestants (up from approximately 20 percent in 2000). While these figures generally mirror tendencies for the Brazilian population as a whole, they show a more rapid erosion of Catholicism among indigenous peoples. These numbers, however, should be taken with a grain of salt, as anthropologists like Robin Wright have pointed to the multiple understandings of conversion among indigenous people, understandings that are often not in line with those of Christian missionaries. Indigenous responses to Christianity run the gamut "from total rejection of the Christian doctrine although expressing a *pragmatic* interest in the assistance offered by the missionaries, to an absolute embodiment of Christian beliefs and practices, providing a field for the reformulation of social and ethnic identity" (Wright 2017: 5). In the meantime, the percentage native Brazilians who declared themselves as followers of "Indigenous traditions" has grown significantly from 1.4 percent in 2000 to 5.3 percent in 2010 (Pissolato 2013: 242). This growth might point to a recovery and revitalization of these traditions.

One last specificity worth mentioning is subregional: *catolicismo mineiro*, the Catholicism of the southeastern state of Minas Gerais. If the Catholicism of the northeast was strongly conditioned by the sociocultural dynamics of the plantation and harsh geography of the *sertão*, Catholicism in Minas was built by fiercely independent settlers, who had come to find riches by prospecting for gold and precious stones, and who eventually amassed the financial resources to address the lack of priests. As the mining economy stabilized, slaves were brought in large numbers and *catolicismo mineiro* organized itself in influential brotherhoods (*irmandades* and *confrarias*) that oversaw their towns' devotions to patron saints. These brotherhoods built ornate baroque chapels and organized lavish festivals

Regional, Urban, and Rural Diversity   111

in honor of the saints. The *irmandades* also reflected and contributed to social divisions and hierarchies, organizing themselves according to race, occupation, and economic status (Ribeiro de Oliveira 1985). Thus, the paradoxical result of this *catolicismo mineiro* was, on the one hand, the reproduction of slavery and, on the other hand, the creation and preservation of Afro-Catholic identities. Black brotherhoods like *Irmandade da Nossa Senhora do Rosário dos Pretos* (Our Lady of the Rosary of the Black Ones), *Santa Efigênia* (Saint Ephigenia, an early Ethiopian convert to Christianity), and *São José dos Homens Pardos e Bem Casados* (St. Joseph of the Colored and Well-Married Men) formed by *negros de ganho*— slaves who were able to earn extra money outside the obligatory work for their masters and thus eventually buy their freedom—gained great prominence. These *irmandades* blended Iberian popular Catholicism with African beliefs, symbols, and practices in creative and dynamic ways that persist to this day (Gomes 2010). As we saw in Chapter 2, these brotherhoods often stood in tension with the clergy and church hierarchy and became vehicles of resistance to the Vatican's attempt to Romanize Brazilian Catholicism (De Theije 1990).

The showcase of Minas Catholicism is the *Estrada Real* (the Royal Road), which links the towns of Ouro Preto and Mariana to Diamantina. With close to eighty colonial chapels, churches, and oratories containing altars sumptuously decorated in gold and the intricate sculptures of Aleijadinho,[13] a famous artist who lived in the eighteenth century, Ouro Preto (literally Black Gold) is singularly striking. It has been designated a world heritage site by UNESCO.

Just as the interpenetration of Catholicism and the plantation economy gave Catholicism in northeastern Brazil a durability that made the region a Catholic stronghold, the tight connection between *catolicismo mineiro* and economic and cultural life in towns like Ouro Preto made this subregion, particularly the smaller and older villages, more resistant to Pentecostalism (Junior 2008).

Having given a descriptive sense of the richness and vivacity of Christianity in the various regions of Brazil, I will go now to delve more deeply into the census to analyze the spatial dynamics of growth and decline of Catholicism and Protestantism by region.

Catholics, Evangelicals, and "No Religion": A Regional View[14]

Antonio Pierucci (2004) argues that the most salient trend in the sociology of religion in Brazil is a process of "detraditionalization," marked by the decline of Catholicism and the diversification of the Brazilian religious field.[15] This decline

112 *Christianity in Brazil*

and diversification, which is most dramatically illustrated by the rapid expansion of Evangelical Protestantism, can be tracked by region.

Table 2 confirms the hypothesis I posed above that accelerated population growth, particularly driven by internal migration, is strongly correlated with the rapid growth of Evangelical Protestantism and the steep decline of Catholicism. Between 2000 and 2010, the two regions that had the highest population growth—the north (22.98 percent) and the Midwest (20.7 percent)—also registered the most significant expansion in Evangelical Protestantism: 8.7 percent for the north and 7.9 percent for the Midwest. Correspondingly, Catholicism had the sharpest declines in the north and Midwest, as well as in the southeast, although the erosion in the latter could be more attributed to the process of secularization and religious fragmentation that normally accompanies large and highly differentiated cities like Rio de Janeiro, São Paulo, and Belo Horizonte. Table 2 also shows that the decline in the proportion of Catholics is slower in the northeast and south than in the rest of the country, confirming the relative resilience of the tradition in these regions.

To have a fuller understanding of the changing place of Catholicism in Brazilian society, we must take a comparative view that includes other (non-Christian) religions and those Brazilians who reported not to have a religious affiliation. Figure 1 compares the absolute numbers (rather than percentages) of Catholics, Evangelical Protestants, and those with no religion nationally and regionally between the last two censuses. The figure shows that the Catholic population grew at a much slower pace than the overall population for every region of Brazil. In contrast, the number of Evangelicals expanded above the population growth rates across all regions. At a finer granulation, we can see that between 2000 and 2010, the number of Catholics fell significantly in the southeast and south, the latter, as we saw, one of the two regions where the percentage of Catholics is still above the national average. In the Midwest and northeast, the growth in the Catholic population was, in absolute numbers, minimal. This once again stands in contrast to the significant growth of Evangelicals in the northeast, considered the stronghold of Catholicism. In other words, while Catholicism shows differential levels of resilience, there is a widespread erosion of Catholic affiliation. This overarching trend is starkly illustrated if we drill deeper, to the municipal level: between 2000 and 2010, the ratio of Catholics to Protestants contracted in 98.3 percent of all municipalities. That is, Catholics only increased their share of the overall population (vis-à-vis *evangélicos*) in 1.7 percent of municipalities (Alves, Barros, and Cavenaghi 2017: 236–7). I will reflect on what this powerful trend and the countervailing Catholic resilience in some regions

Table 2 Percentages of the Population that Self-Declare as Catholic and Protestant in 2000 and 2010 by Region

Region	% of Catholics 2000	% of Catholics 2010	Δ change	% of Protestants 2000	% of Protestants 2010	Δ change	Δ change in the overall population
Brazil (as a whole)	73.6	64.6	−9.0	15.4	22.2	+6.8	+12.33
Northeast	79.9	72.2	−7.7	10.3	16.4	+6.1	+11.18
South	77.4	70.1	−7.3	15.5	20.2	+4.7	+9.07
North	71.3	60.6	−10.7	19.8	28.5	+8.7	+22.98
Midwest	69.1	59.5	−9.6	18.9	26.8	+7.9	+20.74
Southeast	69.2	59.4	−9.8	17.5	24.6	+7.1	+10.97

Source: 2010 Brazilian Census, IBGE.

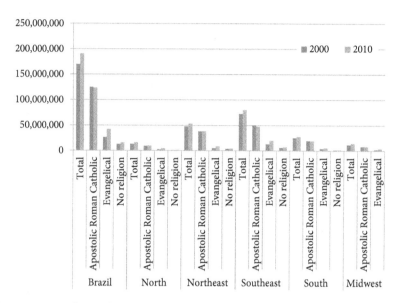

Figure 1 Growth in absolute numbers—population, Catholics, Evangelicals, and those with no religion by Brazilian region, 2000–10. Numbers on the vertical axis are in millions. Source: IBGE; Census 2000 and 2010.[16]

and localities mean for the future of Brazilian Christianity in Chapter 6 and my Conclusion.

Figure 2 shows more clearly the rates of growth of the three groups—Catholics, Evangelicals, and no religion—nationally and by region. While the annual growth rate for the overall population is around 1.01 percent, Evangelicals are growing at a rate of 1.05 percent and those without religion at 1.02 percent. In comparison, the annual rate of growth for Catholics is below 1 percent. In all Brazilian regions, Evangelicals outpace population growth rates. The inverse is the case for Catholics, who had the slowest growth rate in the southeast. Those who did not declare any religious affiliation had the highest rate of annual growth—approximately 1.4 percent—in the north.

Figure 3 gives a good sense of the religious differentiation that Brazil is undergoing at the regional level, showing percentages of religious affiliation for 2000 and 2010. Several dynamics are worth noting. First, Pentecostalism has a greater presence in the north, Midwest, and southeast, the last two regions with Human Development Indexes above the national average, while the north is below. This suggests that while the growth of Pentecostalism is linked to socioeconomic deprivation, there may be other interacting factors, such as the historical and contemporary presence of missions, the availability and kinds of religious innovators involved, the affordances and constraints of the

Regional, Urban, and Rural Diversity

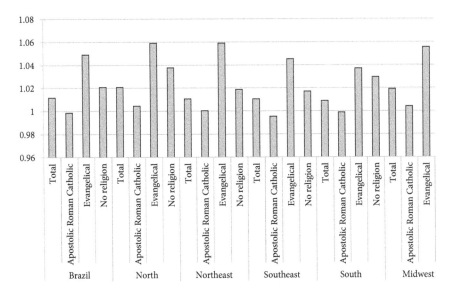

Figure 2 Percentage of annual rate of growth, 2000–10. Source: IBGE (2010).

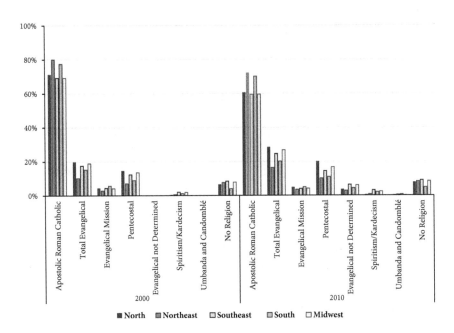

Figure 3 Main religions by region in Brazil, 2000–10. Source: IBGE (2010).[17]

116 *Christianity in Brazil*

Table 3 Religious Breakdown of Rural Versus Urban Brazilians, 2010

	Rural (%)	Urban (%)
Catholic	78	62
Evangelical	15	24
No religion	5	8
Other religion	2	6

Source: IBGE (2010).

region's geography, urbanization, population density, internal, cross-regional, and international migration, and, generally, rapid social change that have affected this growth. For example, Evangelical Protestantism, and particularly Pentecostalism, has grown very rapidly in the north, a region where it has had a long-standing presence, going back to Vingren and Berg, and where there is a more acute dearth of Catholic priests (and even other pastoral agents) who tend to be concentrated in cities or in more developed regions.

Second, the continued predominance of Catholicism not only in the northeast but also the south, which is the second-most densely populated region in the country, as well as the strength of this brand of Christianity in large cities like Fortaleza and Teresina, show that the correlation between rurality and the resilience of Catholicism needs to be handled with some caution. Nevertheless, Table 3 demonstrates that, keeping regional, state, and local variations in mind, this correlation carries some explanatory power.

Whereas more than three-fourths (78 percent) of the rural population consider themselves Catholic (versus only 62 percent of those living in cities), almost one-fourth (24 percent) of urban dwellers in Brazil declare themselves Protestant (as opposed to only 15 percent in the countryside). These statistics dovetail well with my descriptions of festivals, processions, *romarias*, and *irmandades*, which show that Catholicism continues to be practiced with great fervor especially in small towns. Rapid social change, particularly urbanization, threatens to erode these traditional, collective Catholic practices by diversifying and concentrating populations and/or by commodifying these practices, blending them with tourism, capitalism, or other religious traditions. Steil and Toniol (2013: 226) see this detraditionalization as the main cause for the continuous decline in the number of Catholics vis-à-vis Evangelical Protestants. They note that, as Brazil becomes more urbanized, traditional popular Catholicism

> finds less and less resources and traditional local institutions for its reproduction as a religion. A situation that can be attributed both to the changing religious demand of individuals, which has been undergoing an increasing process

of rationalization, as well as to the secularization of many of local religious institutions that often operate in the key of folklore, tourism or even ethnic and social movements.

In contrast, with its emphasis on the individual's voluntary profession of faith and its stress on the scriptures, Evangelical Protestantism finds a fertile environment in the rationalized and secularized city. Indeed, the percentage of Protestants who are urban dwellers quadrupled, going from 6 to 24 percent from 1970 to 2010, while the number of Catholics living in cities decreased by twenty-eight points (from 90 to 62 percent) during the same period (Pew Research Center 2013).

Camurça (2013: 64) puts things well when he states that while Pentecostalism grew in all regions of the country, the fastest expansion took place in the "Pentecostal Ring" constituted by the peripheries of large cities and "the agricultural and mining frontiers of the North and the Midwest of Brazil." Camurça goes on to observe that in these urban peripheries and frontier regions, like the north and the Midwest, the Catholic Church is not well equipped to deal with the dramatic social change. In these areas of Pentecostal growth, "the centralized and bureaucratic Catholic ecclesial structure centered around the parish cannot keep up with the mobility of the population displacements, unlike the agile Evangelical networks" (72). I will have more to say about this in the following two chapters, where I will discuss the dynamics of Catholic decline, Evangelical growth, and religious differentiation.

Third, religious dynamics within the Midwest merit close exploration since the region has not only the highest percentages of affiliation with Evangelical Protestantism, but also registers a growing number of Spiritists or Kardecistas. As the region with the second-fastest rate of population growth in the nation, the Midwest offers a good window into the regional impact of the forces behind the decline of Catholicism, the expansion of Pentecostalism, and the overall diversification of the Brazilian religious field.

Fourth, although the adherents of Umbanda and Candomblé do not yet reach 1 percent of the country's population, they are beginning to have a marked presence in the south, which is surprising given that Candomblé originated in the northeast, in Salvador, Bahia, and Umbanda originated in the southeast, in Rio de Janeiro and São Paulo. This suggests African-based religions are increasingly attracting ethnically differentiated populations, since the south has a considerably higher percentage of Euro-Brazilians by virtue of migration. Alternatively, or perhaps complementarily, Alejandro Frigerio (2013) highlights the importance of Porto Alegre in the revitalization of African-based Brazilian religions and their export throughout the Southern Cone. He shows that there is a dense transnational social and religious field that allows *pais and mães de santo* (religious leaders) to travel among Porto Alegre, Buenos Aires, and Montevideo.

Finally, the category "no religion" continues to show its greatest presence in the southeast and Midwest, both regions with better performance in terms of HDI, suggesting an interesting link between improving socioeconomic conditions and the process of secularization.

Above all, this geographical angle confirms that, while there are significant crisscrossing national patterns stemming from the generative, indigenized matrix of traditional Luso-Catholicism, there is great heterogeneity, complexity, and dynamicity of Christianity in Brazil. Thus, looking at Brazilian Christianity at the regional, urban, and rural levels problematizes any facile overarching predictions about the future: at this level of granulation, the dynamics of growth and decline for various Christian traditions are uneven and mediated by context-dependent variables. Nevertheless, amid this diversity, richness, and fluidity, I have already identified some suggestive correlations, overarching trends, and tentative hypotheses that can help us make sense of the changing face and cartography of Christianity in Brazil and which I would like to explore further in subsequent chapters.

5

A Multifaceted Christianity

A Denominational View

Introduction

Having offered a panoramic view of the history of Christianity in Brazil in Chapter 1 and of its geographical diversity in the previous chapter, I now delve into the paths taken by various Christian denominations, Catholic and Protestant, from their inception to their current standing amid a highly diversified religious field. Thus, this chapter identifies specific dynamics in the development of each expression of Brazilian Christianity that will allow us to compare and contrast forms of sociopolitical involvement in the next chapter. As in previous chapters, the main analytical key for this chapter is the tension between purity and mixture, a tension that has shaped patterns of belief, practice, identity, affiliation, and religious mobility in Brazil. Without discounting powerful processes of institutional consolidation and the construction and implantation of orthodoxy, Brazilian religious formation is primarily characterized by a great deal of hybridity, fluidity, and contestation. Despite the continued hegemony of Catholicism, both at the institutional level in terms of church-state relations, and culturally, Protestant denominations have played a significant role in the articulation of a rich, diverse, and vibrant Brazilian Christianity.

The Process of Inception

As we saw in Chapter 1, the colonization of Brazil took place under a broad regime of patronage concessions the pope made to the Portuguese Crown in order to support the imposition of a universal (catholic) Christianity upon inhabitants of the Americas. Nevertheless, this project was subverted from the

120   *Christianity in Brazil*

beginning by unsuccessful attempts to eradicate Indigenous religious traditions through extermination, segregation, forced evangelization, and miscegenation, as well as by the presence of symbols, beliefs, and practices brought by African slaves, which blended creatively with traditional Luso-Catholicism to give rise to multiple ways of being Catholic at the grassroots. These local popular expressions of Brazilian Catholicism were not always in line with the quest for a universal Christianity. Moreover, the model of a single dominant Christianity had already undergone periods of deep crisis in Europe, including the schism with Eastern churches (1051) and the Reformation, which, starting in 1517, inevitably shaped European Christianity and rendered it more variegated, despite the sustained dominance of Catholicism in Portugal. In other words, Christianity was already diverse when it came to Brazil.

In the same way that Catholicism had many faces, Protestantism was also constituted by several currents and denominations and was often characterized by internal dissidence, which was a consequence of the exercise freedom of conscience entailed in the principles of *sola fides* and *sola scriptura*. And we can connect the introduction of the notion that authentic Christianity is essentially about the individual, fully conscious, and voluntary profession of faith and the personal reading of the Bible without the mediation of the clergy and other forms of religious materiality (i.e., images, embodied rituals, the sacraments, etc.) to the processes of detraditionalization and disenchantment that are at the heart of the religious fragmentation and mobility that we see in Brazil today.[1]

Despite Protestantism's undeniable diversity and tendency toward fragmentation, Antonio Gouvêa Mendonça (2007) reminds us that most Protestant currents in Brazil, except for Lutherans and, to a lesser extent, Baptists and Mormons, who were already Protestants when they came as immigrants, were founded on conversion, not only of Indigenous populations but also of other Christians. According to him, this process of conversion aimed, particularly during the colonial and independence periods, to replace and/or reform a Brazilian Catholic culture permeated with magic and steeped in the cult of saints, miracles, and religious festivals. In its place, Protestants saw themselves as inculcating an ascetic worldview, characterized by an effort to transform the world according to the rational and methodical pursuit of God's designs and by the belief that success and a prosperous life were signs of predestination or divine election. In that sense, despite the theological and organizational heterogeneity, the early Protestant churches in Brazil were carriers of Enlightenment ideas like freedom of conscience and religious disestablishment, which played an increasingly important role in the formation of a secular public sphere in Brazil during the independence period (Mendonça and Velasques Filho 2002).

We saw in Chapter 1 that French Calvinists, called Huguenots, were the first Protestant missionaries to arrive in the country. They settled in so-called Antarctic France (*França Antarctique*, since the colony was located south of the equator), in the Bay of Guanabara, Rio de Janeiro, in the mid-sixteenth century. With support from John Calvin, the expeditioner Nicholas de Villegagnon welcomed Calvinist missionaries to his colony and settled with about 400 men on an island in Guanabara Bay that bears his name. These French settlers were later expelled by the Portuguese in the wake of conflicts related to commercial issues. Portugal saw the French as intruders in the new lands that were the exclusive property of the crown (Abreu 2000: 59–63). Moreover, the French did not pay taxes—the *quintos* (one-fifth)—which gave them an advantage in the European markets. Following the collapse of the colony in Guanabara (which included the return of Villegagnon to Roman Catholicism), Dutch Reformed churches carved a more stable foothold in the country, re-entering through the northeastern state of Bahia toward the first half of the seventeenth century. They also settled in Recife, Pernambuco, and, for about two decades, carried out pastoral activities inspired by a Calvinist theocratic vision. For these Calvinists, bringing life into line with biblical commandments was the central goal. This goal enabled certain rights for enslaved Blacks:

> the black slave could no longer change his owner without his wife accompanying him in the transition. No less significant for the Calvinist theocracy was the commitment to the observance of Sunday rest, a commitment that, in its way, also improved the position of blacks. (Hoornaert et al. 2008: 140)

Just as the Dutch in Amsterdam had been tolerant to Jews who were persecuted by the Inquisition in Iberia, receiving many of them in the city, Recife became a relatively safe space for many Jews expelled from Spain and Portugal. There they founded the first synagogue in the Americas and formed one of the most influential Jewish communities in the region, in constant interaction with other communities in Havana, Córdoba, Jerusalem, and throughout the diaspora (Vainfas 2010).

Following religious and political disputes, the Dutch were finally expelled in the middle of the seventeenth century after twenty-four years in Brazil (1630–54), in an episode called the Pernambuco Insurrection. The conflict was basically generated by a dispute among competing colonial powers interested in the territories held by the Dutch. However, the dispute had strong religious undertones, since it pitted the Protestant or Jewish Dutch against Portuguese

122   *Christianity in Brazil*

Catholics. After all, the seventeen provinces of the Hapsburg Netherlands had been at war with Catholic King Philip II for eighty years (1568–1648) before the Peace of Westphalia divided Europe along ethno-religious lines. Although Dutch presence in Brazil was brief, it left an important legacy. It is worth mentioning the pioneering role of humanist German Mauricio de Nassau, administrator of Dutch Brazil, in encouraging not only religious freedom but also the cultivation of the arts in the Brazilian northeast and the development of the sugar economy.[2]

Following the expulsion of the Dutch, Protestants were not allowed to enter Brazil until the nineteenth century, when the Portuguese king, who had fled Napoleon's invasion of Portugal and established the kingdom of Brazil, opened the doors for the legal entry of English Protestants, the Anglicans. They arrived in Rio de Janeiro in 1816, with Robert Crane as their first chaplain. The Imperial Constitution of 1824 ratified Catholicism as the official religion, but it established freedom of worship, facilitating the entry of other Protestant denominations. The introduction of religious freedom to the constitution took place in the context of the spread of Enlightenment and democratic ideals and the advance of a pluralist and secularist modernity in Europe. Brazil also underwent a process of openness to other religious currents, including Kardecist Spiritism, which put the Catholic Church in a somewhat more fragile situation from the institutional point of view. Kardecist Spiritism emerged in France in the nineteenth century, blending notions like the reincarnation of spirits and karma, which were borrowed from Europe's encounter with the east, with an emphasis on literacy, rationality, and charity.[3] The Catholic Church saw Spiritists, along with Masons and Protestants, as the main threats to its religious hegemony in the wake of the re-articulation of church-state relations.

The so-called freedom of worship had a number of restrictions, such as not allowing Protestant churches to erect their places of worship in the form of a temple or even to use bells in their buildings. In other words, any element that would overtly contradict or defy the official religion was not accepted. Article 5 of the Imperial Constitution stated:

> The Roman Catholic Apostolic Religion will continue to be the religion of the Empire. All other religions are allowed with their domestic cults, or private, in homes intended for that purpose, without taking the external form of a temple.[4]

In 1890, a year after the Proclamation of the Republic in Brazil, the separation of church and state was promulgated. This move came in response to the Catholic bishops' support for the empire and opposition to the republic. From then on, Protestantism had more freedom and legal support to enter the country. It did so through two distinct but often intertwined means: immigration and mission.[5]

A Multifaceted Christianity

German Lutherans led the immigration wave, founding settlements in the state of Rio de Janeiro, in the city of Nova Friburgo, as well as in the south of Brazil, in São Leopoldo and Blumenau. It is estimated that about 250,000 German immigrants arrived in Brazil between 1824 and 1969.[6] To this day, many of these towns retain a great deal of their German character, including the language (mainly *Hunsrückish* from Franconia) and religion. This immigration was the basis for the formation of the Evangelical Church of Lutheran Confession in Brazil (Igreja Evangélica de Confissão Luterana no Brasil—IECLB), established in Nova Friburgo in 1824 and expanding gradually to other states. In 1886, the IECLB became part of the Rio Grandense Synod of the German Evangelical Church.[7] The second major Lutheran Church in the country, the Evangelical Lutheran Church of Brazil (Igreja Evangélica Luterana do Brasil—IELB), founded later, in 1904, stems from the work of American missionary Christian J. Broders of the Missouri Synod, which is generally more conservative than its counterpart, the Evangelical Lutheran Church in America (ELCA), based in Chicago.

In addition to Lutherans, in the late 1800s Brazil also received Baptist immigrants. The first Baptist Church was founded in 1871, by pastors Richard Ratcliff, coming from Louisiana, and Robert Thomas, hailing from Arkansas. Their church performed services in English to minister to immigrants from the southern United States who moved to Brazil following the defeat of the Confederacy in the American Civil War (Dawsey and Dawsey 1995). Seeking to introduce cotton to Brazil, Emperor Dom Pedro II received these immigrants with open arms, offering them land "for as little as twenty-two cents an acre at easy terms" (16). It should be noted that slavery was not officially abolished in Brazil until 1888, although importing slaves was no longer allowed. In truth, Ratcliff and Thomas were following in the steps of Thomas Bowen, the first Baptist missionary who arrived in Brazil in 1860 following his stints in Nigeria. Bowen returned to the United States after just six months due to the precarious conditions of subsistence and diseases he acquired during his short stay in Brazil (Okedara and Ajayi 2004).[8]

The story of the foundation of the Baptist Church in Brazil highlights a common dynamic in the early days of modern Protestantism in the country: first, a few missionaries came on an experimental basis, often self-supported and facing a myriad of obstacles ranging from limited resources and challenging environmental conditions to open hostility from the local communities. Only later, particularly after the 1910 World Missionary Conference in Edinburgh, in which all major Protestant denominations came together and resolved to

124 *Christianity in Brazil*

send missions to the "non-Christian" world, would the process of proselytism be strengthened by the activities of a larger number of missionaries. The story also underlines the transnational dimensions of Brazilian Protestantism, with its reliance on the movement of migrants, missionaries, and resources from abroad, particularly from North America. This transnationalism was always in tension with the process of indigenization of various churches as they began to incorporate local practices and develop Brazilian leadership.

The pioneer church stemming from the missionary roots of Brazilian Protestantism was Episcopalian Methodist, which began to operate in 1835 in Rio de Janeiro under the leadership of Rev. Fountain Elliot Pitts. At that time, the main activity of the missionaries was limited to the sale of Bibles throughout the country and the founding of Sunday schools, efforts that had to be terminated in 1841 due to a lack of resources. The first Methodist parish was established by Rev. Junius Estaham Newman, who arrived in Brazil in 1867, having served as a chaplain to Confederate troops during the American Civil War. As in the case of Baptists Ratcliff and Thomas, initially, Newman ministered in English to North American settlers, who came from a variety of Protestant backgrounds. Newman laid the groundwork for the arrival in 1876 of Rev. John James Ranson, the first permanent and official Methodist pastor charged with learning Portuguese. The first Brazilian converts were welcomed to the church in 1879. Ranson also started the publication of *Metodista Católico*, one of the earliest Protestant papers in the country (Tunes 2009). In the meantime, Newman moved to Piracicaba in the state of São Paulo and founded a college (Reily 1980). Scholars of civil society have argued that newspapers, universities, and coffeehouses—spaces where ideas could be generated, debated, and disseminated—have been central to the emergence of a modern public sphere (Anderson 1983). Especially in light of the anti-modernism and tendency toward centralization (i.e., Romanization) that characterized the Catholic Church in the late 1800s, Methodists and other historic Protestants certainly contributed to the expansion of Brazilian civil society.

Roughly during the same period, in 1855, medical doctor Robert Reid Kalley and his wife Sarah Poulton Kalley (see Chapter 2 for brief biographies), who had introduced Presbyterianism to Portugal a little more than a decade before, founded an autonomous Scottish missionary congregational church in Rio de Janeiro, A Igreja Evangélica Fluminense, thereby marking the return of Calvinist Protestantism to Brazil after two centuries of absence. The Kalleys introduced a minimalist theology, emphasizing hymns as a vehicle for individual conversion (Mendonça and Filho 2002: 34). While the Kalleys' congregationalism was heavily inflected by Calvinism, the first official Presbyterian Church in Brazil was founded in 1862 by Ashbel Green Simonton, an American who had arrived in Rio de Janeiro three years earlier, having just graduated from Princeton Theological Seminary. The young Simonton's work stands out particularly because he created the first evangelical newspaper in Brazil—*Imprensa Evangélica* (*The Evangelical Press*)—in 1864. In 1865, Simonton also ordained the first Reformed Brazilian pastor, José Manuel da Conceição, who was formerly a Catholic priest. Unfortunately, Simonton died shortly thereafter, in 1867, victim to a tropical disease (Shaull 1963).[9] Following the establishment of the first church, Brazilian Presbyterianism experienced multiple currents of dissent, beginning with the formation of the Independent Presbyterian Church of Brazil (IPID) in 1903, led by the Reverend Eduardo Carlos Pereira. He broke with the church due to disagreements over the continued dominance of foreign missionaries in spiritual and educational matters and over his assertion that Freemasonry was incompatible with the gospel. Other dissident churches include the Conservative Presbyterian Church of Brazil (1940), which separated from IPID over issues of doctrinal orthodoxy and whose first president was the Rev. Bento Ferraz; the Fundamentalist Presbyterian Church (1956), established in Recife by Pastor Israel Furtado Gueiros; the Renewed Presbyterian Church (1975), founded by Rev. Palmiro Francisco de Andrade, under the influence of the revivalist, Pentecostal movements that began to touch historical Protestant churches from the end of the 1960s; and the United Presbyterian Church of Brazil (1978), which takes an explicit ecumenical approach and ordains women. The range of branches within Presbyterianism in Brazil—from liberal to fundamentalist and revivalist—is a microcosm of the diversity and dynamism of Brazilian Protestantism.[10]

Increased Protestant missionary presence in Brazil was not only the result of changes in church-state relations in Brazil and the Edinburgh Conference but also due to an intense period of spiritual upheaval in the United States known as the Second Great Awakening, which gave rise to messianic-millenarian movements such as the Seventh-Day Adventists and Latter-Day Saints that believe the end of times is at hand and set up vigorous missions to proclaim this view with corresponding urgency (see alternative Christianities in Chapter 2). As we saw in Chapter 1 regarding the Canudos War and the rebellion at Contestado, messianic and millenarian movements also took place in Brazil toward the end of the 1800s and the beginning of 1900s, as the country became an independent republic and underwent an incipient process of modernization that dislocated many people in the countryside (Queiroz 1965). As a result, ideas about the impending end of times found fertile ground in Brazil.

126   *Christianity in Brazil*

The Seventh-Day Adventists arrived in Brazil in 1893 through the work of missionary Alberto Stauffer in Indaiatuba, in the state of São Paulo. The following year, William H. Thurston was sent to Rio de Janeiro and Adventists spread across Santa Catarina, Rio Grande do Sul, and Espírito Santo (Filho 2004). As alternative Christians, Adventists stand in a relation of nonconformity not only with Catholicism but also with already established mainline Protestant churches, such as Methodists, Episcopalians, and Presbyterians, particularly around the notion of the imminent return of the Messiah. In Brazil, Adventists also experienced internal tensions and dissensions, eventually splitting into the Brazilian Adventist Church and the Adventists of the Promised Church (Filho 2004: 170–1).

Mormons arrived in Brazil with German immigrants Max Richard Zapf and especially with Roberto Lippelt and Augusta Kuhlmann Lippelt and their four children, who settled in Ipomeia in the southern state of Santa Catarina in 1923. The introduction of Mormonism via immigration once again shows that although immigration and mission can be separated for analytical purposes, they are often very tightly intertwined in the history of Protestantism in Brazil. Proselytization only began in earnest in 1928, with the arrival of other elders of German extraction who had been working out of the South American Mission in Buenos Aires (Silva 2008). The dominant language of the missionaries was German until *The Book of Mormon* was translated into Portuguese in 1939. The Second World War interrupted Mormon missionary work in Brazil. It resumed only in early 1951, this time under the initiative of American, English-speaking missionaries. Expansion throughout Brazil might have been hampered by the Latter-Day Saints' explicit restriction against people of African descent holding the priesthood, which was only officially rescinded in 1978. In that same year, Brazil became the first Latin American country to have a full-fledged Mormon temple.

In the early twentieth century, the United States experienced a Third Great Awakening, giving rise to Pentecostalism. Pentecostals came to Brazil very soon after the foundational revivals of Azusa, California and Topeka, Kansas. The pioneer Pentecostal churches were Assemblies of God (AG), which Swedish-American missionaries Gunnar Vingren and Daniel Berg founded in Belém, in the state of Pará, in 1911 (see Chapter 2), and the Christian Congregation of Brazil (CCB), created in 1910 by the Italian missionary and naturalized American Luigi Francescon, who converted first to Presbyterianism and was then baptized into the Pentecostal Church in Chicago. Francescon came from Buenos Aires to São Paulo, basing his pastoral work in the commercial district of Brás. While the AG in Brazil received initial support from Pretus Lewi Pethrus and his Pentecostal movement in Sweden, eventually coming under the sphere of influence of the American Assemblies of God when the Brazilians gained autonomy in 1932, the CCB emerged out of Francescon's ministry among Presbyterians and Italian Catholic immigrants who came to Brazil, especially to the southeast, in large numbers toward the end of the 1800s (Freston 1995).

The distinction between classic Pentecostalism, practiced by the AG and CCB, and other Pentecostal currents that came later is very important because, by the mid-twentieth century, Pentecostalism became the fastest-growing Protestant group not only in Brazil but throughout Latin America. Without a doubt, it is the Protestant group that has most intensely challenged the Catholic Church's institutional and cultural hegemony in the country and the region. As such, it is important to distinguish along a temporal axis the various Pentecostal actors, with their theological, pastoral, and organizational variations, in order to assess more accurately those that have spearheaded this growth. I shall return to this discussion later.

Alongside Roman Catholicism and Protestantism, there are two other forms of Christianity present in Brazil through churches that consider themselves Catholic but are not linked to the Vatican. These are the Brazilian Catholic Apostolic Church, founded in 1945 by Bishop Carlos Duarte Costa, who was excommunicated by the Roman Catholic Church for his critique of the doctrine of papal infallibility, the practice of clerical celibacy, and the Vatican's cozy relations with authoritarian regimes (including that of Getúlio Vargas),[11] and the Orthodox Catholic Church of the Maronite Rite based in São Paulo and established in 1962. The latter is a church of the Eastern Rite in communion with the Apostolic See, which serves Christian immigrants from the Middle East, particularly from Lebanon and increasingly Syria, and their descendants (Pinto 2009).

Contemporary Dynamics within and among Protestant Denominations

Among scholars and the general public, "Evangelical" has become in recent decades an umbrella term used to refer to Protestants as a whole. In the national census, the Brazilian Institute of Geography and Statistics (IBGE) uses the term "Evangelical Mission" to characterize those Protestants who see themselves as spreading the gospel (the good news, *evangelion* in Greek), including those in historic or mainline denominations that trace their origin to the Reformation as well as Adventists. This group excludes Pentecostals, who, although also seeking to proclaim the gospel, have their own characteristics by virtue of their large numbers and internal diversity. To describe the Protestant churches that are most actively proselytizing, the Portuguese term *"crente"* (literally "believer") is also very common among non-academics. It is used by insiders (particularly by Pentecostals themselves, who connect it with the personal, voluntary, and public profession of belief in Jesus as the Son of God and as savior, often marked by baptism in the Holy Spirit) and outsiders (Catholics, who still often couple it with the term *seitas*—sects—to characterize those groups that challenge the church's hegemony most aggressively). Using the term Evangelical, the IBGE tracked the evolution and diversification of the Brazilian religious field.

Figure 4 shows a steep decline in the percentage of Brazilians who self-identify as Catholics, from more than 90 percent in 1950 to 64.6 percent in the 2010 census. During the same period, the proportion of Evangelicals has gone from low single digits to 22.2 percent. Pentecostals, who account for 60 percent of all Protestants, have contributed the lion's share of this growth. The steady decline in the number of adherents to Catholicism also correlates with the growth of the "without-religion" (*sem religião*) population, which has been more pronounced in the last two decades. At present, nearly one in ten (8 percent) Brazilians declare themselves not to adhere to any religion. It should be noted that the "without-religion" identity in Brazil is mostly made up of people who were formerly Catholics and who, while not seeing themselves as members of the church, hold many beliefs and practices derived from Catholicism, often

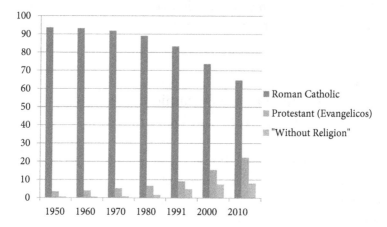

Figure 4 Percentages of religious affiliation by decade. Source: IBGE – 2010 Census.

combining them with African-based and Spiritist symbols and ideas. Recent studies indicate that, while the overall number of "no religion" is increasing, this group is in flux: depending on the life cycle and the situations they face, some of those not religiously affiliated can and do return to the Catholic Church they left earlier (Pitta and Fernandes 2006).

Table 1 does not include African-based religions, Judaism, Buddhism, or other Eastern religions, or the percentages of those who declare multiple religious belongings, since the numbers are quite small and my primary focus is Brazilian Christianity.[12] Table 4 breaks down the percentages by denomination in the most recent census.

The category of "evangelicals not determined" comprises a myriad of "miscellaneous" Protestant churches, such as the Maranatha Church (0.19 percent of the population), the House Blessing (0.07 percent), and the Evangelical Community (0.09 percent). Finally, groups such as Jehovah's Witnesses and the Church of Latter-Day Saints, which in the sociology of religion are normally considered "alternative Christianities" (often as part of New Religious Movements, NRMs; see Chapter 2), were placed in the "Other Religions" category in the Brazilian census. This category contains a multitude of religions with small numbers of adherents, ranging from Buddhism and Islam to African-based religions[14] and NRMs, with the largest group being Spiritists, who

Table 4 Christian Churches/Denominations in Brazil According to the 2010 Census

Churches/denominations	% of the country's population	Number of adherents
Apostolic Roman Catholic	64.63	123,280,172
Evangelical	22.16	42,275,440
Pentecostal	13.3	25,370,484
Evangelical not determined	4.83	9,212,389
Evangelical Mission	4.03	7,686,827
Baptist	1.95	3,723,853
Adventist	0.82	1,561,071
Lutheran	0.52	999,498
Presbyterian	0.48	921,209
Methodist	0.18	340,938
Congregational	0.06	109,591
Other Evangelical Mission	0.02	30,666
Other religions	5.0	9,536,635
Jehovah's Witnesses	0.73	1,393,208
Latter-Day Saints (Mormons)	0.12	226,509[13]

Source: 2010 Population Census by the IBGE, adapted by the author.

130   *Christianity in Brazil*

make up 40 percent of the overall category. Jehovah's Witnesses are the second-largest group within the "Other Religions" category. Mormons, in turn, are the fifth largest, with a smaller membership than Umbanda and Buddhism. From 2000 to 2010, they have experienced a growth of roughly 12 percent, gaining about 27,000 new members, which is comparable to the rate of growth of the overall population in Brazil.

As I stated earlier, given that Pentecostals are the largest and fastest-growing group in Brazilian Protestantism, they require further characterization. According to Freston (1995), Pentecostalism in Brazil has gone through several waves. The first one is constituted by the classic Pentecostal churches founded by foreign missionaries inspired by the revivals in Azusa, which made glossolalia the first and most important evidence of baptism in the Holy Spirit. The second wave refers to indigenized churches created by Brazilians, such as Manoel de Mello's O Brasil para Cristo (Brazil for Christ) and David Miranda's Deus é Amor (God Is Love), that began to develop theological, liturgical, and institutional innovations in response to local conditions.[15] Finally, the third wave includes Neo-Pentecostals, who advance a gospel of health and wealth that often involves spiritual warfare and exorcism (Table 5).

In addition to theological, liturgical, and organizational differences that I have discussed in Chapter 2, each wave correlates with transformations in global Christianity, as well as in social conditions worldwide and in Brazilian society. The first wave is connected with the early stages of globalization in the twentieth century, corresponding to the large influx of immigrants to Brazil in response to economic and political upheavals in Europe and to an incipient process of

Table 5 Classification of Pentecostals According to Freston (1995)

Year of foundation	First wave: classic	Second wave: indigenized	Third wave: Neo-Pentecostal
1910	Christian Congregation		
1911	Assemblies of God		
1951		Foursquare Church	
1955		Brazil for Christ	
1962		God Is Love	
1977			Universal Church of the Kingdom of God—UCKG
1980			International Grace of God Church

Source: Freston (1995), adapted by the author.

A Multifaceted Christianity

industrialization in Brazil. The second wave took place as industrialization and urbanization intensified and became firmly established, even if unevenly distributed throughout the country, while the third one started in and has accompanied the era of electronic communications, mass media, and global consumer culture. Although the largest Pentecostal groups in Brazil continue to be the classical AG and Christian Congregation, the third wave includes some of the fastest-growing Pentecostal churches in the country. Table 6 provides a sense of the size of the main Brazilian Pentecostal churches.

Third-wave Pentecostal churches tend to have thriving global ministries. However, with anywhere from six to twelve million followers across more than 100 countries, the Universal Church of the Kingdom of God (UCKG) stands out as the most successful transnational Brazilian church.[16] The UCKG also used to lead the Pentecostal field in terms of growth within Brazil, while more traditional churches such as the Christian Congregation lost ground. Between 1991 and 2000, "the Universal," as it is known in Brazil (*a Universal*), grew by a whopping 682 percent. Mafra, Swatowiski, and Sampaio (2013: 65) attribute this explosive growth to the UCKG's strategic use of "loose bonds," not based on "localized affiliations but [on] the personal experience of routinized spiritual services made in Brazil but which can be deployed in multiple spaces and sites." These "controlled and predictable services," exorcisms one day, prayers for economic success on another, "give a sense of security and certainty that is much needed in liquid modernity." To hold the dense transnational network of temples together, the UCKG combines these looser bonds with a centralized administrative and marketing structure radiating from Edir Macedo (see Chapter 2 for a brief biography).

The UCKG's strategy of loose bonds might be backfiring, as the Universal is in danger of being outflanked by imitators and other churches that privilege

Table 6 Main Pentecostal Churches in Brazil According to the 2010 Census

Churches/denominations	Brazilian population (%)
Assemblies of God (first wave)	6.46
Other Pentecostal origin	2.76
Christian Congregation (first wave)	1.2
Universal Church of the Kingdom of God—UCKG (third wave)	0.98
Foursquare Church (second wave)	0.95
God Is Love (second wave)	0.44
Brazil for Christ (second wave)	0.10

Source: 2010 Demographic Census by the IBGE, adapted by the author.

the sheer pneumatic experience, endeavoring to produce ever more adrenaline-charged encounters with the sacred. The widespread use of the internet, especially of social media, among young urban Brazilians makes these turbo-charged forms of Pentecostalism more available (Fernandes 2012). The 2010 census shows that the UCKG lost 11 percent of its adherents. This loss might have been simply the result of some of its members marking the "Other Pentecostal Origin" or "Evangelicals not Determined" categories. Nevertheless, we cannot discount the role of the further fragmentation and diversification of the Brazilian Pentecostal scene. Some of the Universal Church's fiercest competitors, such as the International Church of God's Grace and World Church of God's Power, both founded and led by UCKG's dissidents, are included in the catch-all classification "Other Pentecostal Origin." This category also comprises a number of extremely dynamic churches which might be constituting *a fourth wave in Brazilian Pentecostalism*. These churches go beyond the skillful use of electronic media to produce spectacular performances of praise and spiritual warfare, as in the case of the UCKG and its other competitors in the third wave. They make heavy use of the latest developments in social media—Facebook, Twitter, and YouTube which are very popular in Brazil—to forge instantaneous and continuous communication with their followers. These fourth-wave churches also involve the wholesale incorporation, sacralization—in a revival style—and commodification of elements of Brazilian youth subcultures, including music (*funk*) and sports (soccer and *vale tudo*). For these churches, it is the novelty, transgressive force, and emotional edge of the religious experiences that make the looser bonds attractive and enduring, not their predictability and familiarity (as in UCKG). Finally, these churches thrive on the celebrity of their founders and members; their glamorous and excitement-filled lifestyles and images are central ingredients of their churches' national and global brand. In her research on the Australian Hillsong Church, which has a temple in São Paulo and ministers to Brazilian immigrants in Australia, Cristina Rocha (forthcoming) uses the term "Cool Christianity" to highlight the fashion-celebrity-megachurch nexus that characterizes this type of global Evangelical Christianity.

Two good examples of this fourth wave are Igreja Renascer em Cristo (Reborn in Christ Church) and Igreja Bola de Neve (Snowball Church). Founded by bishops Estevam and Sônia Hernandes in the mid-1980s, Reborn in Christ has been described by *The New York Times* as a vast "religious and business structure that includes more than 1,000 churches, a television and radio network, a recording company, real estate in Brazil and the United

States, a horse-breeding ranch and a trademark on the word 'gospel' in Brazil" (Rohter 2007). Reborn in Christ also has the distinction of counting until recently Brazilian soccer superstar Kaká among its members. Kaká is part of what Brazilian sociologist Carmen Rial (2013) calls a new breed of Brazilian religious performer-entrepreneurs, who, taking advantage of the country's world-class prowess in soccer, travel abroad to places as diverse as Japan and Dubai not only to showcase the sport but also to spread Brazilian transnational Pentecostalism.[17] Reborn in Christ has also hosted tournaments of *vale tudo*— literally "anything goes" or better yet "no holds barred"—a very popular style of Brazilian fighting that emerged as early as the 1920s when the martial dance of *capoeira* cross-fertilized with Jiu-Jitsu, brought by Japanese immigrants. *Vale tudo* has now become a subculture among Brazilian urban youth. Igreja Bola de Neve (Snowball Church), for its part, ministers specifically to Brazilian millennials, mixing Christian rock, reggae, and rap with blogging, surfing, skateboarding, and other extreme sports. In fact, Bola de Neve's founding and head pastor, Apostle Rina, preaches from an altar made out of his surfboard. Bola de Neve now has churches in places as diverse as India, Russia (in Moscow), Canada, and the United States (Los Angeles and San Diego, CA, and Pensacola, FL), and Australia (Harbord, north of Sydney, where it takes advantage of the shared culture of the beautiful and buff "beach body" among Australians and Brazilians).[18]

Other churches that could be grouped in the fourth wave of Brazilian Pentecostalism are part of what is known as *funk gospel*, which has been adopted by small congregations in the periphery of large cities that operate and spread through social networks.[19] These churches target primarily young working-class Brazilians, especially those with addiction problems and those who might have been involved in drug trafficking and gangs, and who are part of the urban dance scene in favelas where funk, a hybrid type of music that blends African American and Afro-Brazilian rhythms, is a very visible mark of subcultural identity.[20] As such, "fourth-wave" Pentecostal churches are not just a phenomenon among urban, middle-, and upper-class cosmopolitan millennials and post-millennials. Funk gospel's stronghold is Rio de Janeiro and one of its most popular groups is Bonde do Tigrão (Big Tiger's Tram). The lyrics of Bonde do Tigrão's *passinho do abençoado* (the little step of the blessed one) demonstrate the blend of poor urban youth culture and Pentecostalism:

> And he was a "crack-head" [*cracudo*],[21] but then he returned, he is now our municipal guard, urban orders, Wilson goes along the little step, in little step, small step in the blessed one, the little step of the blessed one.

As Mariano (2005) argues, Brazilian Pentecostalism has never been homogeneous and internal disagreements and schisms have been a key feature of its evolution. It should be noted that many small, storefront evangelical, especially Pentecostal, churches open every year, particularly among poor sectors of the population, those with low levels of education, and among those living on the margins of large cities. Very often, these churches are located in temporary and precarious facilities: sheds or garages are commonly adapted, equipped with plastic or folding chairs and makeshift altars. The names of these churches are announced by crude handmade posters and there is no official record of their existence at City Hall.

Brazilian Pentecostalism's enormous diversity, especially at the grassroots level, its ongoing cross-fertilization with other Brazilian religions, like Umbanda, and popular culture, as well as with global religious and cultural trends, have made more arduous the task of constructing useful analytical typologies. We can safely say that understanding the richness, complexity, and dynamism of Brazilian Pentecostalism is an unfinished task, one that is bound to occupy scholars for years to come. It is hard to predict whether the accelerated growth it has experienced in recent decades will continue. Even bearing in mind all the difficulties in developing a comprehensive and systematic view, Cecília Mariz and Paulo Gracino (2013: 162) argue that the pace of growth of Pentecostalism in Brazil might be cooling down. These researchers show that while some churches may have grown numerically, the overall rate of Pentecostal growth has slowed down in comparison to previous decades, as churches begin to draw adherents not just from Catholicism but from rival Pentecostal congregations. Mariano (2013), for example, states that while Evangelicals grew 61 percent between 2000 and 2010, the number of those declaring themselves Pentecostals expanded only by 44 percent. This growth is still quite robust, especially when compared with the 12.3 percent growth for the country's population. However, it is far lower than the blistering rates in 1991 (112 percent) and 2000 (115 percent). Moreover, while Pentecostals continue to constitute the largest group within Brazilian Protestantism, they are now only 60 percent of all Evangelicals, down from 68 percent in 2000 (Mariz and Gracino 2013: 161). For Mariano, Mariz, and Gracino, it is too early to declare an ebb in the expansion of Pentecostalism in Brazil. Before making any solid prognostications, the categories "Evangelicals—Not Determined" and "Other Pentecostal Origin" will have to be examined at a much finer granulation, since at present they hinder a fuller and more accurate analysis of trends in Brazilian Christianity. For instance, some Pentecostals surveyed may have reported that they are "Evangelical—Not Determined," thus

A Multifaceted Christianity 135

accounting for the decrease of Pentecostals' share of Evangelicals in the last census.

Contemporary Dynamics within Brazilian Catholicism

Even in the context of growing religious pluralism and the erosion of religious belonging, Catholicism continues to be the dominant religion in Brazil. Furthermore, we saw in the previous chapter that the weakening in Catholic affiliation is regionally uneven, with the northeast and the south continuing to be relative Catholic "strongholds." And just as there is religious diversity among evangelical churches in the country, Brazilian Catholicism also offers multiple expressions, although they are not the result of schisms. At the risk of simplifying a vast, heterogeneous church, one could say that there has been a persistent tension in Brazilian Catholicism between conservatives and progressives. Whereas conservatives have generally sought to uphold doctrinal orthodoxy and liturgical tradition and sustain and even fortify the church's internal hierarchies vis-à-vis challenges of other religions and of the outside world, progressives have attempted to adapt the church's universal message to local conditions and to transform its organization to engage current religious and sociopolitical contexts. I will examine the sociopolitical implications of the ongoing tensions between conservative and progressive Catholics, from the grassroots to the clergy and bishops, in the following chapter. Here, I simply offer a general characterization of these two currents within Catholicism, identifying their composition and relative influence within the church.

As seen in Chapter 1, while there have been reformist figures and movements throughout the history of Brazilian Catholicism, the progressive wing of the church gained prominence from the late 1960s on, as the *aggiornamento* (updating) called for at the Second Vatican Council (1962–5) began to permeate the Latin American Catholic Church with the meeting of its bishops in Medellín, Colombia in 1968. Heeding Medellín's call for a preferential option for the poor and influenced by the emerging liberation theology, Brazilian progressive Catholics began to undertake a series of pastoral initiatives at the grassroots (Fernandes 2010). Arguably, the most important of these was *comunidades eclesiais de base* (base ecclesial communities, CEBs), which grew mainly in rural areas and some urban peripheries and were coordinated by pastoral agents—priests and nuns—influenced by and in conversation with liberation theologians. These small communities of neighbors read the Bible and Catholic social teaching in the context of the social, economic, and political conditions their members encountered in their everyday lives. Out of this faith-life link, they identified conditions that were incompatible with Christian values of love, solidarity, justice, and the common good and reflected on, and sometimes even engaged in, the actual implementation of actions that could transform those conditions.

There is some debate as to the scope and influence of progressive Catholicism. At their height in the 1980s, surveys conducted by the National Conference of Brazilian Catholic Bishops (CNBB) and scholars associated with progressive Catholicism reported that there were 100,000 CEBs throughout the country, a number that has been disputed by some researchers who have been critical of the overly positive way in which these communities have been portrayed in academia (Hewitt 1991; Daudelin 1992; Valle and Pita 1994). Even taking that number at face value and assuming that each CEB consists of thirty to fifty people, the total number of participants would be three to five million—2 to 3.3 percent of Brazil's population in 1990.[22] By comparison, in 1991, Pentecostals were 6 percent of the country's population. Despite their centrality, CEBs are not the only component of progressive Catholicism. The latter is more like a dense cluster of interlocking networks of pastoral initiatives, ranging from Catholic Action in its various expressions among workers, students, peasants to the Pastoral Land Commission (CPT), which deals with land tenure and social justice in the countryside and was very influential in the rise of the Movimento dos Sem Terra (the Landless Movement—MST), and the Indigenous Missionary Council (CIMI), focusing on the rights, culture, and language of native Brazilians. In the next chapter, I shall argue that the influence of progressive Catholicism is more widespread and enduring than the estimated number of Brazilian Christians who participate in CEBs suggests. Furthermore, like Pentecostalism, Brazilian progressive Catholicism is also a key player in global Christianity, connected with other liberationist movements throughout the world through the transnational circulation of theologians, pastoral agents, bishops, books, and other pedagogical materials such as Paulo Freire's *Pedagogy of the Oppressed* and Leonardo Boff's *Church: Charisma and Power*. The election of Pope Francis, who has made service to the poor a central aspect of his papacy, also seems to have revitalized progressive Catholicism in the Americas, including Brazil, at least when it comes to the promotion of social justice, even if Francis seems to hold the line on thorny issues like the ordination of women, celibacy, and reproductive rights. On the other hand, the election of President Jair Bolsonaro in 2018 has energized ultraconservative Catholics and given them more public visibility and influence in policy matters. In contrast to Pope Francis's calls to address social inequalities and follow scientific advice in eradicating Covid-19, these conservatives have not only denounced changes that they fear will undermine the church's magisterium, particularly in matters of liturgy and sexuality, but they have also sided with Bolsonaro's denial of the seriousness of the pandemic and his reluctance to adopt a national policy of quarantining and social distancing. I will have more to say in the next chapter when I discuss the social, political, and religious factors that led to the election of Bolsonaro. Suffice it to say that there has been a sharpening of the polarization between progressives and traditionalists.

Parallel to and in tension with progressive Catholicism, the Catholic Charismatic Renewal (CCR) arrived in Brazil at the end of the 1960s through Jesuit priests Harold Rahm and Edward Dougherty, both of whom had come into contact with the movement in North America, where it was spreading rapidly following an outpouring of the Holy Spirit in the spring of 1967 at Duquesne University in Pittsburgh—known as the "Duquesne Weekend." Radiating from the city of Campinas, São Paulo, the movement introduced yet another way of being Catholic in Brazil, one that, like CEBs, allows for increased laity involvement, as called for by Vatican II, but focuses more on the spiritual edification and moral renewal of nominal Catholics. It carries out these tasks through an emphasis on the intense, emotive, and personal experience of the Holy Spirit in small, intimate prayer groups (*grupos de oração*), Sunday Masses, and large and often lavish assemblies that bring together Charismatics at various levels, from the diocese and the state to the nation and the international scene. Just as in Pentecostalism, healing, as well as collective and heavily mediatized expressions of religious effervescence like singing, clapping, and ecstatic praising are part and parcel of the CCR's modus operandi and appeal. I discussed in Chapter 2 how, in contrast to progressive Catholicism, Brazilian Charismatic Catholicism does not make social justice a priority (Fernandes 1996). For this reason, these two strands of Catholicism are often seen in tension with each other: often Catholic Charismatics take more conservative stances, expressing a greater concern with the struggle against abortion and for the preservation of traditional family structures and gender roles rather than with challenging the social conditions that lead to poverty in the name of Catholic social teaching. Moreover, the CCR's stress on healing seems to bear a strong elective affinity with Neo-Pentecostalism's gospel of health and wealth. It is important to note, however, that while the differences in pastoral emphasis and the institutional and theological strains are real and significant, on the ground there is quite a

138   *Christianity in Brazil*

bit of cross-fertilization between progressive and Charismatic Catholics (De Theije 1999). Conversely, Mariz and Souza (2015) argue that there are limits to the "symbolic exchanges" taking place between Catholic Charismatics and Pentecostals. We shall see in the next chapter that alliances between these groups are more instrumental, built around perceived shared social and political goals, such as the elimination of abortion and the implementation of religious education, than theological or institutional.

As in the case of CEBs, it is difficult to ascertain the exact number of Catholic Charismatics in Brazil. The first social scientific attempt to survey them by Pierucci and Prandi (1996) placed their number at 3.8 million. More current estimates by Carranza and Mariz (2013: 137) put that number at ten million, "organized in 20,000 prayer groups, diocesan, state, and national coordinations, countless programs to train youth and leaders, in addition to missionary programs." This number, while greater than those for progressive Catholicism and more comparable to the 13.3 million Pentecostals, is still far from constituting the majority of Brazilian Catholics. Nevertheless, just as in the case of CEBs, the CCR punches above its numerical weight. Beyond the boundaries of institutional membership, Charismaticism has become a ubiquitous style of being Catholic in Brazil, a performative style that is particularly appealing to young urban Brazilians and those in the until recently growing middle class whose lives are imbued with electronic media and consumer culture. According to the Pew Forum (2013), 57 percent of Brazilian Catholics considered themselves Charismatic. Moreover, it is estimated that there are close to 800 *novas comunidades de vida consagrada e aliança* (new communities of consecrated life and covenant) in Brazil, including Canção Nova (New Song), Shalom, Comunidades de Vida e Aliança (Covenant and Life Communities), Pantokrator, and Toca de Assis, which, as we saw in Chapter 2, disseminate their Charismatic style at both the national and international levels through various electronic media, carrying out transnational ministries in Africa, Europe, the United States, and Israel.[23]

The labels progressive and conservative, liberationist and Charismatic, in the end, are very limited in trying to capture the richness and fluidity of Catholic identities in Brazil. The same survey conducted in the mid-1990s by Pierucci and Prandi that found that there were 3.8 million Charismatic Catholics in Brazil (versus 1.8 million CEB members) reported that there were 61.4 million "traditional" Catholics. Here traditionalism should not be seen as necessarily synonymous with the views of the conservative Catholics that have supported Bolsonaro. Despite the dynamism and innovation of CEBs and the CCR, most Brazilian Catholics continue to live their religiosity through the cult of the saints, Marian devotions, and religious festivals. Alternatively, Brazilian Catholics blend this traditional popular Catholicism with the Tridentine focus on the sacraments and with post–Vatican II Catholicism. They may even add to this mixture elements of African-based religions, Spiritism, and New Age religions. In such conditions, a Brazilian Catholic may claim a double or even triple belonging. S/he may call himself/herself a "Spiritist Catholic" or "Catholic and evangelical" without experiencing contradiction. Anthropologist Marcelo Camurça (2013: 74) speaks of a "customized Catholicism," a Catholicism tailor-made by the individual to address his/her needs and longings out of fragments of the multiple expressions of Christianity and of other religions in an ever more pluralistic and fluid religious field.

I have documented on the ground the perceptions that *evangélicos* have of Catholics—that they are "spiritually careless" (*espiritualmente descuidados*), "permissive" (*permissivos*), and "lacking commitment" (*descomprometidos*).[24] These perceptions, which dovetail with the notion of "customized Catholicism," are shared also many by Charismatic Catholics who are critical of their fellow Catholics. In response, Charismatics have engaged in campaigns to promote Catholic identity and pride through large festive gatherings in which people proclaim "*Sou feliz por ser católico!*" (I am happy to be Catholic!), as well as through Catholic radio, TV, social media, and material culture (e.g., t-shirts, car stickers, posters, hats, rosaries, etc). In Guerra's words, the response by Catholic Charismatics has been to construct

> a Catholic identity characterized by the "pride" (*o orgulho*) of being Catholic, in opposition to the ostentatious presentation of evangelical identities in general, which defines the "believers" (*crentes*) as "different," "pure" in a world of impure [people], "renewed" (*renovados*) and "children Of God," as opposed to a dwindling majority, classified by [these believers] as just God's creatures. (Guerra 2003:16)

Notwithstanding the claim to revitalize the core of Brazilian Catholic identity, which is inextricably tied to the structures of feeling and experience in traditional Luso-Catholicism (see Chapter 2), these campaigns carry their own forms of rationalization and disenchantment, being often deeply intertwined with the logic of the market, especially with consumerism and the promotion of subcultural lifestyles and individual well-being (Fernandes 2019). And if we consider the proliferation "fourth-wave" Pentecostal congregations, which feed off the adrenaline produced by "cool" youth lifestyles and the showmanship and celebrity of their leaders, it is possible to hypothesize that the customization of faith is a widespread phenomenon in the Brazilian religious field, affecting all Christian denominations in one way or another.

On the Way to Some Conclusions

What are the implications of these denominational dynamics for the future of Christianity in Brazil? I will tackle this challenging question in the book's conclusion; however, for now, I can say that while Catholicism continues to occupy a leading place in Brazil in terms of numbers as well as institutionally (i.e., church-state relations—more in the next chapter) and culturally, as a key ingredient in the matrix of a Brazilian minimal religiosity, Brazilian Christianity has become greatly differentiated and fluid, both across and within denominations. Across denominations, Evangelical Protestantism, particularly Pentecostalism but also the "alternative Christian churches," such as Adventists, Jehovah's Witnesses, and Latter-Day Saints, has grown dramatically, stamping Christianity with a strong pneuma-centric flavor that the still numerically dominant Catholic Church has incorporated in its own liturgical and pastoral style via the Catholic Charismatic Renewal Movement and the new communities of consecrated life. While there has always been circulation among religions and dynamics of multiple religious affiliation and identification—for example, the permeability between Catholicism and African-based religions—this shared pneuma-centrism adds another channel to flow back and forth among various churches and denominations. This fluidity is reflected in the expression "customized Catholicism."

In response to a pluralistic and simultaneously competitive and cross-fertilizing religious field, there is also growing differentiation within denominations. We have seen in the previous chapters that Catholicism has always been internally diverse, characterized not only by the imposition of orthodoxy, but also by resistance, syncretism, and transgression, especially at the grassroots. In this chapter, we saw how Protestantism too has witnessed considerable dissidence and fission, as shown most clearly by the example of Presbyterianism. We also have seen that Pentecostalism is highly fragmented, marked by multiple waves of innovation in response to competition, the activities of missionaries and religious entrepreneurs, and changing social, political, and cultural circumstances, including transformations in the economy and media. Before I draw conclusions about the future of Christianity in Brazil, I want to explore more precisely those circumstances to see how various forms of being Christian in Brazil interact with sociopolitical dynamics.

6

Brazilian Christianity, Politics, and Society

The Legacy of Traditional Catholicism

Any analysis of the relationship between Christianity and Brazilian society and politics must begin with the Royal Patronage (O Padroado Real), for, as we saw in Chapter 1, it set structures and dynamics that still shape contemporary Brazil. By giving the Portuguese Crown the duty and power to Christianize the newly acquired territories through the nomination of priests and bishops and the construction and administration of churches, monasteries, and seminaries, Pope Leo X (1513–21) in effect tied the Brazilian Catholic Church's fortunes to the colonial status quo. The Padroado established the hegemony of Catholicism in Brazil at the institutional level, with the church being recognized by the state as the only legitimate religious institution to the exclusion not only of a rich variety of Indigenous traditions but also of Protestantism, Judaism, Islam, and African-derived religions, which were present early on.

More importantly, the church was also dominant culturally, inculcating a tiered worldview populated by *beatos*, priests, bishops, saints, angels, and archangels located in different levels of holiness and influence that dovetailed with colonial hierarchical organization. In other words, dependence upon local, regional, and national saints for miracles that could address the harsh conditions confronted by those who were not among the Portuguese elites mirrored the dependence on local, regional, and national political *patrões* (bosses), who could use their positions in the civil administration to bestow protection and favors in exchange for service, loyalty, and eventually, when democracy was established, votes. During the Old Republic (1889–1930), this system of political patronage consolidated, especially in the countryside, into what came to be known as *coronelismo*, a term derived from "*coronel*" (colonel), a title originally given to leaders of the National Guard who were charged with protecting the empire but which was in time honorifically bestowed to large landowners to signify their command over local resources (Leal 2012). In *coronelismo*, the connection between spiritual and political hierarchies was mediated, reinforced, and mirrored by the institution of godparenting (*empadrinhamento*), whereby those at the bottom of the social order sought to form religiously sanctioned bonds of kinship with *coroneis* by giving them the duty of ensuring the religious education and well-being of their children.

From the beginning, then, Christianity in Brazil was heavily inflected by a patriarchal and corporatist ethos that has contributed to and interacted with patrimonial and personalistic politics based on the strategic mobilization of dense spiritual and social networks. We have seen, however, that Catholic dominance was never complete and that there was considerable diversity within Brazilian Catholicism, despite the efforts to institute orthodoxy in the wake of the Council of Trent. Still, the Royal Patronage did set in motion particular patterns of church and state relations and, more broadly, particular modes of interaction between Christianity and politics that have persisted even up to the impeachment of President Dilma Rousseff in 2016 and the election of Jair Messias Bolsonaro in 2018.

In Chapter 1, I discussed how independence and the transition to the national period in the late nineteenth century brought a realignment of church and state relations. With the church structurally invested in the maintenance of the empire, the emerging republican elites actively sought to undermine its influence. Thus, the constitution of 1891, promulgated just a couple of years after the revolution, clearly proclaimed the separation of church and state, guaranteed freedom of worship, and declared that "no religion [*culto*] or church will enjoy official financial support nor will they have relations of dependence or alliance with the federal or government" (Article 72 #7). However, despite this pledge, republican authorities encouraged and facilitated the entry of missionaries and immigrants from non-Catholic countries to counter the continued cultural influence of Catholicism. We saw how this period marked the growing presence in Brazil of mainline Protestants, such as the Lutherans, Methodists, Presbyterians, and Baptists, who built schools, seminaries, and hospitals, expanding civil society and the public arena beyond the Catholic compass. With some exceptions, such as the case of Richard Ratcliff, a deeply conservative Baptist committed to the preservation of slavery, Protestants introduced more congregational forms of organization that, at the very minimum, challenged traditional hierarchical politics. In other words, the increased religious pluralism ushered in by independence and the national period had important long-term implications for Brazilian society and politics.

Brazilian Christianity, Politics, and Society　　143

The separation of church and state fed into regional and national conflicts such as those of Canudos (1896–7) in Bahia and Contestado (1912–16) in the southern states of Paraná and Santa Catarina. In these conflicts, religious issues like the recognition of civil marriage and the state's control of public education and cemeteries mixed with struggles over land tenure. These struggles were generated by the forcible displacement of share croppers and small farmers produced by the introduction of new crops, such as coffee, for global capitalist markets, and of new technologies like the railroad, as well as by the attempts of elites in Rio de Janeiro and São Paulo to take power from local bosses. Many peasants perceived all these religious and sociopolitical changes as undermining the kinship-based fabric of rural traditional Luso-Catholicism (see Chapter 2). In response, they took up arms against the secular state, almost always with tragic consequences.

The separation of church and state also set the stage for the Romanization of Brazilian Catholicism, with the Holy See rather than the Portuguese Crown or the emperor becoming its main point of reference and support. In practice, this meant a modernization of Brazilian Catholicism through the standardized formation of priests and the introduction of a reinforced Vatican orthodoxy, often at the cost of controlling and even suppressing local beliefs, practices, and organizations. Romanization thus represented a period of Catholic consolidation and centralization, which was accompanied by tensions with popular devotions and groups like *irmandades* (brotherhoods) that had developed through syncretism since the beginning of the colonial period. These tensions, in turn, laid the groundwork for the further diversification of Brazilian Catholicism that would come with the Second Vatican Council. As discussed in Chapter 1, even with the Brazilian Catholic Church increasingly turning to Rome for direction, Catholic elites sought re-accommodation with the new secular republican authorities. As a result, the hierarchical, corporatist, and personalistic political structures and dynamics generated during the colonial period were left fairly intact. The persistence of *coronelismo* during the Estado Novo (New State, 1937–45) attests to this fact: President Getúlio Vargas, who rose through the patronage networks in Rio Grande do Sul, could be said to represent a new version of the *coronel-caudilho*, with more centralized powers based on the modern state.

The Socio-Economics and Politics of Brazilian Pentecostalism

It is only with the explosive growth of Pentecostalism beginning in the 1960s that the fate of traditional sociopolitical structures and dynamics hung in the balance. This growth accompanied an uneven model of capitalist development anchored on industrial poles located in the peripheries of large cities like São Paulo and Rio de Janeiro. Buffeted by unpredictable cycles of boom and bust in the global prices of agricultural commodities—from sugar and rubber to oranges and coffee—and by persistent natural disasters like droughts in the countryside (particularly in the northeast), Brazil began to experience rapid and disorderly urbanization that threatened to break the fabric of the hierarchical, corporatist, and personalistic Catholic order. In their pioneering works, Emilio Willems (1967) and Christian Lalive D'Epinay (1968) drew from sociologist Emile Durkheim's concept of anomie to explain the accelerated growth of Pentecostalism in Brazil and Chile. Durkheim had observed that as small, relatively simple agrarian societies based on "mechanical solidarity"—social cohesion based on low levels of differentiation—evolve into large, complex industrial societies characterized by "organic solidarity," in which social integration is the result of the interdependence among highly differentiated parts, a situation of lawlessness (*a-nomos*) occurs. In this anomic condition, the individual is unable to rely on the old norms that have been upturned or the new ones that have not yet consolidated. Applying the concept of anomie to the Brazil in the 1960s, Willems and Lalive D'Epinay hypothesized that Pentecostalism held a particular appeal for people migrating to large cities. Faced with an intense, disorderly, and highly diversified environment, migrants from the countryside experience a dramatic sense of disorientation, unable to navigate the dangers and unpredictability of urban life without the cohesion and guidance provided by the shared collective representations they left behind. With its emphasis on the immediate experience of the sacred in the intimate setting of the congregation (as opposed to the large, impersonal Catholic parish), an ascetic lifestyle, and a personal relationship with Jesus, Pentecostalism offered the best antidote to anomie.

Complex social phenomena like the decline of Catholicism and rapid growth of Pentecostalism in Brazil cannot be reduced to a single social or religious variable. Rather, they are the outcome of the entanglement of many religious, socioeconomic, and historical factors. Nevertheless, there are clear correlations between Catholicism's relative resilience and "rurality," and between Pentecostal growth and rapid urbanization. Indeed, the percentage of rural Catholics is higher than the average percentage of households in the countryside for Brazil, while the percentage of Evangelicals dwelling in cities exceeds the proportion for the country as a whole, suggesting that Evangelical Protestantism, particularly Pentecostalism, may be well adapted to the challenges of city life (see Table 4 in the previous chapter). Mariz and Gracino (2013: 168) note, along the lines of

Lalive D'Epinay and Willems, that "Pentecostalism has advanced more sharply in regions receiving migrant populations, while in regions that send these [migrant] groups Catholicism is still strong."[1] And as these sending regions become more touched by migration, urbanization, and, more generally, globalization, the long-standing social relations and moral cohesion that undergirded Catholic hegemony will continue to weaken (Steil and Toniol 2013: 226).

Willems and Lalive D'Epinay differed on the long-term political consequences of the growth of Pentecostalism. For Willems, it signaled the collapse of the hierarchical, corporatist, and personalistic Catholic rural order, opening the way for the rise of individual autonomy supported by the Protestant principles of *sola scriptura* and *sola fides*, that is, by direct access to the sacred through God's word and through one's faith. Adapting sociologist Max Weber's thesis of the Protestant ethic, Willems saw this stress on the exercise of individual conscience, together with the emphasis on the total transformation of a person, particularly the rejection of the vices of the world (e.g., alcoholism, gambling, marital infidelity and strife, vices which often go along with the migration of single men to the city), as inculcating an ethos more in line with democracy and capitalist development. In contrast, Lalive D'Epinay argued that Pentecostalism's reliance on tightly knit and strongly emotive congregations led by charismatic pastors represented a transplantation to the city of the patriarchal and personalistic Catholic patterns in the countryside. When confronted by the diversity, anonymity, volatility, and risks of city life, migrants were, in effect, re-deploying in their Pentecostal congregations the authoritarianism of the traditional Catholic order, with pastors as the new *patrões* (bosses) and mediators vis-à-vis urban political elites, providing security and services in exchange for votes.

Ever since Willems's and Lalive D'Epinay's groundbreaking work, there has been an ongoing debate about the sociopolitical impact of Pentecostalism. Echoing Willems, David Martin (1990) argued that Pentecostal asceticism could contribute in the long run toward the economic improvement of poor Latin Americans by stimulating literacy (to read the Bible), ability to speak, voluntarism, grassroots leadership formation, and autonomy (as part of self-sustaining congregations). In Brazil, evidence for Martin's claim is at best contradictory, suggesting that both Willems and Lalive D'Epinay may have a point. In contrast to historical Protestants who consistently have incomes and levels of formal education higher than the average Brazilian, after 100 years of presence, Pentecostals continue to be at "the base of the social pyramid," with 64 percent of them earning no more than the minimum wage and with only 42 percent of them (older than fifteen) having completed elementary school

(Mariano 2013: 125).[2] In fact, the 2010 census shows that Pentecostalism is growing particularly "in poor, unassisted areas where from 1980 violence among the youth became epidemic and where gangs and armed groups spread; these are places where the presence of both the Catholic [Church] and the apparatuses of the state [os poderes públicos] is rare" (125). As such, Pentecostalism might be more about protecting the most vulnerable sectors of the Brazilian society from the "pathogens of poverty" (Chesnut 1997) and the most deleterious contradictions of Brazilian capitalism than about upward economic mobility.[3] Moreover, the dominance of Neo-Pentecostalism's gospel of health and wealth may be ushering in a consumerist outlook, a strong desire to rely on gifts of the Holy Spirit to become economically successful in an instant, that has little in common with the Protestant Puritan asceticism that Weber described (Kramer 2001). More on the confluences between Neo-Pentecostalism and current sociopolitical dynamics later.

Similar ambivalences are found in debates about whether Pentecostalism is politically progressive, marking a break from the traditional way of doing politics inflected by colonial Catholicism, or politically conservative, giving old authoritarian patterns a new lease on life. Some of the most nuanced ethnographic work shows that Pentecostals can and do evince a wide range of political attitudes and behaviors, from political apathy to conservatism on cultural and social issues and progressivism when it comes to economics. This is not surprising given Pentecostalism's great diversity and fluidity. Ireland (1992) distinguishes between two ideal types of *crentes* (Evangelicals). "Church crentes" are primarily concerned with proselytism and the growth of their congregation. To achieve these goals, they are more willing to form alliances with established secular groups, particularly local bosses, to secure the resources that allow them to advance their earthly mission. As a result, church *crentes* tend to have a conservative political outlook.[4] In contrast, "sect crentes," the second ideal type of Brazilian Pentecostal constructed by Ireland, emphasize the inherent sinfulness of humanity and all human creations, including politics and even churches, and the need to prepare for the impending second coming of Jesus Christ, who will overturn all secular orders and bring a new reign of peace and justice. Thus, sect *crentes* are deeply suspicious of politics, often articulating a radical critique of entrenched patronage networks.

Ireland contends that Pentecostalism's condemnation of human institutions as corrupt and its focus on salvation at the end of times leaves it with few theological and ethical resources to imagine the construction of more just institutions and structures in the now. Thus, the potential for transformative politics among sect *crentes* tends to remain focused on the local level, on the moral regeneration of individuals, families, and, at best, particular neighborhoods or communities. In Ireland's view, this is particularly the case when Pentecostalism is compared to progressive popular Catholicism, whose liberationist politics I will discuss later on.

There is indeed considerable evidence that Pentecostalism has a transformational impact on the politics of identity and everyday life. Brazilian scholars such as Cecília Mariz and Maria das Dores Machado (1997) have shown how Pentecostalism's asceticism—the emphasis on abstinence, thrift, and hard work—as well as its redefinition of manhood away from public displays of sexual prowess toward being a strong, righteous, and reliable husband and father, gives Brazilian women a measure of security and power. As Machado (2005: 389) puts it:

> Pentecostalism combats the predominant masculine identity in Brazilian society, stimulating in the men that join the movement forms of conduct and qualities traditionally associated with femininity. Just like women, [men] must be docile, tolerant, loving, caring, etc., living an ascetic life ruled by a rigid sexual morality. Beyond that, they are expected to worry about family well-being, being more dedicated to the education and care of their children. All these expectations reveal a reconfiguration of male subjectivity, creating the possibility of more egalitarian family arrangements.

In other words, while Pentecostalism might not overturn existing gender roles and hierarchies—in fact, it seems to reinforce them by commanding *crente* women to respect and obey their husbands as the legitimate heads of their households—it curbs some of the most damaging habits associated with masculinity, such as womanizing, drinking, gambling, and domestic abuse, allowing many households to cope better with the "pathogens of poverty" (Chesnut 1997). This domestication of male chauvinism may help account for why Pentecostalism is particularly attractive to women. The 2010 census showed that 55.6 percent of Pentecostals are women (Mariz and Gracino 2013: 170).

Along the same lines, Pentecostalism's emphasis on the direct experience of the Holy Spirit who moves in mysterious ways and can baptize anyone regardless of his/her class, gender, and color of skin has unexpected consequences for Brazilians of African descent. Despite the myth of racial democracy—the national narrative that Brazil has not experienced a system of sharp racial segregation as in the United States and South Africa—Afro-Brazilians continue to be discriminated against and excluded.[5] Anthropologist John Burdick (1993) argues that in contrast to Catholicism, which is a "cult of continuity" that draws its lay leadership from the most established, invariably lighter-skinned local groups, Pentecostalism, along with African-based religions like Candomblé and Umbanda, are "cults of affliction" constituted by people who come together seeking to address common predicaments like addictions and illnesses that the precarious national health care system fails to resolve. This "we-are-all-in-this-together" condition mitigates any social and racial distinctions. Incorporating debates on gender and Pentecostalism with the analysis of racist attitudes that denigrate the bodies of black Brazilians as either ugly or over-sexualized, Burdick (1998: 22) writes:

> By conceiving of women's bodies as vessels into which the Holy Spirit can be poured, Pentecostalism effectively shifts the gazes from without to within. Pentecostalism has its own female aesthetics, but it is an aesthetic designed to draw attention to the space within, to the part unseen . . . . This is a body that is released from the male gaze, from its status to the satisfier of male desire.

As compelling as this argument is, it must be counterbalanced by the fact that Neo-Pentecostal Brazilian churches such as the Universal Church of the Kingdom of God have taken an aggressively proselytizing stance vis-à-vis Candomblé and Umbanda, advocating "spiritual warfare" against them. The demonic spirits that UCKG pastors bind and expel in their weekly *cultos de libertação* (liberation services) as the sources of sickness and misfortune are Pomba Gira, Zé Pilintra, Tranca Rua, and other ancestor spirits that occupy a central place in Umbanda's and, to a lesser extent, Candomblé's pantheons. Pastors and members of the UCKG have gone as far as picketing Umbanda and Candomblé houses, running afoul of Brazil's constitution which guarantees freedom of religion and leading to charges that the church seeks to destroy African heritage in Brazil. There is, however, rich irony in the Universal's combat of African-based spirits: all the time and energy devoted to exorcizing them seems to confirm their efficacy. In a kind of symbiotic relation, African-based religions are recognized as potent competitors within the market for pneuma-centric religions, religions centered around the powerful experience of spirits, whether they are ancestor spirits from Africa or the Holy Spirit (Chesnut 2003).

On the other side of the coin, progressive Catholicism and historical Protestantism have incorporated African instruments like drums, rituals like dance, and images like Zumbí and Martin Luther King into "inculturated" Masses and theologies (Selka 2009). While these incorporations may at times appear essentialist, imposing simplistic and static notions of African traditions in Brazil and the Americas, they do represent earnest efforts to condemn racism and to recognize and empower the often-ignored voices of Afro-Brazilian Christians.

Beyond the micropolitics of gender, race, and everyday life, Brazilian Evangelicals also participate in electoral politics. Paul Freston sees the legislative elections of 1986, immediately following the transition to civilian rule, as a "turning point," with Pentecostals "exchang[ing] their apolitical slogan 'believers don't mess with politics' for the corporatist 'brother votes for brother,' electing a numerous and vocal caucus" (2001a: 12). Thus, whereas there were only twelve Protestants elected to the 1983–7 legislative cohort (of 594 members), thirty-two came in for the 1987–91 period, a number that held steady until 1999, when forty-nine were elected. The majority of the Protestants elected during that period—61 percent—identified themselves as Pentecostal. This stands in sharp contrast with previous affiliation of Protestant congressmen: from 1933 to 1987, only 6 percent were Pentecostal and 94 percent came from historical churches, such as Lutherans, Presbyterians, Methodists, and Baptists (Freston 2001a: 19). As of September 2016, there were a total of ninety Protestant congressmen (that is, 15 percent of the legislative body), the majority of whom are affiliated with the Assemblies of God, the Pentecostal Church that has historically been the chief Protestant force in congress.[6]

Party affiliation for Protestants in congress is diverse and highly fragmented.[7] Thus, it is hard to generalize, but while many Pentecostals belong to center-right parties like the Brazilian Republican Party (PRB) and the PP (Progressive Party) or the centrist MDB (Brazilian Democratic Movement Party), which was instrumental in the impeachment of President Dilma Rousseff (Workers' Party—PT), mainline Protestants tend to be affiliated with center-left parties, as is the case of Benedita da Silva, formerly from the Assemblies of God but now a Presbyterian, who has been active in the PT. A clear exception to this rule of thumb is Marina Silva, formerly of the Partido Verde (Green Party) and now leader of the Rede Sustentabilidade (Sustainability Network), who was strongly influenced by liberation theology and was an activist in the base communities and the Catholic Pastoral Land Commission before becoming a Pentecostal.

What is clear is that the *bancada evangélica* (the Evangelical caucus), often working with Charismatic Catholics, has coalesced into a strong single political force, the Frente Parlamentar Evangélica (FPE—Evangelical Parliamentary Front), to advance social and cultural issues such as opposition to abortion, same-sex marriage, and recognition of the civil rights of the LGBT community.[8] FPE's focus on morality, its reliance on the principle of "brother votes for [and with] brother," and pragmatism have been particularly evident in presidential politics. After accusing Luiz Inácio "Lula" da Silva and his hand-picked successor Dilma Rousseff of being "Satan worshippers" (*satanistas*) during their campaigns, once elected, the FPE supported their left-wing governments. Nevertheless, in the wake of a deepening economic crisis, the Front had a new about-face and supported Rousseff's contentious impeachment and the installing of a right-of-center regime. These shifts show that the FPE's key interest is "to be on the side of who is strong [at a particular juncture] and who can certainly favor their cherished conservative agendas" (Cunha 2016). An alternative, less instrumental reading of this shift might be that the FPE was concerned with the corruption that had embroiled the governing PT, since, after all, corruption is a moral issue. However, many members of the FPE have themselves been implicated in corruption scandals as part of persistent patterns of patrimonial politics in Brazil.[9]

Neo-Pentecostal churches, like the UCKG, have definitely tilted Evangelical politics to the right, advocating dominion theology, a geopolitical view that goes beyond carrying out the Great Commission, Jesus's injunction to his disciples to "go therefore and make disciples of all nations, baptizing them in the name of the Father and of the Son and of the Holy Spirit, teaching them to observe all that I have commanded you" (Mt. 28:19-20).[10] Operating through dense transnational networks of missionaries and through the expert use of electronic media, these churches seek to capture territories and liberate souls throughout the world in a veritable cosmic battle against the Devil and his minions, in the process making Brazil a religious power in the shift of Christianity's center of gravity to the Global South. Arguably, the most visible illustration of UCKG's dominion theology is the Temple of Solomon in São Paulo, with which I introduced the book. Macedo sees the colossal and sumptuous building as the material apotheosis of a geo-spiritual project that makes Brazil the epicenter of Jesus Christ's coming reign and places the country at the center of a vast "globally integrated network" (Mafra, Swatowiski, and Sampaio 2013). This network inverts the country's peripheral place in the capitalist world system, in effect mirroring Brazil's rise as one of the BRICS, that is, one of the emerging new economies along with Russia, India, China, and South Africa.

The rise of the right-wing populist politician and former army captain Jair Bolsonaro and his election as president may have marked a watershed for Brazilian Evangelicals (Bailey 2017). Although he is a Catholic, Bolsonaro is married to a Baptist. His marriage ceremony was celebrated by Pastor Silas Malafaia, a prominent Neo-Pentecostal televangelist, whose net worth was estimated by *Forbes* (2013) at $150 million and who has publicly condemned homosexuality, same-sex marriage, and abortion. During the ceremony, Malafaia declared that the union between "male and female" (*macho e fêmea*) is a "principle of God."

Brazilian Christianity, Politics, and Society 151

Bolsonaro also made a point of getting baptized in the waters of the River Jordan by prominent Assemblies of God pastor Everaldo Dias, just as the Brazilian senate was proceeding to vote on impeaching Dilma Rousseff. A short video of the event was widely circulated on social media. Social media, especially Facebook, YouTube, and WhatsApp, also played an important part in demonizing the Workers' Party and its presidential candidate, Fernando Haddad, for trying to undermine the traditional family as the irreducible and irreplaceable nucleus of Brazilian society. During the Rousseff administration, Haddad had been minister of Education, at a time when an anti-discrimination and anti-bullying program for a junior high school named Escola sem Homofobia (School without Homophobia) was proposed.[11] This proposal was met with fierce resistance from the *bancada evangélica*, as well as many (Neo)Pentecostal churches and social media. They began to spread conspiracies about the contents of what they dubbed "The Gay Kit" (*o Kit Gay*) and about communist plots to indoctrinate children with politically correct ideology friendly to deviant sexuality like pedophilia. Romancini (2018) sees this as the "construction of a moral panic" by a "mediatic populism" led by conservative Christian actors well seasoned in the use of electronic media.

Parallelly, conservative Christian networks, which prominently included Edir Macedo's TV Record, disseminated a well-crafted image of Bolsonaro as the candidate committed to "the values of the Christian family" and protector of the interests of "*o cidadão de bem*" (the good citizen) against the social and political chaos facing the country following a sharp economic downturn that took place during the Rousseff administration.[12] With the motto "*Brazil acima de tudo! Deus acima de todos!*" (Brazil above all! God above everybody!), Bolsonaro advanced a nationalist and populist platform that included the liberalization of restrictions to the ownership of guns and the attempt to re-read the legacy of the military dictatorship in a positive light, as an idealized patriarchal past of order and progress, when the nation was "at peace" and unified under the strong arm of the military, a military that protected the motherland from the rapacious hands of international and godless communists. If in the process, a few of these communists had to be tortured or "disappeared," that was the price to pay. He also pledged that he would single-handedly clean the corruption eating at Brazilian democratic institutions and society at large.

As we will see below, Bolsonaro's reading of the military regime does not correspond to facts about the widespread repression they perpetrated. Nevertheless, the enormous vacuum left by the crisis of traditional parties, including the Workers' Party, which became embroiled in Lava Jato (Cash Wash), a multi-billion dollar scheme by large multinational corporations (Petrobrás and Odebrecht) to bribe government officials in exchange for lucrative contracts, created the conditions under which Bolsonaro's image as a valiant anti-corruption fighter not beholden to any established political party could gain traction. More specifically, Lula da Silva, the leader of the Workers' Party who up until that point had been the leading presidential contender, was convicted and imprisoned for receiving kickbacks he used in the construction of a seaside luxury apartment as part of Lava Jato. Eventually, he was also prohibited from being a presidential candidate under questionable judiciary maneuvers.[13]

With Lula out of the way, Bolsonaro successfully tapped into the generalized sense of insecurity and anger among the citizenry following the economic recession and the various political scandals. Violent crime was a particular concern for Brazilian voters. This is not surprising, given that, at 30.8 homicides per 100,000 people, Brazil had one of the highest murder rates in the world in 2017.[14] That's 64,000 killings (an increment of close to 50 percent in the last decade) to go along with more than 60,000 reported cases of rape. Transnational drug syndicates that now control vast territories in cities throughout Brazil play a major part in violent crime, which disproportionately affects poor young Brazilians of African descent. Bolsonaro's proposal was to give police more punitive powers, to relax gun-control laws, and to encourage strongman vigilantism.[15] His law-and-order stance played well not only with men but also with women who saw him as protecting their families, despite his repeated sexist comments (Sims 2018).[16] The stance also resonated with the emphasis on asceticism and on spiritual warfare against the Devil's minions in many Pentecostal churches. After all, these churches do not just combat the ravages of drug addiction, producing re-formed, God-fearing citizens; they also battle the evil spirits who cause it. Neo-Pentecostal churches like the Universal Church of the Kingdom of God imagine these spirits as Umbanda's *povo da rua*—spirits of color representing life in the *"brega,"* the rough-and-tumble streets of poor neighborhoods—mercurial rogues like Zé Pilintra, Tranca Rua, Sete Facas, and Pomba Gira. Drawing from Weber, we can say that the physical violence and the stress on incarceration behind Bolsonaro's politics of law and order has a strong "elective affinity" with the spiritual and symbolic violence of exorcism and being "slain in the Holy Spirit."[17]

On October 28, 2018, in the second round, Bolsonaro was elected president of Brazil with 55.13 percent of the vote, that is, 57.7 million votes. In one of the first in-depth scholarly analyses of Bolsonaro's election, Carvalho and Junior (2019) rightly remind us that his triumph was not the result of a single factor, but rather a combination of multiple variables. They emphasize the role of geographic inequalities: "the exacerbation of social and regional polarities" between the poorer northeast and north and the wealthier south and southeast. Bolsonaro won the latter by wide margins, while he lost the northeast by a significant percentage (almost forty points).[18] While Carvalho and Junior do not explain the reasons behind these regional differences, it is worth pointing out that the northeast was one of the regions most benefited by the poverty reduction programs of the Workers' Party. Such a redistribution of wealth might have produced a backlash in the wealthier regions of the country.

Carvalho's and Junior's point about the importance of regional and urban-rural dynamics is well taken.[19] I have suggested that these scales need to be considered more seriously in the study of the changing character of Christianity in Brazil. Nonetheless, from the sociology of religion viewpoint, there are important national and global variables that contributed to Bolsonaro's election. I already hinted at them in my comment on the elective affinity between his image as a strongman coming to cleanse Brazil with an uncompromising law-and-order stance and theological-moral visions within Christianity, both Catholic and Protestant. I have argued that messianism and millenarianism, condensed in the figure of King Sebastião who would come to vanquish infidels and re-establish a golden age, have been central to the underlying structures of feeling and experience inculcated by traditional Luso-Christianity as it took root in Brazil. While the media and the context have changed, this time involving electronic networks and a heavily urbanized Brazil, patrimonial politics persist.[20] And to borrow from Ireland's dichotomy, the message of traditional morality and gender roles not only appealed to traditional and conservative Catholics (more on them later) but also resonated particularly strongly with "church" *crentes*. According to Datafolha, 70 percent of *evangélicos* voted for Bolsonaro, while only 49 percent of Catholics voted for him (versus 55 percent of the overall population). As the above figure shows, while *crentes* are without a doubt an important part of Bolsonaro's electoral base, almost one-third of Evangelicals did not vote for him, a fact that once again demonstrates their relative diversity when it comes to politics. These might be Ireland's "sect" *crentes*.[21] At the very least, Bolsonaro divided Evangelicals in similar ways to the deep discord he generated in the Brazilian public at large. More broadly and in terms of underlying trends, Bolsonaro's election can be read at least on two interrelated levels. Nationally, it may represent a realignment of politics: the alliance of Evangelical Christians, large landowners, and the military is likely to push back against the expansion of civil rights and protections for Indigenous people, peasants, the landless, the urban poor, Brazilians of African descent, the LGBTQI+ community, and the environment, which had begun with the transition to civilian rule in 1982 and seemed to have consolidated, albeit with some contradictions, in the PT's administrations. For all their shortcomings, these administrations, particularly Lula da Silva's, had managed to reduce poverty indexes and redistribute some of the wealth.[22] As we saw in Chapter 1 and as I will examine later, progressive Christians, both Catholics and historic Protestants, were very much protagonists in this expansion of civil society and in advancing visions of social justice that they felt were central to the gospel. The fact that almost half of Catholics voted for Bolsonaro may indicate that the ideals and ethos advanced by liberation theology and CEBs still have fragile, shallow roots—more about this later—and it remains to be seen if these progressive forces can muster resistance to the authoritarian turn. In addition, there are vocal Catholic groups formed by priests, bishops, and lay people that are deeply critical of progressive agendas and left-leaning parties and social movements. They believe that these institutions want to establish communism in Brazil and are anti-family. These traditionalist groups are extremely supportive of Bolsonaro's "pauta de costumes" (the "good habits" agenda), which includes "measures such as the Family Statute that limits the definition of the family nucleus to the union of a men and a woman; School without a Party, which seeks to prohibit professors from expressing 'ideological' opinions; the fight against the 'ideology of gender.'"[23]

At the global level, the election of Bolsonaro may be seen as part of a nationalist reaction against the superficial and commodified cosmopolitanism, mobility, socioeconomic dislocation, and detraditionalization brought about by the current episode of globalization, as also exemplified by the presidency of Donald Trump in the United States and by Brexit.[24] Zygmunt Bauman (2006) has argued that late modernity is characterized by "a liquid fear," a terror of the unknown and the uncontrollable, ranging from market volatility to terrorism, climate change, and environmental catastrophes, to which globalization has made us more vulnerable. As we saw when I wrote about violent crime and social upheaval in today's Brazil, certain dimensions of this fear are well founded and not just a form of false consciousness. And a skillful charismatic leader like Bolsonaro can readily tap into the real longing for security and stability of the population. Yet, this diffuse fear very often coalesces into a visceral loathing of the Other, which uncritically conflates terrorists, drug traffickers, and violent gang members with immigrants, asylum seekers, or those who live in poor neighborhoods or do not share our religious or sexual identity. That is why the recognition of the contingency and fluidity of identities and the valuing of difference that has been part and parcel of the progressive agenda is seen as an existential threat, spelling the end of (Christian) civilization.[25] Any form of alterity must be eliminated, excluded, or controlled through surveillance, incarceration, or the implementation of draconian laws or derogatory categories. Social media with its ever-presence and vulnerability to conspiracies and "fake news" have only heightened this fear and made it more viral. In turn, this terror triggers the desire for order and the nostalgia for an imagined past of harmony through uniformity and clear identities (often in an us-versus-them template). This past is often imagined as one in which (white) men were real men, with no gender fluidity and no women, racial minorities, and immigrants to contest their privilege. In this idealized past of peace and order, as opposed to the uncertain and messy present, men had full authority over families in the same way that God is sovereign above everything ("*Deus acima de todos!*"). Here Bolsonaro's conservative politics have, once again, elective affinities with the Neo-Pentecostal vision of the world as imbued by evil spirits that need to be defeated and bound under the universal leadership of a muscular, successful Jesus Christ. A concrete example of this convergence is Bolsonaro's decision to recognize Jerusalem as the capital of Israel as a way to reward his Evangelical base. Many of his supporters hold a dispensational theology that sees the restoration of Israel as a prelude to Jews accepting Jesus Christ as their rightful Messiah and, then, to the second coming (Schreiber 2019).[26]

Arguably, no one has expressed the geopolitical vision of Bolsonaro's administration and its elective affinities with a conservative Evangelical Christian agenda more eloquently than Ernesto Araújo, his minister for Foreign Affairs. In his blog, he writes:

> I want to help Brazil and the world free themselves from globalist ideology. Globalism is economic globalization that has come to be piloted by cultural Marxism.[27] Essentially, it is an anti-human and anti-Christian system. Faith in Christ means today to fight against globalism, whose ultimate goal is to break the connection between God and man, making man a slave and God irrelevant. The metapolitical project essentially means opening oneself to the presence of God in politics and history.[28]

The question here is whether we might be seeing a new deployment of Christendom that is no longer limited to forging a new concordat between church and state and is symbolized by the iconic statue of *O Cristo Redentor* extending his arms over the heart of Brazil, as was the vision of Cardinal Leme in the early 1900s (see Chapter 3). It would be a Christendom that sees a fully converted Brazil as the main protagonist in the Christianization of the world

156 *Christianity in Brazil*

through the export of Brazilian Christianity by transnational churches like the UCKG and the IMPD. I will have more to say about this in my conclusion.

These reflections offer a good point of departure to understand the implications of the election of Bolsonaro for Brazilian Christianity. Nevertheless, we need to recognize that this is still an unfolding story.[29]

Brazilian Catholicism and Politics

Parallel to the socioeconomic changes that framed the growth of Pentecostalism during the 1960s and 1970s, the Brazilian Catholic Church was also undergoing radical transformations. The Second Vatican Council (1962–5) spurred a process of *aggiornamento* (updating) of Catholicism, following a century of opposition to modern ideas and projects like democracy, socialism, and freedom of religion. The council enjoined Catholics to "read the signs of the times," that is, to engage contemporary society and to value modernity's contributions to the advancement of humanity, even as it also asked them to grapple with the challenges it posed through the application of the social teachings of the church. In 1968 in Medellín, Colombia, the Latin American bishops came together to flesh out the implications of the council for the region. Reading the signs of the time—the widespread social inequalities maintained by repressive military governments and the rise of revolutionary movements challenging the status quo—the bishops adopted a preferential option for the poor that had dramatic consequences for church-state relations in Latin America. After centuries of allying with the dominant political groups, a relationship shaped by the Royal Patronage and left fairly intact by independence, the bishops made the vast sectors at the margins of society the locus for pastoral action, implementing a series of initiatives at the grassroots, such as base ecclesial communities (CEBs), for theological reflection. The task was to start with the experiences of poor Latin Americans, experiences which very often include hunger, lack of adequate housing and health care, unemployment and underemployment, as well as political repression, and consider what the gospel and the church's magisterium would say about those experiences. What does this thinking disclose? In the words of Brazilian liberation theologians Leonardo and Clodovis Boff,

> in the light of faith, Christian see in [the poor] the challenging face of the Suffering Servant, Jesus Christ. . . . The Crucified in these crucified persons weeps and cries out: "I was hungry . . . in prison . . . naked" . . . . Here what is needed is not so much contemplation as effective action for liberation. The

Brazilian Christianity, Politics, and Society

Crucified needs to be raised to life. We are on the side of the poor only when we struggle alongside them against the poverty that has been unjustly created and force on them. Service in solidarity with the oppressed also implies an act of love for the suffering Christ. (Boff and Boff 1987: 4)

The focus on the poor and, more specifically, on combating the "structural sin" inherent in economic oppression led some progressive Brazilian Catholics to borrow from Marxist class analysis, which during the late 1960s had emerged as an alternative to capitalist models of development that were not only inadequate to address the country's widespread poverty but also seemed to justify it. Since 1959, the Cuban Revolution provided inspiration for armed insurrections throughout Latin American, offering an alternative political project. In Brazil, some Catholic student activists and leaders working among peasants became radicalized and took up arms against the military dictatorship. However, there was not a guerrilla movement of the dimensions of those in Nicaragua, El Salvador, or Colombia. And while Marxism's reductionism and atheism would become points of contention in the Vatican's upbraiding of liberation theology with the election of John Paul II and his successor Benedict XVI, its use was not prevalent among progressive Catholics. Nevertheless, Vatican II and Medellín ushered in a new political imagination in Latin America, more specifically in Brazilian Catholicism, one that in the strong advocacy for the common good, particularly as it applies to the most disadvantaged sectors of society, stands in contrast not only to traditional systems of political patronage but also to Pentecostalism's focus on the spiritual and moral transformation of the individual, in his/her personal relationship with God. Whether this Catholic liberationist sociopolitical vision actually translates into transformative practices at various levels, from the grassroots to social movements and political parties, is more uncertain.

As we saw in Chapter 1, building on the groundwork of progressive leaders like Hélder Câmara, the Brazilian Church was at the forefront of implementing the conclusions of Medellín. This commitment was strengthened by the military coup of 1964, which installed a repressive dictatorship that killed and "disappeared" more than 400, detained, tortured, and exiled upward of 50,000 dents, suspended all constitutional rights such as habeas corpus, and shut expressions of political opposition, from independent unions to political lling a widespread apparatus of surveillance, cultural and moral ntrol (Filho 2012). The most brutal period of the dictatorship to be known as *os anos de chumbo* (the years of lead), and it ional coordination with other authoritarian military regimes in Argentina, Uruguay, Paraguay, Chile, and Bolivia in the "Condor Operation." As many as 60,000 people, most in neighboring Argentina, were killed during that US-backed plan (Rohter 2014).

The church's hierarchy was initially supportive of the coup, feeling that it would neutralize the threat of communism. However, as the military regime grew more brutal, the church eventually became one of the few institutions in civil society with the moral legitimacy and national and transnational organizational resources to stand up to the repression. While there were divisions within the Catholic hierarchy regarding the extent to which the church should become directly involved in protests, the case of the archdiocese of São Paulo, under the leadership of Cardinal Paulo Arns, shows that the church acted as a major advocate for human rights, extensively documenting and denouncing abuses by the military regime. This opposition led to the harassment, detention, and torture of lay Catholic activists and members of the clergy (Bruneau 1982; Mainwaring 1986). In addition, during the *abertura* (literally, the "opening," the gradual transition to civilian and democratic rule from 1974 to 1985), the church was one of the strongest voices in support of direct elections (*diretas já*) (Della Cava 1988).

The overall and long-term sociopolitical impact of Brazilian progressive Catholicism has been subject to debate. Some scholars point to the small number of Catholics involved in CEBs. As I discussed in Chapter 5, even at the height of their prominence, there were at best 100,000 base communities, perhaps comprising 3–5 percent of all Brazilian Catholics (Hewitt 1991; Daudelin 1992; Valle and Pitta 1994). This stands in sharp contrast to a large number of Pentecostals participating in ever-proliferating churches. This contrast has led to the claim that while "the Catholic Church opts for the poor because it is not a church of the poor . . . Pentecostal churches do not opt for the poor because they are already a poor people's church. That is why poor people are choosing them" (Mariz 1994: 80). Along the same lines, Burdick (1993) has argued that the strong focus in CEBs on developing a critical social consciousness and engaging in political activism paradoxically tends to reproduce hierarchies within the poor: this focus privileges the most educated and financially stable sectors of that population, those that have the literacy, time, and economic security to be able to sustain that kind of engagement. If we add to this reprod entrenched socioeconomic hierarchies the fact that CEBs often de on priests and other pastoral agents to function, the politically force of grassroots progressive Catholicism appears overstate would seem to be the continuation of Catholic patriarchal p of this stands in contrast to Pentecostalism which offers a less intellectualized, more visceral religion that, especially in its Neo-Pentecostal versions, can be experienced without mediation by the faithful and addresses the urgent needs of the poor for health and economic survival, the need to be cured and protected from the ravages of alcoholism, drug addiction, and violence. In that sense, Pentecostalism would truly be *"a religião popular,"* the most grassroots version of Brazilian Christianity.

We have seen above, however, that Pentecostalism is diverse and politically multivalent. The same goes for post–Vatican II progressive Brazilian Catholicism. Not all CEBs were explicitly involved in capital "P" politics. As political scientist Daniel Levine (1989) observes, "they range in emphasis from highly pietistic and devotional to socially activist, in structure from authoritarian to democratic, and in status from autonomous to utterly reliant on guidance from external elites and dominant institutions." Vásquez (1998) has shown that the charges of elitism and failure to connect with the masses leveled against CEBs have to be greatly nuanced by an understanding of the structural and institutional transformations and constraints faced by Brazilian progressive Catholicism and, more generally, by Brazilian society as a whole, as it underwent a democratic transition from the late 1980s on. First, due to Brazil's deeper insertion in the processes of globalization, there were dramatic changes in the economy that rendered vast sectors of the working poor more vulnerable and compelled them to focus primarily on survival, thus making political organization more difficult and liberation theology's vision of beginning to build the reign of God here on earth less plausible. Second, with the election of Pope John Paul II in 1979, the Vatican became openly hostile to liberation theology, naming conservative bishops that withdrew support from and even severely curtailed progressive Catholicism's grassroots initiatives.

Despite the contradictions within progressive Catholicism and the social and religious obstacles it faced, its contributions to contemporary Brazilian society cannot be denied. The church offered safe spaces to undertake political activism at a time when Brazilian civil society was still inchoate and under severe strain (Krischke 2001). In the words of a CEB activist, during the military dictatorship "people didn't have the right to speak, people were repressed, and [in the base communities] there was a place where people had very similar identity, so we felt stronger as a group, as a people. We felt the force of knowing that we were going to conquer something greater" (Drogus and Stewart-Gambino 2005: 44). Within the spaces of solidarity afforded by grassroots progressive initiatives, poor farmers and city dwellers alike gained valuable leadership skills, such as the capacity to speak in public, to analyze social phenomena critically, and to organize. In particular, "women began to have their rights to participate in things outside the home, because before I didn't even know these things existed. Then I began to see that I could do more than clean house, sew. *We became real people*" (2). Linking private and public spheres meant that women "started talking about local problems, for example, the lack of asphalt, sewage, day care, difficulties at school, and the health post. Then, women became conscious that to improve the neighborhood it was necessary to be making demands and to make things happen in the neighborhood" (2–3).

As the transition to democratic rule took place, many of these Catholic activists went on to become leaders in the expanding civil society. In fact, many of the founders of the Workers' Party (1978) were progressive Catholics, heavily influenced by liberationist pedagogical methods and religiopolitical philosophy. This is certainly the case with former President Lula himself, whose involvement in the *pastoral operária* (the Catholic pastoral initiative toward industrial workers) and the newly formed independent union Central Unica dos Trabalhadores (CUT) nurtured his leadership skills (Bourne 2008). Furthermore, progressive Catholicism's visions of the common good and of the earth and its fruits as gifts from the creator that must be handled with care, as well as its ethos and goals, have permeated vibrant social movements such as the Movimento dos Trabalhadores Rurais Sem Terra (Movement of Landless Rural Workers—MST), which political scientist Miguel Carter (n.d.: 1) calls "Latin America's premier grassroots organization and one of the most significant social movements for land reform in world history."[30] According to Carter (2015: 397) "the MST's public activism has been instrumental in reinstating land reform on Brazil's national agenda. It has played a decisive role in the creation of over 2,000 agricultural settlements . . . benefitting an estimated 135,000 landless families through the distribution of 3.7 million hectares of land, an area the size of the Switzerland or state of West Virginia."

Thus, it is possible to conclude safely that while the number of those involved in CEBs and other progressive Catholic initiatives might have been small, the nature of this involvement and the context in which it took place greatly magnified their sociopolitical impact. This is what Burdick concludes when he highlights three "legacies of liberation": "the formation of new leadership cohorts, the transmission of those cohorts' values and views to new social contexts, and the new perspectival inflections of popular consciousness that result" (2004: 142).

From the 1980s on, the combination of the disorderly transition to democracy, the restructuring of the Brazilian economy along neoliberal lines, and the

Brazilian Christianity, Politics, and Society 161

election of Pope John Paul II put progressive Catholicism's lasting legacy to the test. In particular, the Vatican summoned the Catholic Church in Latin America to shift its focus toward a "new evangelization," toward a sustained effort to reach out to nominal Catholics to preach the gospel to them and make it the centerpiece of their lives within and outside the church. As John Paul II told the Latin American bishops in Haiti in 1983,

> grave problems weigh on this [Latin American] people from the religious and ecclesial point of view: the chronic and sharp scarcity of vocations, priestly [as well as of] nuns and other pastoral agents with the concomitant result of religious ignorance, superstition, and syncretism among the humblest; the growing indifference, if not atheism, due to the current secularism, especially in the big cities and in the most educated layers of the population; the bitterness of the many, *who because of a wrong option* [una opción equívoca] *for the poor*, feel abandoned and unattended in their aspirations and religious needs; the advance of religious groups, many times lacking a true evangelical message and with methods of acting that show little respect for a true religious freedom, which place serious obstacles to the Catholic Church's mission and even to those of other Christian confessions. (John Paul II 1983, emphasis added)

In practice, the new evangelization meant de-emphasizing the political involvement around issues of social justice that characterized the 1960s and 1970s and instead increasing a stress on the spiritual and moral regeneration of the individual and his/her family. It is in this context that the Catholic Charismatic Renewal (CCR) movement gained increasing prominence in the Brazilian Catholic scene. It is not that CCR is apolitical; it is just that, as in the case of Pentecostalism with whom it shares a focus on the experience of the Holy Spirit, Charismatics adhere to "a traditional formula: first change the individual and then society by consequence will change. Any social change is always conceived of as a project of moralization, of the individual's morality, of sex and the most internal family relations" (Prandi and Valentin 1998: 171). This understanding of politics has translated into high-profile public campaigns, such as *Por hoje não, por hoje não vou mais pecar* (From now on, from now on I am not going to sin anymore) and *Hosana Brasil*, which particularly target young, urban middle-class Brazilians through big rallies and the skillful use of electronic media, entertainment, and music. The aim of these campaigns is to "live, promote, and proclaim chastity" and to keep "the goal of being saintly in modern times" (Carranza and Mariz 2013: 143). The CCR has also created a "Ministry of Faith and Politics" that seeks to "evangelize politics from the experience of the baptism in Holy Spirit. The objective is not to form political parties or to stage political

162 *Christianity in Brazil*

campaigns, but raise consciousness among Christians so they can use the vote in a just manner."[31] As I discussed above regarding the Evangelical caucus, Catholic Charismatics have joined Pentecostals in advancing policies that support the project of the remoralization of Brazilian society, strengthening and preserving traditional family roles and values in the face of rapidly changing gender identities.[32] Machado (2015) argues that in this coalition, Charismatic Catholics have focused more on infusing Brazilian politics and society with pro-life and conservative values, while Pentecostals have stressed the political formation of pastors and congregation members who can run for office and implement policies that serve the interests of their churches.

The emphasis on the new evangelization, the continued rapid growth of Pentecostalism, and the ascendency of the CCR as the preferred Catholic strategy to counter this growth led some in the late 1990s to declare that liberation theology was dead. However, I have been insisting that we must be careful not to overdraw the opposition between, on the one hand, a conservative, individualist, and spiritualist CCR, and on the other hand, the politically progressive and socially engaged CEBs, just as it is perilous to see progressive Catholicism and Pentecostalism in dualistic terms. "Consciousness-raising" materials from the CCR's Ministry of Faith and Politics state that the profile of a legitimate "charismatic political candidate" includes commitment "to the changes necessary for the effective realization of social justice in the country," "defense of the common good," "promotion of social inclusion," and a commitment to "the cause of the neediest and the struggles of his/her people," alongside the "defense and promotion of life" in "a path [*caminhada*] in consonance with the Church" (CCR 2012: 6). In other words, progressive Catholicism's language of consciousness-raising, social justice, the defense of the common good, and the struggle on behalf of the people has been incorporated by the CCR movement. This integration is not surprising, given that they are both offspring of the Second Vatican Council and are both influenced by Catholic social teaching. As we saw in Chapter 1, "at the local level the ideological differences between liberationist and Charismatic Catholicism are far less important that often assumed" by scholars and national religious leaders (De Theije 1999: 118). There are not only strong similarities but a great deal of cross-fertilization between the CCR and CEBs, such that both groups "create opportunities for ordinary men and women for voice and leadership." From the parishioners' point of view, "the differences between CEBs and CCR groups are more a matter of style than content. The idea that the two movements are fundamentally opposed to each other finds little support at the local level" (De Theije 1999: 118).

Prognostications of the demise of Brazilian progressive Catholicism proved premature with the election in 2013 of Pope Francis, who has made engagement with the poor a key element of his papacy. Whereas under John Paul II, the Congregation for the Doctrine of the Faith condemned certain aspects of liberation theology and silenced or censured several of its proponents, including Brazilian theologians Leonardo Boff and Ivone Gebara (see their biographical profiles in Chapter 3), following the election of Francis, Cardinal Gerhard Müller, the new Prefect of the Congregation, welcomed Gustavo Gutiérrez, considered the founder of liberation theology, to the Vatican. Müller went as far as declaring liberation theology "one of the most significant currents of Catholic theology of the 20th century" and co-authoring a book entitled *On the Side of the Poor: Liberation Theology* with Gutiérrez. Leonardo Boff sees these developments as signs of "the end of the war between Rome and liberation theology," a truce that may allow for a recognition that "some vehement mobilizations of ecclesial sectors against Liberation Theology were more motivated by some preferences in political orientation than by the desire to safeguard (*guardar*) and affirm the Apostles's faith." For Boff, the election of Francis confirms the continued relevance of progressive Catholicism and the validity of its preferential option for the poor:

> That which was true during the turbulent days when we were persecuted by the security apparatuses of the military and publicly defamed by our own brothers in the faith continues to be true now and hopefully always: the poor scream because they are oppressed [and] it belongs to the Christian faith mission to listen to those screams and to do what we can so that [the poor], organized and with the consciousness raised, can get out of that infamous situation that does not please anyone, including God. (Boff 2013)

Francis's groundbreaking encyclical on the environment *Laudato Si: On Care for Our Common Home* is further powerful evidence of the renewed influence of liberation theology in the Vatican and global Catholicism. The encyclical echoes many of the themes articulated by Boff two decades before in his *Cry of the Earth, Cry of the Poor* (1995), such as St. Francis of Assisi's deep appreciation for the interconnectedness and sacredness of all life and the liberationist insights that socioeconomic oppression is intimately linked with the degradation of the environment and that capitalism's unfettered quest for progress and wealth is at the heart of this oppression and degradation. In Francis's words, "The human environment and the natural environment deteriorate together; we cannot adequately combat environmental degradation unless we attend to causes related to human and social degradation. In fact, the deterioration of the environment

164   *Christianity in Brazil*

and of society affects the most vulnerable people on the planet" (Francis 2015: #48, p. 33).[33]

While it is true that Pope Francis has spurred a positive re-evaluation of progressive Catholicism with his clear denunciations of the excesses of global capitalism,[34] it is important to highlight the subtle ways in which he reinterprets the category of the poor. Francis thinks of poverty primarily as a virtue, as a marker of service, frugality, honesty, purifying suffering, and loyalty at a time of general indignation toward the excesses and wastefulness of contemporary capitalism. Poverty above all implies a call for moral and spiritual conversion in the midst of a church that has lost a great deal of its moral standing. This view is clear in his first encyclical *Lumen Fidei*, co-authored with Benedict XVI, which cites Francis of Assisi and Mother Teresa of Calcutta as models for work among the poor:

> They understood the mystery at work in them. In drawing near to the suffering, they were certainly not able to eliminate all their pain or to eliminate every evil. To those who suffer, God does not provide arguments which explain everything; rather his response is that of an accompanying presence . . . . Suffering reminds us that faith's service to the common good is always one of hope—a hope which looks ever ahead in the knowledge that only from God, from the future which comes from the risen Jesus, can our society find solid and lasting foundations. (Francis 2013: #57)

In other words, the primary pastoral task is to mitigate the effects of poverty and to offer the poor hope of a better life, not to accompany them in their struggles to build societies that reflect Catholic social teaching. These struggles are not directly connected with God's salvific work, as they were for liberation theology and other movements inspired by progressive Catholicism like the MST.

Francis's very successful visit to Brazil in 2013 offers an instructive window into the pastoral and political implications of his understanding of the poor and social justice. The visit took place right after mass protests against the persistence of inadequate social services like public health, education, and transportation, as well as the deepening of economic inequalities in the face of a recession, all while the country was spending millions of dollars to prepare for hosting the World Cup (2014) and the Olympics (2016). In this context, Francis visited Varginha, one of the poorest communities in Manguinhos, an area of Rio de Janeiro popularly known as "the Gaza Strip" for its high levels of violence among drug traffickers and between them and the police. Francis not only gave a speech in the local soccer stadium but also walked the streets of the neighborhood. In his speech, he asked "those who have more resources, public authorities, and all people committed to social justice: do not tire of working for a more just and empathic [*solidário*] world. No one can remain insensitive to the persistent inequalities. May each and everyone understand the need to give his/her contribution to end social injustices." Francis also critiqued the forcible "pacification" of *favelas* program advanced by the Brazilian government in preparation for the World Cup and Olympics, affirming that "no amount of pacification will be able to last, nor will harmony and happiness be attained in a society that ignores, pushes to the margins or excludes a part of it."[35]

At his speeches celebrating World Youth Day in Copacabana Beach, Francis asked young Brazilians and other pilgrims "Are you ready to enter the wave of revolution?" and encouraged them to "stir things up . . . to make a mess, to disturb complacency." Nevertheless, Francis's call to revolution is different from the street protests that preceded his visit. While the pope acknowledged the right of the people to protest in "an orderly, peaceful, and responsible fashion," he referred, rather, to a revolution of the heart, one that can bring more faith, love, and solidarity to a world in which "young people who have lost faith in the Church or even in God because of the counter-witness of Christians and ministers of the gospel . . . . So many young people who have lost faith in political institutions, because they see in them only selfishness and corruption." In other words, the call to revolution is primarily and fundamentally a call to evangelization, not to be afraid "to take Christ to all environments, even to the existential peripheries, including those who seem most distant, most indifferent." "Where does Jesus send us? There are no frontiers, there are no limits: he sends us to all people."[36] In this sense, Francis's theology has clear continuities not only with his conservative predecessors Benedict XVI and John Paul II's project of new evangelization but also with the Great Commission that has been so essential to Pentecostalism's global imagination. On the other hand, Francis's emphasis on poverty and his condemnation of the "culture of selfishness and individualism" in contemporary capitalism could be considered as a direct critique of the gospel of health and wealth, as articulated by Edir Macedo's IURD and other Neo-Pentecostal churches like Reborn in Christ (Almeida 2013).

If the visit to Brazil is an indication, Francis might be bridging two powerful pastoral approaches that have been at odds with each other in the Global South, a feat that eluded his two predecessors. He has taken the preferential option for the poor, which is central to progressive Catholicism—minus its more radical political implications and in-depth analysis of the social roots of injustice—and blended it with the embodied intimacy and cathartic affectivity of the CCR movement—but without the showiness that often accompanies this movement.

It is a charismaticism read through the grammar of simplicity, following the Jesuit tradition. The long-term pastoral impact of this synthesis vis-à-vis the growing diversity of Christianity in Brazil is an open question.

Certainly, the rise and election of Bolsonaro have made the synthesis more challenging. Progressive Catholics overwhelmingly supported PT's Fernando Haddad, as did a slight majority of Catholics (51 percent). A couple of weeks before the second round of the elections, on the feast of Nossa Senhora Aparecida, Haddad made a point of receiving communion, a highly symbolic act given Our Lady's centrality in Brazil's Catholic identity. This act prompted an angry backlash from conservative Catholics who objected to the "sacrilege" of giving the sacrament to a "communist" and " supporter of abortion and gay ideology."[37] Just a day before, Haddad had met and appeared in public with Bishop Leonardo Ulrich Steiner, the then General Secretary of the Brazilian Conference of Catholic Bishops (CNBB), where in the words of the bishop they discussed issues of common concern: "the legalization of abortion, the protection of the environment, special attention to the indigenous and *quilombola* issues [afro-descendants], the defense of democracy and the strict fight against corruption" (Domingues 2018b). While Bishop Steiner did not explicitly endorse Haddad, the latter declared that his agenda was pro-life. "All my actions are in line with the principles presented by the CNBB. I am open to receive new suggestions from them" (Domingues 2018b). However, just a few days after, the archbishop of Rio de Janeiro met and was photographed with Jair Bolsonaro. Standing next to the archbishop, Bolsonaro stated: "We are committed to the defense of the family, the innocence of the child in the classroom, in defense of religious freedom, contrary to abortion, contrary to the legalization of drugs. Those commitments are in the heart of every good Brazilian" (Domingues 2018b).

Conservative Catholics have continued to flex their muscles during the Bolsonaro administration. On May 21, 2019, the Frente Parlamentar Católica (Catholic Parliamentary Front) organized a public consecration of Brazil to Our Lady of Fatima's Immaculate Heart at the Planalto Palace, Brasilia. Bolsonaro attended the event, lending it legitimacy. The Virgin Mary's apparition at Fatima in Portugal in 1917 is associated with three secrets that, as they have become revealed, have to do with Mary's warning about the dangers of war, secularization, and communism (requesting the consecration of Russia to rectify her "errors," including atheism).[38] With the *#OrePeloBrasil* (#PrayForBrazil) handle, promoters of the event expressed support for Bolsonaro and his Justice Department's effort to pass a tough anti-crime bill (Tunes 2019). Thus, they made a clear connection between conservative Christian values, shared by Catholics and *evangélicos*, and the government's law-and-order agenda. They see both these values and this agenda as critical to the conversion of Brazil, especially after fifteen years of control of the presidency by the Workers' Party (PT).

While there are some overlaps between conservative and progressive Catholics in terms of current politics, particularly around the opposition to the legalization of abortion, their split support of Haddad and Bolsonaro shows an unresolved tension between two pastoral-political emphases—one on the defense of traditional moral values and another on the promotion of social justice—at the heart of Brazilian Catholicism. The first emphasis on the defense of the traditional family and the promotion of a pro-life agenda dovetails with the Catholic Charismatic effort to preserve the doctrine and authority of the church and to strengthen Catholic identity in a pluralistic society through the use of electronic media. The second more in line with the progressives' vision of a more inclusive and egalitarian church, which prophetically denounces abuses against the most vulnerable (with the vulnerability of the unborn as the point of overlap). How this tension is negotiated will shape the ways in which Brazilian Catholicism positions itself nationally and globally and looks to the future.

Coda: Covid-19 and the Deepening Polarization of Brazilian Christianity

I wrote above that Bolsonaro's political rise as part of a coalition of landowners and economic interests seeking to accelerate the exploitation of Brazil's natural resources, Evangelical Protestants and conservative Catholics, and the military is an evolving story. The coming of Covid-19, commonly known as the coronavirus, is a case in point.

Identified in Wuhan, China in December 2019, the virus has not only killed and sickened many throughout the world, but it has also had an enormous social and economic impact, forcing distancing and isolation to prevent its spread. Even with these measures, the virus spread very rapidly across the globe, with Europe, particularly Italy and Spain, becoming a hotspot. We could see the hypermobility of Covid-19 as an expression of the intensifying global connectivity and interdependence which have made many localities vulnerable to baffling and uncontrollable forces, precisely the same forces that have motivated nationalistic reactions such as the rise of Bolsonaro. Preliminary reports indicate that the virus entered Brazil in late February 2020 through urban, well-to-do Brazilians returning from vacations in Italy. Once in the country, it has spread rapidly to working-class and poor areas, such as the Baixada Fluminense in the outskirts of Rio de Janeiro, where the health infrastructure is precarious and many of the cases and virus-related deaths are not reported.

In Brazil, as in other parts of the world, the debate has been between the need to save lives through quarantining and social distancing and the desire to keep the economy going. Bolsonaro has pursued the latter, denying the danger of the pandemic as a ploy by the media to generate "fear" (*pavor*) and dismissing the virus as a "measly flu" that Brazilians' immune systems would easily counter, since they are used to swimming in raw sewage, and nothing happens to them.[39] In a statement on national television, Bolsonaro drew from Brazil's patriarchal structures of feeling that link male strength with the health of the nation:

> The virus has arrived. We will face it and it will soon pass. Our lives have to go on; we need to keep our jobs; we must preserve our families' livelihood. Indeed, we should return to normality . . . ninety percent of us will not have any manifestation, if we become contaminated . . . . In my particular case, because of my history as an athlete, if I were infected by the virus, I would not need to worry, I would not feel anything, or would be, at most, affected by a little flu or cold [*uma gripezinha ou resfriadinho*].[40]

Bolsonaro's denialist attitude was supported not only by economic elites but also by many conservative Christian leaders, concerned about keeping their churches open for massive events and, at a deeper level, about the role of the secular state in dictating their actions. Bolsonaro's position, however, contradicted the guidelines of the World Health Organization (WHO) and his minister of Health, Luiz Henrique Mandetta, who is trained in medicine. Mandetta took to the airways to disseminate scientific information about Covid-19. At the same time, in his interviews, he articulated a Catholic philosophy and ethics, citing from Antonio Vieira, who we encountered in Chapter 3, and even from the Lebanese poet Khalil Gibran that "we are the sons and daughters of the longing of life for itself."[41] Acknowledging that "faith is an element for improvement of the soul, of the spirit . . . [and that] people need it,"[42] Mandetta advocated that churches be kept open, but without large gatherings and that pastors and priests should make use of the internet to preach and provide spiritual direction to the faithful. In several situations, more than just recognizing the relevance of religion in times of a global health crisis, the minister seemed to express his own religiosity and devotion. For example, in the run-up period to Easter Week, Mandetta affirmed his Catholic identity to show solidarity with this religious segment of the population, who would have to social distance:

Brazilian Christianity, Politics, and Society   169

Easter, Holy Week, I'm Catholic, I'm really Catholic, I go, I pray, I like it: the processions, the Easter Mass, the family gatherings, Easter lunch, the chocolate, the bunny, this will all mess with the emotions of all of us. And we are going to have to be very resilient.[43]

In other words, the tensions around how to respond to the virus in Brazil are not so much between a secularist, technocratic, globalist, and "Leftist" approach and a religious, conservative, and nationalist perspective, but between two moral, religiously inflected discourses. In fact, with a conservative and anti-PT background, Mandetta supported the impeachment of former President Dilma Rousseff and opposed the hiring of Cuban doctors to work in Brazil during the PT government. Mandetta's charisma and his ability to communicate effectively with his medical team, the congress, the press, and the population at large represented a growing threat to Bolsonaro, who as we saw, depends heavily on his media image for his authority and legitimacy.

National surveys indicated that approximately 80 percent of the Brazilian population approved the minister's measures and recommendations to respond to the pandemic, while Bolsonaro's position eroded significantly, with 39 percent disapproving of his stance to end social isolation in favor of the economy.[44] Moreover, the governors of twenty Brazilian states supported Mandetta's recommendations, ordering the closure of schools, universities, commerce, and services in general. João Doria and Wilson Witzel, the governors of Brazil's two most prominent states—São Paulo and Rio de Janeiro, respectively—became vocal critics of Bolsonaro's denialism, further undermining the president's position.

In response, Bolsonaro engaged in high-profile symbolic acts meant to signal his disagreement with Mandetta and the state governors. He appeared publicly shaking hands with his supporters in the streets, called for massive demonstrations in favor of returning to work, and tweeted about the centrality of the economy's health. While Mandetta's popularity offered him a measure of protection, he was eventually fired by Bolsonaro. The immediate trigger was an interview he gave to a popular program on Rede Globo, an outspoken opponent of Bolsonaro, stressing the need for Brazilians to hear a unified voice so that they would not be confused and divided on whom to trust regarding the pandemic. In his farewell to his team, Mandetta once again drew from his Catholicism by recounting a story of a visit he paid to a hospital created by Saint Dulce, the nun canonized by Pope Francis in October 2019.

When I went to Salvador to see the hospital of Sister Dulce's charity, I was with Mayor ACM Neto and he knelt down. I decided to kneel too and pray that she

170 *Christianity in Brazil*

> would illuminate the country. And he said: "Sister Dulce, if become a saint, I will go to the Vatican." I thought it was going to take 30 years [to] pay the promise up front, but I went. Getting there, what I asked was: protect the SUS [*o Sistema Único de Saúde*—the public health care system], because by protecting the SUS, you protect many people.[45]

Here we see once again how Christianity, in this case, Catholic notions of the common good, inform social issues and political positions in Brazil. Considering the central role that Evangelical Protestants had in Bolsonaro's election and the influence of the Evangelical Parliamentary Front during his administration, it would not be risky to assume that Mandetta's overt expressions of his Catholicism may have displeased certain religious leaders and supporters of the president, making it one of the likely factors for the minister's dismissal. On the eve of Mandetta's firing, a conversation was disclosed between Onyx Lorenzoni, former Chief of Staff for Bolsonaro and a member of the Evangelical Lutheran Church of Brazil, which is affiliated with the conservative Missouri Synod, and the minister of Citizenship Osmar Terra, in which they analyzed Mandetta's disagreements with Bolsonaro. Lorenzoni stated emphatically that he would have "already cut off the minister's head," if he had been in Bolsonaro's position.[46]

More generally, pitting health versus economics has foregrounded diverse forms of being Christian in Brazil. Pastor Silas Malafaia, founder of the Assembly of God Victory in Christ, declared that he would not close his churches during the pandemic, as they would be "the last stronghold of faith and hope for the people."[47] In line with President Bolsonaro's denial of the seriousness of the pandemic, Pastor Silas cautioned that to focus too much on the virus's repercussions would be to "enter into neurotic craziness" (*entrar numa neura louca*). "[This] is a dammed little bug that we can't even see [but] causes a mess in the world, in the economy. People are terrified. We believe that God is in control of all things. And we believe in the power of prayer. Because that is our weapon, people! It is what we have."

Other religious leaders, such as Catholic Bishop Odilo Scherer, initially advocated that more Masses be held in order to avoid full churches.[48] But as soon as Pope Francis directed people to stay at home, the collective celebrations were suspended in Catholic temples.

Another illustrative religious point of inflection regarding the pandemic was Bolsonaro's call to hold a national day of fasting to fight the coronavirus in response to a request from Pastor William Ferreira of the Church Assembly of God Crusade of Fire Ministry, located in the state of Minas Gerais. With this call, Bolsonaro was trying to appeal to traditional Catholics, as well as to Charismatics and Evangelical Protestants. Although the original idea for the fast came from a pastor, reactions among Evangelicals were varied, as they sought to justify it in theological terms, while being skeptical about the president's intervention in a sphere that, in their eyes, is the purview of religious leaders. Thus, at stake in Bolsonaro's call for a national day of fasting was the same concern for separating churches from the power of the state that informed the Evangelical resistance to quarantining and social distance. According to Pastor Guilherme de Carvalho from the Neo-Pentecostal Hope Church: "The president can ask religious authorities to pray and cooperate with the country. But the president does not summon religious authorities or evangelical pastors. He has no authority to do so. We have here a clear violation of the principle of the sovereignty of the spheres."[49]

Bolsonaro's position has been furthered weakened by the resignation of his widely popular minister of Justice, Sérgio Moro. Judge Moro had played a key role in the investigation and prosecution of Lava Jato, the anti-corruption campaign that embroiled the Workers' Party, leading to the impeachment of Dilma Rousseff and the imprisoning of Lula da Silva. In joining Bolsonaro's administration as a "super-minister," Moro had lent gravitas to the president's pledge that he would rid the country of political corruption, organized crime, and criminal violence, a pledge that, as I discussed above, greatly enhanced his popular appeal in the face of an acute and generalized crisis of legitimacy of established political parties and other traditional institutions. Upon resigning, Moro accused Bolsonaro of political interference in the judiciary, arbitrarily firing the general director of the Federal Police and seeking to replace him with a loyalist who would keep the president informed about the multiple ongoing criminal investigations against him and his family. In turn, this accusation prompted the attorney general to demand a formal investigation, as calls for impeachment proliferated. As a final parting shot, Moro declared that he is no longer confident that Bolsonaro is committed to fighting corruption.[50]

Brazil's situation in the midst of the pandemic is chaotic and the future looks rather grim: left unchecked, the virus may not only kill thousands of poor Brazilians in densely populated *favelas* and dormitory cities, which lack even basic health care services, but it can also decimate Indigenous populations in the Amazon, just as they are under the increasing pressure of Bolsonaro's aggressive pro-development policies. And Bolsonaro's trademark bravado and personalistic and performative politics point in potentially (self-)destructive, anti-democratic directions. We see here the re-emergence of long-standing patterns of political authority—inflected by religion, whether it be messianism, millenarianism, or traditional patronage—that have contributed to the persistence and even exacerbation of socioeconomic inequalities. Thus far, the diversity of voices within Brazilian Christianity has meant a fragmentation of moral visions, some of them contrasting, as to how to respond to the pandemic.

Conclusion

Quo Vadis Brazilian Christianity?

From the beginning, as the Apostle Paul's letters to the diverse Christian communities emerging in the Greco-Roman world demonstrate, Christianity has evinced a prodigious capacity for "global localization" or "glocalization" (Vásquez and Marquardt 2003; Roberson 1992), that is, the capacity to adapt creatively a message of universal salvation to the particular local conditions it encounters.[1] This capacity has greatly facilitated its mobility across various lands. In Brazil, that capacity is enormously heightened. To the extent that one can heuristically speak of a "Brazilian Christianity," rather than simply "Christianity in Brazil," one can point to a protean, multilayered intermingling of traditional Luso-Catholicism (with its particular themes like Sebastianism), African and Indigenous religions, Evangelical and Charismatic Protestantism, and modern and postmodern New Religious Movements. This poly-faceted Christianity is richly material, thoroughly characterized by what Robert Orsi (2016) has called "holy intimacies," the strong longing for and drive to make the sacred abundantly present in the now, in the natural world, in everyday life, even while holding fast to the ardent desire and anticipation of a fully transfigured world. This is true whether we speak of mysterious apparitions of images of the Virgin Mary in the wilderness, hosts that miraculously turn into Christ's blood, the "mud-hut Jerusalem" of Canudos, the *caminhada* of CEBs, or of baptisms in the Holy Spirit, with its accompanying embodied gifts of glossolalia, divine healing, and exorcism. Because of its strongly material, affective, embodied, and performative modulations, Brazilian Christianity is not only endlessly creative but also highly portable in the age of globalization.[2]

Now that I have completed the journey across various aspects of Brazilian Christianity and have offered a fuller sense of the shifting yet relatively stable assemblies of actors, forces, processes, worldviews, and scales that have been involved in its construction, we can ask: What will the future face(s) of Brazilian Christianity be? What role is it likely to play in world Christianity? Perhaps the

174   *Christianity in Brazil*

best way to answer these complex questions is to go back to the vignettes with which we started our voyage.

Pope Francis's trip to Brazil was enormously successful. He attracted huge ecstatic crowds. This stands in contrast to his predecessor Benedict XVI's visit in 2007 to open the fifth general meeting of the Conference of Latin American Bishops at the famed sanctuary of Aparecida, São Paulo. That visit had a much lower public profile, with Benedict XVI spending most of his time at small events and the meeting of the Latin American bishops, though he did canonize Friar Galvão, a Franciscan who lived in colonial Brazil, before a crowd of approximately a million people. The contrast between Benedict XVI and Francis highlights the challenges faced by Catholicism in Brazil, as in the rest of Latin America and the Global South, as well as the debates on how to meet these challenges. The economic, social, and cultural transformations of a thoroughly globalized world, including the rapid spread of pneuma-centric religions through electronic media and transnational networks, pose difficult tests for the Catholic Church, which has long seen itself as *the* global actor, the vessel of a universal message.

From the beginning of his visit, in an interview on his way to Brazil, Benedict sketched the picture of a defensive church, suspicious of the outside world, strongly concerned with the purity of the doctrine, and beset by "a certain weakening of Christian life in the whole of society and of even affiliation to the Catholic Church due to the secularism, hedonism, indifferentism and proselytism of numerous sects, animist religions and new pseudo-religious expressions" (Benedict XVI 2007a). In the face of these challenges, Benedict emphasized the need to focus on moral issues, Catholic doctrine and values, and spiritual conversion. The interview stood out for his agreement with some bishops in the region that Catholic politicians who promote legislation approving abortion deserve excommunication. In addition, when asked about liberation theology, Benedict declared:

> I would say that with the transformation of the political situation[,] the situation of liberation theology has also profoundly changed, and now it is evident that these facile millenarianisms, which promised immediately, as a consequence of revolution, the complete conditions for a just life, were wrong. Everyone knows this today. Now, the question is how the Church should be present in the struggle for the necessary reforms, in the struggle for more just living conditions. On this, theologians are divided, in particular the representatives of political theology. We, with the timely Instruction emanating from the Congregation for the Doctrine of the Faith, have tried to promote a work of discernment, that is, we have tried to free ourselves from a mistaken mixture between Church and

politics. And we have tried to show the specific part of the mission of the Church, which consists precisely in responding to the thirst of God and therefore also in educating for the personal and social virtues.(Benedict XVI 2007a)

He reiterated this message more sharply in his inaugural speech to the CELAM meeting at Aparecida, when he stated that "political work is not the immediate competence of the church." He continued: "Only by being independent can you teach the great criteria and the irrevocable [*inderrogáveis*] values, guide the consciences and offer a life option that goes beyond the political scope. To form consciences, to be the advocate of justice and truth, to educate in the individual and political virtues, is the fundamental vocation of the Church in this sector" (Benedict XVI 2007b).

Contrast all of this with Pope Francis's call to youth in Copacabana not to be afraid to go out in the world "to stir things up . . . to make a mess, to disturb complacency," to make a "revolution." We saw that the revolution called for by Francis is not by any means a violent or even a nonviolent uprising against the status quo; it is, like Benedict's, a revolution of the spirit. Nevertheless, Francis advocates a church open to the world, not afraid to engage with it, to transform it. And in light of the massive protests against corruption and socioeconomic inequalities that immediately preceded Francis's visit, the political dimensions of this engagement cannot be ignored. This attitude of creative engagement is also reflected in the concluding documents of the Aparecida meeting, which Francis, then-Cardinal Jorge Mario Bergoglio, had a significant hand in crafting (Cavassa 2013):

> The church is called to a deep and profound rethinking of its mission and relaunch it with fidelity and boldness in the new circumstances of Latin America and the world. It cannot retreat in response to those who see only confusion, dangers, and threats, or those who seek to cloak the variety and complexity of situations with a mantle of worn-out ideological slogans, or irresponsible attacks. What is required is confirming, renewing, and revitalizing the newness of the Gospel rooted in our history, out of a personal and community encounter with Jesus Christ that raises up disciples and missionaries. (CELAM 2007: #11)

Contrast also Benedict's skeptical posture toward liberation theology with Francis's embrace of progressive Catholicism's strong concern for social and environmental justice. Moreover, as part of his visit to the poor neighborhood Varginha, in Rio de Janeiro, Francis stopped in front of a temple of the Assemblies of God and, to the pastor's surprise, prayed with the members of the congregation who were at the door. They even asked him to bless them.[3] Here,

Francis might be accepting the inevitable pluralism of the Brazilian religious field, while simultaneously encouraging the church's mission to confidently proclaim the gospel in the midst of this fragmentation.

Pope Francis's re-appropriation of progressive and Charismatic Catholicism and his ecumenical engagement with local Pentecostals show the church's ability to respond creatively to Brazil's changing religious and sociopolitical conditions. Catholicism continues to be the dominant expression of Christianity in Brazil. With more than 120 million Catholics (approximately 12 percent of the world's Catholics), Brazil still has the largest Catholic population in the world. The Catholic Church also continues to be very relevant to Brazilian society, despite the growing religious pluralism that threatens its hegemony. With virtually all of the major political forces and governmental institutions tainted by corruption and in disarray, the church, despite scandals of sexual abuse, consistently polls as one of the most trustworthy and respected organizations in the country. For example, in a survey by the Getúlio Vargas Foundation, 57 percent of Brazilians indicated that they trusted the Catholic Church, a percentage well above the police (25 percent), unions (24 percent), the president (11 percent), the congress (10 percent), and political parties (7 percent). Only the armed forces were trusted by more Brazilians (58 percent).[4] Even the judiciary, especially the Supreme Court, whose independence was expected to provide a moderating check on Bolsonaro's more authoritarian instincts, has lost credibility, trying to suppress the publication of an article investigating possible corruption by one of its magistrates (Casado and Andreoni 2019). And it remains to be seen whether the military's active participation in the Bolsonaro administration in key cabinet positions will also taint it.

The National Conference of Brazilian Bishops (CNBB) has been a key interlocutor in the debates about the future of Brazil, maintaining a high-profile critical attitude toward the neoliberal reforms that began in the deeply unpopular administration of Michel Temer (who replaced Dilma Rousseff after she was removed from power) and are likely to intensify under Bolsonaro, arguing that these reforms would be harmful to poor and working-class Brazilians. More specifically, the bishops have strongly voiced their opposition to Temer's proposal to dismantle the pension system, warning that this proposal would lead to "social exclusion." The CNBB has insisted that "society has to participate in the debate to help suggest and build a lasting pension system. We call attention to people who do not have the means to express themselves and to the people who will be most affected, who will always be the poorest."[5] Moreover, as allegations of Temer's involvement in a bribery scheme have emerged, allegations that have

Conclusion 177

generated widespread protests, Bishop Leonardo Ulrich Steiner, formerly the Secretary-General of the CNBB, stated in no uncertain terms that the "ethical conditions for him to continue [in power]" are not there (Fellet 2017).[6]

The CNBB has continued to project its moral voice in the Bolsonaro administration. As part of the 2019 Campanha da Fraternidade, entitled *Fraternidade e políticas públicas—Serás libertado pelo direito e pela justiça* (Fraternity and Public Policies—You Will be Liberated by Rights and Justice), the CNBB critiqued the government's effort to weaken gun-control laws as a way to deal with the structural problems that lead to high indices of criminality and violence. It also called for a defense of the rights of the "people who suffer the most" (*o povo mais sofrido*), specifically a defense of the rights "to life, to land, and to culture by indigenous people," as well as miners (Camporez 2019). Bolsonaro has been keen on opening the Amazon to national and transnational corporations so they can extract its mineral riches, and he sees protected Indigenous lands as one of the main obstacles. Thus, the CNBB and CIMI's defense of Indigenous rights is particularly galling to him. He has gone as far as calling these organizations the "rotten part" (*a parte podre*) of the Catholic Church.[7] But the CNBB is standing firm. "Just because we have new situations, we will not stop announcing what has been the guiding criterion of the action and the pronouncement of the episcopal conference itself" (Modino 2018).

Moreover, as I discussed in the previous chapter, many of the Catholic bishops have stood against President Bolsonaro's attempts to minimize the danger of Covid-19 in order to keep the economy running. The CNBB Secretary-General, Joel Portella, affirmed the importance of maintaining social distancing and criticized the politically constructed dilemma pitting life against economy. Furthermore, a group of 152 bishops and archbishops signed a letter that was sharply critical of the Bolsonaro government and received the support of numerous progressive priests. The letter passed to the Council of Bishops of Brazil to be analyzed but did not become the official position of the church, which remains politically divided.[8]

If it is true, as I hypothesized in the previous chapter, that the election of Bolsonaro represents a tentative realignment of Brazilian politics toward an authoritarian narrowing of civil society, could progressive Catholicism come to play a similar role to what it did during the military dictatorship? Just as those repressive years coincided with the transformative effects of Vatican II and Medellín, so too may the populist nationalism of Bolsonaro, which places a strong emphasis on conformity to a hierarchical past, on order and progress, run up against the prospects of a revitalized progressive Catholicism, both in

Brazil and worldwide. Or does the fact that almost 50 percent of Catholics voted for Bolsonaro signal a turning away from the ideals and methods of progressive Catholicism, just when it seemed to be coming back to the world stage with Francis's papacy? A lot will depend on the impact on everyday life of Bolsonaro's politics and on progressive Catholicism's creativity in fulfilling "the preferential option for the poor," that is, in adapting its theology and pastoral approaches to respond more effectively to the material and spiritual needs, longings, and dreams of the majority of Brazilians in a highly pluralistic religious arena and an increasingly globalized Brazil.

As I have demonstrated throughout the book, Catholicism's continued relevance in Brazilian society is not limited to the thoughts, pronouncements, and actions of the bishops or the church's various institutions. In fact, this relevance is built on Catholicism's historical and ongoing contributions to Brazilian popular religiosity and culture, from architecture to music. Despite the pluralization of Brazilian Christianity, these contributions are likely to endure. However, Protestantism, present in the country since the colonial period, has experienced exponential growth since the 1980s, spearheaded by the dramatic expansion of Pentecostalism, all part of a process of increasing diversification in the Brazilian religious field. Close to one in four Brazilians are now Protestants. If current trends hold, there are a couple of potential scenarios. The first envisions the loss of Catholic hegemony, with Catholics becoming less than 50 percent of Brazil's population by 2030 and Protestants becoming the majority religion (42 percent versus 40 percent Catholic) by 2040. As Brazil becomes "more urban, more feminine, more mixed (with a growing population declaring [themselves] black and brown)," Evangelical Protestantism will continue to expand since it has proven to be particularly attractive to women, city dwellers, Afro-Brazilians, and the young (Alves, Barros, and Cavenaghi 2012: 20).

A 2018 survey by the reliable Datafolha indicates that we may not have to wait until 2030 to witness Brazilian Catholicism's loss of numerical supremacy. This survey showed that Catholics only represented 52 percent of adult Brazilians, while Evangelical Protestants are now edging up to 30 percent.[9]

At the theoretical level, this scenario fits well with the detraditionalization hypothesis, which proposes that with globalization, particularly with the relentless "time-space" compression and disembedding produced by processes of rapid and uneven urbanization, internal and transnational migration, and instantaneous global connectivity through electronic media (Vásquez and Marquardt 2003), everyday life has become deeply unsettled and baffling, dramatically fraying the sociocultural (rural, or at least strongly locally based) fabric woven since colonial

Conclusion 179

times by traditional Catholicism—the Catholicism of saints, Marian devotions, apparitions, and miracles—hampering the transmission and reproduction of Brazilian Catholicism as a whole. Rather than automatically inheriting religious identity from one's ancestors or maintaining affiliation to Catholicism as the historical religion of Brazil, individuals buffeted and networked by global forces feel free to pick and choose among a thickening profusion of religious beliefs, practices, and organizations that address the existential challenges they face (Steil and Toniol 2013: 229). With its stress on individual this-worldly renewal (the gospel of health and wealth) and other-worldly salvation and its sectarian approach vis-à-vis competitors, Pentecostalism is especially well suited to benefit from the process of detraditionalization. And since the process is cultural and structural, the Catholic Church has very limited pastoral and liturgical options in terms of improved outreach to arrest it. Indeed, the 2015 Datafolha survey revealed that 44 percent of those who currently declared themselves Evangelical Protestants were once Catholics.

Despite compelling empirical evidence and theoretical arguments, the detraditionalization scenario is too simplistic. Empirically, internal surveys by CERIS—a respected social research institute associated with the CNBB—found that the number of priests in Brazil increased by 11 percent from 2014 to 2017, reducing the ratio of priests to inhabitants from one in 8,130 to one in 7,802 (Balloussier 2018).[10] In 2000, that ratio stood at one in 10,124. This steady decline suggests that pastoral attention to communities might improve, shrinking the personnel advantage that Evangelical Protestants have by virtue of their priesthood of all believers. However, priests are unevenly distributed, concentrated in the southeast and south, rather than in the northeast and Midwest, where, as we saw, Pentecostalism is growing the fastest.[11] In one stark case, the largest Catholic district in the country which is located in the Amazons has only 27 priests for 800 congregations (Soloway 2014). Moreover, the presence of more priests might not be the silver bullet that halts the decline in the number of Catholics and the growth of Pentecostalism, if the process of detraditionalization is indeed breaking the "chains of memory" and undercutting the transmission of Catholicism through the family and immediate community because of accelerated urbanization, migration, and dramatic socioeconomic change. And if Pentecostalism's structure of feeling and experience continues to resonate strongly with the reality that the majority of Brazilians face on the ground, in everyday life, it is likely to continue growing even if the church is institutionally strengthened. Perhaps more promising is the growth in the number of deacons, which jumped 116 percent from 2004 to 2014.[12] Deacons can perform many of the liturgical functions of a priest, such as baptism, marriage, and celebrations of the word without consecration of the Eucharist. And, as they are more likely to be members of the communities they serve, they can bring the church closer to the grassroots. Nevertheless, to the extent that the church continues to privilege the authority of priests as being vested with the original and exclusive power to perform the Eucharist, the sacrament that marks a sharp difference between Catholicism, which believes in trans-substantiation, and other forms of Christianity, the impact of these deacons will be limited.

Finally, in my work among youths in Rio de Janeiro's periphery, I found that 90.7 percent of those surveyed had inherited their Catholicism from their mothers (Fernandes 2013). Thus, I conclude that "if there is detraditionalization, it is not (yet) a key explanatory and determining variable for the decline in the number of Catholics in Brazil" (Fernandes 2015: 191–2).

On a more theoretical note, we have to recognize that, like secularization, the weakening of traditions is not a linear, totalizing process; it is likely to have different intensities depending on the region. The rural-urban tension, discussed in Chapter 4, is particularly significant in this regard. Roberta Campos's work on Ave de Jesus (see Chapter 3), a millenarian movement of penitents in Padre Cícero's Juazeiro do Norte, demonstrates that there is a vital rural Catholicism built around the *culto do santo protetor*, the strong public yet profoundly personal devotion to one's protector saint, which is deeply rooted in locality and long-standing traditions. This Catholicism displays great creativity and a capacity to move individuals and groups in powerful ways, and thus these potent, affective devotions and forms of sociability are very likely to perdure (Campos 2009). In a country that has effectively become a "risk society," to borrow from sociologist Ulrich Beck (1992), a society in which citizens feel besieged by all sorts of dangers in their daily lives and as they circulate in the streets, there is a greater need for this kind of supernatural protection.[13] Certainly, we can read Neo-Pentecostalism's and Charismatic Catholicism's emphasis on the exorcism of capricious evil spirits and on divine healing as a way to navigate this widespread risk and insecurity.

On the basis of her fieldwork, Campos makes valuable observations that should inform our understanding of the history, present dynamics, and potential future of Brazilian Christianity. According to her, because the sociology and anthropology of religion in Brazil have tended to focus primarily on cities, particularly in the southeast (Rio de Janeiro and São Paulo), they have not only missed the creativity of rural popular Catholicism but also rendered the north and northeast invisible (Campos and Reesink 2011). We saw in Chapter 4 how

Conclusion 181

Catholicism, particularly traditional Luso-Catholicism, shows greater resilience in the northeast. And I argued that as "frontier" regions, the north and the Midwest offer strategic windows onto the social and religious transformations that take place with the pressures of urbanization and economic development. Campos goes on to argue for a truly pluralistic social science of religion in Brazil that places regional differences and comparative patterns front and center. I wholeheartedly endorse the need to develop empirically and analytically these levels of granulation and to cross-fertilize them with the already excellent work on local communities (such as Burdick 1993; Ireland 1993) and global processes (Vásquez 1998; Rocha and Vásquez 2013).

As a second caveat to the detraditionalization scenario, I can point to the fact that the sharp decline in numbers of followers is not just affecting the Catholic Church, but also all institutionalized forms of Christianity, including historic/ mainline/mission Protestantism, which stresses individuality (i.e., voluntary affiliation and exercise of freedom of conscience encouraged by *sola scriptura* and *sola fides*). Indeed, Brazilian Protestantism's overall growth is primarily due to Pentecostalism. The most established, bureaucratized Pentecostal churches might eventually experience pressures similar to those besetting the Catholic Church and historic Protestant churches. In fact, from 2005 to 2011, the portion of "non-practicing" Evangelicals jumped from 0.7 to 2.9 percent of the total Brazilian Evangelical population (a total of four million Brazilians) (Cardoso 2011), creating a significant socio-religious category that used to apply just to Catholics. Especially among young Brazilians between the ages of fifteen and twenty-nine years old, I found (Fernandes 2017) that in Rio de Janeiro, one of Pentecostalism's strongholds, the tendency toward breaking all links with established religions is stronger than becoming Pentecostal. In addition, we saw how, despite the extravagant inauguration of the Temple of Solomon by the Universal Church of the Kingdom of God, a sign that the church has finally made it as part of the establishment, it has lost more than 200,000 followers or 10 percent of its membership. Late modernity, with its overwhelming reliance on electronic media, its commodification of culture (including religion), and widespread global flows and networks, favors those religions that are the nimblest, most capable of innovation amid the relentless pace of change, complexity, and connectivity. "Fourth wave" Pentecostal churches and customized Christianities, which thrive on the excitement generated by youth subcultures, extreme sports, fashionable lifestyles, hip music, and the celebrity of their leaders and followers—all promoted twenty-four-seven through social media, appear in the best position in this regard. Typically, these churches do not promote a sectarian affiliation or operate through strong bonds. Quite the contrary, they are popular because of their informality and flexibility, because they allow participants to come as they are to try something new and different, enjoy a great show, and feel good about themselves.

The defining logic of the Brazilian religious field is one of intense mobility, circulation, and experimentation. For example, the census category of "without religion," while growing in numbers, might also be provisory, contingent on a particular phase in the life cycle. Approximately, 23 percent of Catholics indicated that they had considered themselves without religion before (Fernandes 2006: 24). We may thus be witnessing processes of de-adherence and re-adherence that in the long run complicate the prediction that Brazilians will turn Protestant.[14] As Pentecostals compete with each other more fiercely than ever and as Catholicism borrows creatively from Pentecostalism, blending some of its pneumatic aspects (in the Charismatic Renewal's "virgophilic" version) with traditional popular devotions and a less politically overt appropriation of progressive Catholicism's focus on social justice, as in new communities of consecrated life like Toca de Assis, Evangelical Protestantism's growth may slow down and eventually plateau, and Catholicism may thus maintain its demographic hegemony, even if substantially diminished.[15]

On the other hand, while some leaders in the church had hoped that the growth of the CCR would stem the hemorrhage of Catholics to Pentecostalism, this has not happened thus far. John Paul II was an enthusiastic supporter of the Catholic Charismatic Renewal Movement, seeing it as the quintessential instrument to carry out a new evangelization. However, his successor Benedict XVI was more suspicious of the movement because of its propensity to become a deterritorialized end unto itself at the expense of parish life and structures built around the authority of the priest to perform the sacraments. Francis was initially even more negative toward the CCR's showmanship, which, in his eyes, make it more like a "school of samba" than a serious spiritual organization.[16] As we saw in Chapter 3, these suspicions translated into Marcelo Rossi, a leading face in the CCR, not being able to play a central role in Benedict's and Francis's visits to Brazil. *Novas comunidades* have also had a mixed record. Despite their rapid growth, several of these organizations, including Toca de Assis and Heralds of the Gospel, have been under investigation for doctrinal questions and internal issues of power (Mariz and Medeiros 2013; Fernandes and Souza 2014). Pope Francis has been generally supportive of these communities, which is not surprising since they reflect some of the values and goals he articulated in his sermon at Copacabana. Nevertheless, he has expressed concern that some

Conclusion

of these groups "are not born of a charism of the Holy Spirit, but from a human charism, a charismatic person who attracts by [his/her] human qualities of fascination. Some I might even say, are 'restorative:' they seem to give confidence/security [*segurança*] but, on the contrary, only give rigidity."[17] Francis's concerns seem directed at groups like Heralds of the Gospel, whose leadership is linked to the ultraconservative group Sociedade Brasileira de Defesa da Tradição, Família, e Propiedade (Brazilian Society for the Defense of Tradition, Family, and Property—TFP).[18]

While it is true that global capitalism and media undermine the worldview of traditional Luso-Catholicism, they also create their own "economies of the occult" (Comaroff and Comaroff 2001) and "spectral realities" (Vásquez 2017), with commodities and capital seeming to take a life of their own, controlling the fate of individuals and even entire countries. In other words, the processes of detraditionalization and "de-magicking" are not inexorable one-way streets. Rather, and this is a point that often gets lost in discussions about absolute affiliation and church attendance numbers, they are coupled with processes of re-enchantment and re-traditionalization that shape religious life (Heelas, Scott, and Morris 1996; Vargas 2012). This is amply demonstrated by the return or re-affirmation of "old" identities and cultural systems in the midst of late modernity, such as so-called fundamentalisms and other "strong religions," including rectificationist Islam and Hindu and Christian fundamentalisms (Almond, Appleby, and Sivan 2003). Within Brazilian history, we saw this in the case of Canudos and Padre Cícero's Juazeiro. Both were significant collective mobilizations in response to the establishment of Brazil as a modern secular republic. However, while Canudos was obliterated, Padre Cícero and his Juazeiro became the subjects of one of the most popular and vital devotions in Brazil, and more recently, St. Dulce, a Catholic nun from Bahia, has been canonized on October 13, 2019. These differential outcomes evince how difficult it is to speak with certainty about the future of Christianity in Brazil—structural trends are always mediated by multiple factors in the conjunctures in which they operate. And, despite its reliance on decentered "postmodern" electronic media, the rise of Bolsonaro could be construed as an attempt to re-traditionalize the increasingly fragmented Brazilian civil society, as new and fluid identities come to the fore and contest long-standing power asymmetries.

Indeed, Bolsonaro's case also points to another aspect of re-traditionalization: the invention of new hybridized traditions like the hyper-syncretic Valley of the Dawn which combines elements of Christianity, ideas of imagined indigeneity, and the spirits of Umbanda with science fiction and UFOs (Vásquez and Souza

Alves 2013).[19] These new-old traditions are now projected at transnational and global scales, whether through migration, tourism, or the electronic media, as people seek to resituate themselves and carve out viable spaces of meaning and livelihood amid the turbulence of globalization. In its exorcisms of demonic spirits that create misfortune, life-changing baptisms by the Holy Spirit, practice of tithing in exchange for God's material blessings, and intense collective experiences of the sacred in small tightly knit congregations and large spectacular gatherings, all bearing a strong affinity with neoliberal capitalism, Pentecostalism contributes to and reflects a re-enchantment and re-traditionalization. In parallel ways, Catholicism may be able to creatively redeploy its non-dualistic, "magical" worldview to adapt and even thrive in the current age. We have seen how Brazilian Catholicism is already doing this with charismatic singing priests, massive assemblies, extensive electronic networks, and colossal temples of its own.

In that sense, a more likely scenario in Brazil is what Pierucci (2006: 49) called an "almost binary religious pluralism" and what Camurça (2013: 70) has termed a "channeled diversity" (*diversidade acanhada*), with Christianity constituting almost 87 percent of the Brazilian population and a much narrower slice made up of other religions and those without any religious affiliation.[20] Among the various tributaries within each major channel, and, to some extent, across different channels, there will be increasing religious experimentation that fosters circulation in multiple directions and changes in the self-identification of the faithful through creative juxtapositions and adaptations of religious practices and beliefs. Particularly, young Brazilians are vigorously experimenting with religion, testing and moving among different options, in search of those that offer meaning and depth to their increasingly wired lives. This intense mobility challenges established religious institutions, which can no longer rest on their laurels and simply count on the strength of inherited bonds and received cultural identities. In a chaotic and uncertain globalized Brazil,

> many factors can catalyze or discourage religious bond[s]: the loss of a loved one, illness in the family, a child who uses drugs. Religion is sought as a refuge in the present to live the here and now. God cannot be a figure of the past or a distant being. The faithful say that they seek him and want to find him on a daily basis. This is the challenge for the religious narratives embraced by traditional institutions. (Fernandes 2017)

This may point to yet a third scenario (as a corollary of the second) in which firm, exclusive institutional affiliations and identities, as well as sectarian

Conclusion 185

outlooks, may in the long run decrease in importance, particularly among young Brazilian Christians who are more open to ecumenism (Mariz and Souza 2015). For these young Brazilians, the shared this-worldly mysticism of popular and Charismatic Catholicism and of Pentecostalism (cross-fertilized with African-based, Indigenous, and New Age religions) may serve as a rich and fluid matrix in which all religions would interact with each other in shifting relations of tension, accommodation, and hybridity. In this case, the language of winners and losers in the religious field may not tell the whole story of the complex, multidirectional dynamics of Brazilian Christianity. And here a thoroughly variegated and hybrid Brazilian Christianity would both mirror and contribute to the coming of a polyglot, but strongly pneuma-centric world Christianity (Phan 2012; Tan and Tran 2016).

How these scenarios play out will not only have significant implications for Brazil, but may also shed light on the future of global Christianity, as many countries in the "Global South," which is increasingly the religion's center of creativity (Jenkins 2008, 2011; Sanneh 2005), are undergoing the same processes—de- and re-traditionalization, cultural and religious pluralization, tighter embeddedness in transnational networks and global flows of capital, media, and peoples—that Brazil is experiencing. In either of the scenarios—the conversion of Brazil into a Protestant country in tension with the enduring but decentered legacy of Catholicism, or the continued pluralization of the religious field, with pneumatic Christians, both Catholic and Protestant, converging in their styles, political aims, and theological and moral outlooks amid growing numbers of followers of other religions and of those not affiliated to any religion—it is likely that country will continue to play a central role "as a key center of religious creativity and innovation within an emerging, polycentric global religious cartography" (Vásquez and Rocha 2013: 1; see also Koschorke 2016). With dynamic transnational churches like UCKG and para-churches like the Charismatic Catholic Canção Nova leading the way, Brazilian Christianity will greatly contribute to this new cartography.

At eighty-two million, the population of Renewalists (combining Pentecostals and Charismatics, in their classic and new waves) in Brazil is the second largest in the world, just behind that in China (95.3 million) and ahead of American Renewalists (seventy-six million) (Johnson 2009: 480). Furthermore, between 1910 and 2010, Brazilian Renewalists had the highest annual average growth in the world (17.26 percent) (Johnson 2009: 481). More importantly in terms of international projection, Brazil already sends the second-largest group of Christian missionaries—only behind the United States—to the world at large. In 2010, Brazil sent 34,000 missionaries and received 20,000 (also occupying

186   *Christianity in Brazil*

second place in this category behind the United States), showing how globally networked Brazilian Christianity is.[21]

Of particular importance here is the role that Brazilian missionaries are having in south-south flows, shaping Christianity throughout the Americas, from Peru and Haiti to the United States, and in Africa, particularly in South Africa and Lusophone countries.[22] Linda van de Kamp (2011: 2) argues that Neo-Pentecostal Brazilian churches like the Universal Church and God Is Love that have a widespread presence in Mozambique, Angola, and South Africa, "are not necessarily part of a [deterritorialized and abstract] Western globalized modernity," as many anthropologists of Christianity claim. Instead, offering a case of glocalization, these churches see themselves as taking the battle directly to Satan, going back to the home turf of the "evil spirits" that haunt Umbanda and Candomblé. With their talk of fighting "*macumba*," a pejorative word that in Brazil designates various forms of "black magic" but that does not exist in Mozambique (but that, once introduced, gets re-signified by upwardly mobile Mozambican women to explain and transcend their trials and tribulations), "Brazilian-Mozambican Pentecostals have created a specific Christian, or even Pentecostal, transatlantic space of interaction and exchange" (5). This transatlantic sociocultural field has enabled Brazilian churches to compete successfully in Lusophone Africa against other transnational Pentecostal titans, such as the Nigerian Redeemed Christian Church of God (RCCG) and the Ghanaian Lighthouse Chapel International, which operate in English and without the shared spiritual imagery (Van de Kamp 2015).[23] At the same time, with their gospel of health and wealth, Neo-Pentecostal Brazilian churches carry images of success, of making it to the middle class in the developing world, reinforcing the messages of prosperity and fun the "Brazilian way" that the widely popular *telenovelas* from TV Globo bring to Africans caught in cycles of civil war and economic stagnation. In turn, these images may encourage migration from Africa to Brazil, which transnational church networks may facilitate, further enhancing the multidirectional south-south flows.[24]

The potential global impact of Brazilian Christianity goes beyond the growing numbers of missionaries and the activities of powerful transnational churches. Brazil has consolidated itself as a prominent pole of theological, pastoral, and ecclesiological innovation. For example, we saw how Brazilian liberation theologians like Leonardo Boff and Ivone Gebara are helping to reinvigorate global Catholicism, bringing a renewed emphasis on outreach and service to the poor and marginalized and addressing global issues like climate change and environmental justice. As part of the Synod of Bishops for the Amazons in 2020,

Pope Francis considered a proposal made by local Catholic leaders to ordain as "elders—preferably indigenous, respected and accepted by the community—even if they have an established and stable family" as priests and women as deacons in order to respond to the acute shortage of priests in the region. The proposal generated great excitement among liberals and progressives because it could signal a dramatic shift in the church's long-standing organization and modus operandi. Conversely, traditionalists fretted that adopting this proposal would lead to the elimination of clerical celibacy. Eventually, although the proposal was approved by more than two-thirds of the synod, Pope Francis did not take it up in his apostolic exhortation following the event.[25] That a proposal with such far-reaching consequences and that generated worldwide attention emerged from Brazil demonstrates the global relevance of Brazilian Catholicism.

The potential global impact of ideas, theologies, symbols, and practices originating in Brazil is also evident for Brazilian Protestantism. In the previous chapter, I considered whether Edir Macedo's dream that, one day, all nations of the world would bow down before his colossal Temple of Solomon bears elective affinities with Bolsonaro's populist and patriarchal nationalism as it recalibrates Brazil's position in the Americas and the world. His minister of Foreign Affairs Ernesto Araújo has written that Brazil "needs a foreign metapolitics so that we can situate ourselves and act on that cultural-spiritual plane in which the destinies of the world are defined more than in the field of trade or military-diplomatic strategy. Destinies that we need to study, not only from the point of view of geopolitics, but also from a 'theopolitics'" (Araújo 2017: 355). In view of late modernity's uncertainties and discontents, could churches like the Universal Church of the Kingdom of God and Catholic groups like those who organized the consecration of Brazil to Our Lady of Fatima's Immaculate Heart in Bolsonaro's presence be providing the transnational infrastructure and theological and ritual bases for that global politics, with born-again/spiritually renewed Brazil at the heart of a worldwide salvific project of re-traditionalization? The mere fact that this question is posable demonstrates the increasing global relevance of Brazilian Christianity.

Notes

Introduction

1 See Fernandes and Vásquez (2013). Argentinean Jesuit Jorge Mario Bergoglio was chosen as pope on March 13, 2013. He took the name of Francis, in honor of Francis of Assisi, the founder of the Franciscan Order and a saint known for his vows of poverty and his love and care for all living things.
2 Watts (2013).
3 "Pastor da Universal Chutando uma 'Santa.'" Available online: https://www.youtube.com/watch?v=VpPwWEsk0OY (accessed August 22, 2020).
4 See also Mafra et al. (2013), the special issue on "Pentecostalism in the Lusophone World" in *PentecoStudies* (Zawiejska 2018), and Martjin Oosterbaan, Linda van de Kamp, and Joana Bahia (2019).
5 According to the United Nations, in 2014, about one-fourth of the world's population—1.8 billion people—were aged between ten and twenty-four years. The great majority of them (nine in ten) live in developing countries in the Global South, and while the countries with the largest and fastest-growing young populations are in Asia and Africa, Brazil has the seventh largest number of young people in the world (fifty-one million). See UNFPA (2014).
6 "*Brasil acima de tudo, Deus acima de todos*" (Brazil above everything, God above all) was the slogan Jair Bolsonaro used in his electoral campaign. He was elected president in 2018. More about the religious underpinnings of this event in Chapter 6.
7 For a good critique of reductive and simplistic readings of the globalization paradigm as applied to religion, see Glick-Schiller (2005).
8 On glocalization, see Robertson (1995), Vásquez and Marquardt (2003), Swyngedouw (2004), and Roudometof (2016).

Chapter 1

1 The term "millenarianism" is connected to Christian eschatology (matters related to the end times—*eschaton*). It is the belief based on the Book of Revelation that Jesus Christ will return to earth to defeat the powers of evil and inaugurate a thousand-year (thus, millennium) reign of the just, as a prelude to the final judgment. Jesus's

190   *Notes*

imminent second advent will be foreshowed by miraculous signs amid deepening iniquities. On Sebastianism, see Myscofski (1988) and Quéiroz (1965).

2 The quip "Brazil is the country of the future . . . and always will be" is attributed to French general and president Charles de Gaulle, but it has become part of the tragicomic popular wisdom that Brazilians have about their national character.

3 In fact, the whole process was called "*limpeza de sangue*" (blood cleansing).

4 See Hemming (1978) and Denevan (1992).

5 See Eltis (2001).

6 Gilberto Freyre (1987) in his magisterial treatment of the genesis of Brazil, *Casa Grande e Senzala*, argued that mixing was central not only for Brazilian Christianity but for Brazilian culture and character as a whole. Freyre had an essentialist view of cultures and racial identities, seeing the Portuguese, African, and Indigenous peoples as self-contained, homogeneous entities, with fixed traits that would eventually combine. This static view is problematic. Nevertheless, Freyre's insight that encounter, difference, conflict, and hybridity are central in the Brazilian experience remains vital.

7 See Hoornaert (1977: 46).

8 Luke Clossey (2015: 4) argues that, for all Jesuits' global pretentions and "the idealized view of the Society of Jesus as a tightly centralized and smoothly running military machine," the trajectories of knowledge production and dissemination were more often than not entangled, not going through Rome, but across "peripheries" and "semi-peripheries" of the empire (such as among China, Germany, and Mexico).

9 See Antônio Vieira in Chapter 3.

10 Literally "reductions" for their aim to gather Indigenous peoples spread throughout vast tracks of land. Wilde (2015b) observes that reductions generated "highly polarized" reactions in Europe. "While apologetic stances defended the missions as a noble experiment of civilizing the indigenous people who resided in the forest, the anti-Jesuit position perceived the religious order as exploiters of the natives who sought to create a kingdom independent from the Spanish and Portuguese crowns."

11 By then the Jesuits had achieved great prominence, numbering 474, 44 percent of whom were Brazilian.

12 For Langfur, this resistance shows how Indigenous peoples helped define the limits of state power, since this resistance forced the state to modify its aggressive policies toward ones that stressed trade and negotiation vis-à-vis populations not fully incorporated into the nascent nation.

13 Some progressive Catholic theologians interpret the experience of reductions as an incipient example of "inculturation" of the gospel, that is, the adaptation of Christianity to the context and culture of the Natives rather than its dogmatic imposition by force. For more on the divergent assessments of the emancipatory nature of reductions, see Peterson and Vásquez (2008: 142–6).

Notes

14 Caicedo (2014) suggests that because the Jesuits focused heavily on the education and technical training of the Natives, their missions among the Guaraní have had a more lasting impact in terms of developing human capital than those established by Franciscans, who tended to stress charity and taking care of the poor and sick. Conversely, the less regulated nature of Franciscan reductions might have provided the space for more religious and cultural experimentation at the grassroots.

15 Azzi attributes this reticence not only to patriarchal Lusitanian attitudes, but also to the crown's pressing goal of ensuring "the permanence, growth, and hegemony of the Portuguese minority in the conquered lands" (1983: 25). Portuguese women were in Brazil to reproduce.

16 In contrast to first orders, constituted by male religious clerics, such as Franciscans, Dominicans, and Benedictines, and second orders, the female counterparts of first orders, tertiary orders are lay associations "whose members share in the spirit of some religious institute while in secular life, lead an apostolic life, and strive for Christian perfection under the higher direction of the same institute are called third orders or some other appropriate name." See the Catholic Church's *Code of Canon Law*, 298–329.

17 In English, a beatified person. The Catholic Church has a formal process to declare someone blessed, but in popular Catholicism, exemplary and strongly devout persons who may be associated with miracles may be venerated as intercessor saints, even if the church has not officially recognized them.

18 This is not to ignore that many of those places had been already invested with meaning by Indigenous people through their myths and stories of creation. Working on colonial New England, historian Jean O'Brien (2010) shows how "firsting," claiming that places only came to be after Europeans named and settled them, was one of the main strategies to "write Native Americans out of existence." This was clear in the case for the apparition of our Lady of Guadalupe in Tepeyac, in colonial Mexico, on a hill that had been associated with the Aztec fertility goddess Tonantzín. And certainly, Tupi groups had been fishing in the Paraíba River before the arrival of the Portuguese.

19 The events have been dramatized in the movie *The Mission* (1986).

20 The society would also be suppressed by Pope Clement XIV in 1773 and would only be restored in 1814. The Távora affair, named for a prominent noble family in Portugal that was publicly executed in the wake of the accusations, allowed Pombal not only to dispose of the Jesuits but also to curb the influence of the Portuguese aristocracy, which he perceived as threatening the consolidation of his power. See Leitão and Romeiras (2015).

21 On Canudos, see Levine (1995); on the Muckers, see Biehl (2008); on Contestado, see Diacon (1991); on Padre Cícero, see Della Cava (1970); and on Pedro Batista, see Pessar (2004).

192 *Notes*

22 Aquino notes that these orders were far more open to indigenization than their male counterparts, spurring a rapid growth in the number of Brazilian nuns. He concludes that "with their institutes and with their welcoming of Brazilian women in their organizations . . . these sisters contributed to growth of education in Brazil and also to the beginning of the transformation of social role of women in Brazilian society, albeit through the prism of conservative Catholic morality—a 'Catholic feminism' [that was] in competition with the liberal and anarchist models of the period" (2014: 412).

23 On Romanization, see Azzi (1974) and Oliveira (1985).

24 A Brazilian priest who was supportive of the cause to have the miracle in Juazeiro recognized by the Holy See expressed his exasperation with the French Lazarist priests who dismissed the event in the following terms: European priests think that "Our Lord does not leave France to work miracles in Brazil" (Della Cava 1970: 48). Here we see the paradoxical effects of Romanization. While the project was meant to shift the center of gravity of Catholicism toward Rome, it ends up giving rise to Brazilian Catholic nationalism. According to Della Cava, Brazilian priests advancing the validity of the miracle felt that this event meant that "Brazilian Catholicism had come of age, and that the Brazilian church was now comparable to any in Europe" (Della Cava 1970: 48).

25 A concordat is a negotiated agreement between the Holy See and a sovereign state that gives the Catholic Church a privileged place in matters of worship, morality, and/or civil society (e.g., education and marriage) vis-à-vis other religious groups.

26 Many Catholic Action activists, especially those involved with the Catholic University Youth (JUC) suffered violent persecution by the military regime, with some of them having to go underground or leave Brazil. For a good history of the movement, see Souza (1984). For an abbreviated version in English, see Souza (2002).

27 Conference of Latin American Bishops—Medellín (1968), *Document on Justice*, #7.

28 In contrast to modernization theories that hold that the underdevelopment of Latin America and other countries in the so-called Third World is the product of their cultural (and religious) and social backwardness, that is, their failure to follow in the steps of the developed countries, dependency theory referred to the "development of underdevelopment"—to the fact that the underdevelopment of nations in the periphery of the world capitalist system is generated by their exploitation by developed nations (like the United States) at the core of that system. In light of dependency theory's critique of the notion of development, theologians like Gustavo Gutiérrez adopted the term "liberation" to characterize the construction of self-actualized individuals who have affirming relationships with God and their fellow human beings. The key text in Brazilian dependency theory is Cardoso and Faletto (1979, though the book was originally published in Spanish in

Notes

1969). Sociologist Fernando Henrique Cardoso would go on to become president of Brazil (1995–2002) and basically to disown his views.

29 Conference of Latin American Catholic Bishops—Medellín (1968), *Poverty of the Church*, #10.

30 *Documento de Puebla. III Conferencia General del Episcopado Latinoamericano (1979), #79.* In the bishops' words, "this option does not imply the exclusion of anyone, but [it does mean] a preference for and drawing closer to the poor."

31 For a discussion on CEB numbers in Brazil, see Hewitt (1991), Valle and Pitta (1994), and Vásquez (1998).

32 For a good study of the range of grassroots organizations associated with the progressive diocese of Nova Iguaçu, under the leadership of Adriano Hypólito, see Mainwaring (1986).

33 See Burdick (2004).

34 I will have more to say about Boff in Chapter 3.

35 The same can be said about the Brazilian religious field as a whole. For example, so-called *religiões ayahuasqueiras*, like Santo Daime and União do Vegetal, emerged in the Amazon region, as *seringueiros* (rubber tappers) came into contact with Indigenous shamanic worldviews and rituals, and blended them with Christian, African-based, and Spiritist elements. From Acre, these religions extended to cities in Brazil (and throughout Europe and Japan) through networks of affluent, cosmopolitan youths involved in the counterculture movement (Labate and Cavnar 2014). As *a cidade da Nova Era* (the city of the New Age), Brasilia in Goiás has also been a prolific pole of religious creativity in the country's interior, birthing new religious movements like Valley of Dawn (Vásquez and Souza Alves 2013). The global rise (and fall) of Spiritist healer John of God in the small city of Abadiânia, Goiás is yet another example (Rocha 2017b). While the circulation of these religions has been facilitated by the vectors of late modernity, that is, religious tourists, the global media, the self-help industry, transnational immigrants, and so forth, they seem to be rooted in a powerful nostalgia and desire for the (imagined) simplicity, innocence, authenticity, naturalness, "mysticism," and more communitarian way of life in the hinterlands (as opposed to the consumerist, hyper-rationalist, instrumentalist, uprooted, and artificial individualism of city life in Western late modernity). See Vásquez and Rocha (2013).

36 See Carranza (2000).

Chapter 2

1 I add the notion of experience to Williams's term to stress not just the powerful role of affects, but also of the senses and the lived body in these ways of being Christian.

194 *Notes*

Borrowing from Pierre Bourdieu (1974), I adopt a "structural dynamism" that sees religious practices as the relatively stable outcome of the tensile interplay between agency and structure, individual and group, and symbolic and social processes.

2 Weber associated mysticism with contemplation, in contrast to asceticism which entails systematic activity upon the self in the form of discipline and restraint. In that sense, he saw asceticism as "disenchanting," as transforming the religious subject and world according to the methodical implementation of human designs, while mysticism tends to operate with a "magical" understanding of reality that sees it as thoroughly informed by the supernatural. The mystic sees himself/herself as a vessel for the indwelling of the sacred and ultimately seeks a total union with God. It is in this latter sense that we use the term mysticism here. TLC does have contemplative dimensions, often resulting in the defense of sacralized hierarchies against the revolutionary work of the ascetic, but it is certainly not passive. See Weber (1963).

3 On Nossa Senhora Aparecida, see Macca (2003); on Padre Cícero, see Della Cava (1970). It is worth noting that the "miracle at Juazeiro" follows logically from the notion of transubstantiation affirmed at the Council of Trent, according to which the consecration of the bread and wine turns them—in reality and substance—into the body and blood of Jesus Christ.

4 Wilkinson (2017) makes a good point that the revised notion of animism is a construct that may reflect more modern Western concerns and desires (about the environment, for example) than the actual lived practices and experiences of Indigenous peoples. But then again, what is not a construct in the study of religion? Even the concept of religion itself has been shown to be the product of colonial and orientalist interests. The issue is not the search for value-neutral, "innocent" concepts, as if they were possible, but to construct analytical tools that allow for richer, more capacious and dynamic approaches to the complexity of the realities we encounter, including religion(s).

5 For a study of the construction of *feitiçaria* in the Portuguese encounter with West African peoples, see William Pietz (1987). Sansi-Roca (2007) argues that this concept circulated widely in the Luso-Atlantic world. It has additional connotations of something false, including artificiality (from the Latin root *facticium*), that is, the thing is not real or natural; it is false and scandalous.

6 In response to the iconoclasm of the Reformation, Catholic apologists suggested that in contrast to the crude materialism and immanentism of fetishists, who saw the agency of their sacred objects as issuing directly from their material essence, the Catholic venerates images, crosses, and relics because they point to something beyond them, to the transcendent. Nevertheless, Caroline Walker Bynum (2011) shows that in medieval Catholicism, sacred materiality was "self-referential." "Rather than passing beyond in quiet meditation, the medieval devout frequently

treated such images as a locus of the divine." These devotees "responded to the overtly tactile appeal of such object. They kissed and fondled them" (65). In their "insistent materiality," "these objects seem[ed] to articulate a power not so much beyond as within themselves" (105), demonstrating the real presence of Christ or the divine.

7   On millenarianism in Brazil, see Pessar (2004).

8   On Canudos, see Levine (1995).

9   For one of the best treatments of traditional popular Catholicism in Brazil, see Brandão (1980).

10   Ribeiro de Oliveira (1985).

11   De Theije (1990).

12   Kiddy (2005).

13   On this controversy, see Verger (2018), Bastide (1978), and Capone (2010).

14   Bourdieu (1991).

15   In fact, it was common in home altars in the countryside to turn the statue of the saint upside down if s/he failed to fulfill the believer's petition as a way to "punish" the saint. Here, we are back to our discussion of the efficacy of Christian materiality. Drawing from the materialist turn in religious studies and creatively appropriating Rudolf Otto's characterization of the sacred as *mysterium tremendum et fascinans*, Scheper Hughes (2012) refers to *Mysterium Materiae*, the uncanny potency of matter *qua* matter to be generative of the experience of the sacred.

16   For an excellent comparative study of religious worldviews in Brazil, see Ireland (1992).

17   The intertwining of the supernatural and natural realms, or better put, of the visible and invisible worlds, of humans and nonhumans was, of course, also central to Indigenous "structures of experience" (Descola 2013). A key example here is the widespread presence among Indigenous religions of the figure of the *pajé*, the shaman or spiritual leader who could travel across different realms and assume the identities of nonhuman kin through chant and dance and often with the assistance of psychoactive substances, to heal, cause harm, hunt, and/or prophesize. These Indigenous structures of experience or understandings of "sociality" (Vilaça and Wright 2016: 6) should not be underestimated in their contributions to the formation of Brazilian Christianity and to the fluid and contested matrix of minimal Brazilian religiosity.

18   For an analysis along these lines, see Ribeiro de Oliveira (1985).

19   See Mariz (1994) and Vásquez (1998).

20   Boff (1978).

21   Gebara and Bingemer (1989).

22   Boff (1997).

23   Santiago-Vendrell (2010).

Notes

24 Shaull (1966).

25 R. Cardoso (n.d.). Various churches like UCKG and Reborn in Christ have issued their own credit/debit cards that can be conveniently used to tithe during the service.

26 Costa (2016). Proponents of prosperity theology justify their practices of tithing by citing biblical texts like Solomon's Prov. 3:9–10: "Honor the LORD with your substance and with the first fruits of all your produce; then your barns will be filled with plenty, and your vats will be bursting with wine."

27 Chesnut (2003).

28 De Theije (1999: 118).

29 Carranza, Mariz, and Carmurça (2009).

30 See https://tocadeassisirmaos.org.br/ (accessed August 22, 2020).

31 "Pope Francis: Humanity's Future is in the Hands of the Poor." July 9, 2015. https ://www.catholicnewsagency.com/news/pope-francis-humanitys-future-is-in-the-hands-of-the-poor-66764 (accessed August 22, 2020).

32 Turner (2013).

33 For an analysis along these lines, see Fernandes and Vásquez (2013).

Chapter 3

1 Foucault (1978).

2 See Hall (1997) and Orsi (2005). In Latin America, there is also a rich tradition of scholarship focusing on "popular" voices—those at the grassroots—which dovetails with the lived religion approach in the United States. See for example, Levine (1992) and Peterson (1997).

3 For an excellent collection of letters from the first Jesuits in Brazil, see Leite (1940).

4 The term *France antarctique* refers to the French colony in the Guanabara Bay leading into Rio de Janeiro. It was known as Antarctic because it was south of the equator.

5 On the shrine, see https://www.santuariodeanchieta.com/ (accessed August 22, 2020).

6 On Vieira, see Besselaar (1981) and Barros (2008).

7 The literature on Villegagnon is extensive, but most works rely heavily on reports by Jean de Léry, the Calvinist shoemaker and traveler who recorded in detail the experience of the French colony. See Jean de Léry (1961).

8 Née Jean de Cointac, a French Dominican who converted to Protestantism and was a member of Villegagnon's expedition.

9 For a good source on Conselheiro, see Silva (2001). On his religious worldview, see Otten (1990).

Notes

10 The *cangaceiros* or *jagunços* (bandits and gunmen for hire) that accompanied Conselheiro and defended Belo Monte could be plausibly read as "primitive rebels" (Hobsbawm 1965), loosely organized forms of peasant resistance against abusive *coroneis*, landowners, and their own gunmen and paramilitary gangs. However, care must be taken not to romanticize these figures, for they reproduced patterns of patriarchal violence and, in that sense, they reinforced the hierarchical status quo.

11 See Cunha (1902). The work was translated to English with the title *Rebellion in the Backlands* (Chicago 1944). The Canudos campaign has also been fictionalized by Mario Vargas Llosa in *The War of the End of the World* (1981).

12 For an alternative reading, see Ventura (1997).

13 The literature on Father Cícero is vast. For two good sources in English, see Della Cava (1970) and Slater (1986).

14 This is a reference to the Marian apparition in Lourdes, France in 1858, which served to cement Catholicism as part of national French culture. Among other things, Romanization involved the substitution of Vatican-sanctioned European devotions for local ones.

15 For an anthropological analysis of the construction process of popular devotion to Padre Cícero, see Braga (2008). For images of the sanctuary, see http://maedasdoresjuazeiro.com/ (accessed August 23, 2020).

16 "Padre Cícero Viveu, 'Fé Simples,' Diz Carta do Vaticano; Lei Resumo." *Globo: Ceará*, December 13. Available online: http://g1.globo.com/ceara/noticia/2015/12/padre-cicero-viveu-fe-simples-diz-carta-do-vaticano-lei-resumo.html (accessed August 23, 2020). Emphasis in the original.

17 For a biography of Macedo that draws heavily from interviews with him, see Lemos and Tavolaro (2007).

18 See the report prepared by Rede Record posted on YouTube: Pires (2014).

19 Tsuriel-Harari (2014).

20 This section draws from Fernandes (2003). For a sympathetic biography, see Marra (2015).

21 Rossi cited in Arêas (2007: 60).

22 iBest awards are given by Brazil Telecom based on popular vote or through selection by a jury of Brazilian media providers and experts.

23 "Padre Marcelo Revela Dieta, 'Alface, Cebola, e Tres Hambúrgers por Dia,'" *Globo: O Fantástico*. June 12, 2013. Available online: https://goo.gl/xDb1CI (accessed August 23, 2020).

24 "'Sou Um Desses Loucos que Caiu em Dieta Maluca,' Diz o Padre Marcelo Rossi," *Globo: O Fantástico*, July 12, 2013. Available online: https://goo.gl/xDb1CI. https://goo.gl/ymuYgK (accessed August 23, 2020).

25 See the interview: "Do altar ao palco: quem são os astros da Igreja Católica," *Zero Hora* 08 August 2015. Available online: https://goo.gl/l7QwlJ (accessed August 23, 2020).

198   *Notes*

26 Interestingly, Ratzinger participated in the examination of Boff's thesis, even offering financial support to publish it.

27 Congregation for the Doctrine of the Faith. "Notification on the Book: 'Church: Charism and Power' by Father Leonardo Boff OFM," March 11, 1985. Available online: http://www.vatican.va/roman_curia/congregations/cfaith/documents/rc_co n_cfaith_doc_19850311_notif-boff_en.html (accessed August 23, 2020). For a fuller account of Boff's conflict with the Vatican, see Cox (1988).

28 Interview (1997), *Programa Roda Viva*. January 25, 2018. Available online: https://www.youtube.com/watch?v=NkaHURNRPwQ (accessed August 23, 2020).

29 Cited in Baptista (2007: 398). Burle Max (1909–1994) was a Brazilian landscape architect.

30 Sociologist François Hourtart, who used Marxism to study the interplay between religion and society, was particularly influential at Louvain. He served as a *peritus* (expert) at the Second Vatican Council and trained prominent Latin American sociologists of religion such as Pedro Ribeiro de Oliveira and Otto Maduro.

31 See the interview at https://goo.gl/bqNZsM; UNIVESP TV, May 26, 2018 (accessed August 23, 2020).

32 For instance, when I have interviewed young novices (Fernandes 2005b) I found that they were consistently not in favor of the ordination of women, fearing that belonging to the hierarchy would blunt their prophetic power, their power to demand change. Moreover, they expressed the opinion that the demand for the ordination of women came more from theologians who had embraced secular strands of feminism.

Chapter 4

1 In two high-profile cases, union leader and environmental activist Chico Mendes and American-Brazilian nun Dorothy Stang, an activist in the Pastoral Land Commission, associated with progressive Catholicism, were brutally murdered at the behest of big landowners, cattle ranchers, and loggers for defending the rights of poor farmers and landless agrarian workers and for advocating for land reform. Mendes was killed in Acre in 1988 and Stang in Pará in 2005.

2 Umbandistas and Candomblecistas celebrate St. Sebastian, the patron saint of the city of Rio de Janeiro, as the Catholic correlate of Oxossi, the spirit of the forest and West African divinity of hunting (with bow and arrow). St. Sebastian's hagiography tells us that he was martyred tied to a tree and shot by arrows. This once again demonstrates the fluidity of Brazilian religions.

3 Unless noted otherwise, all tables and charts were created by the author, drawing from the sources.

4 Just for reference, the HDI for the United States is 0.915. IDHM—Human Development in Macro Brazilian Regions: 2016 (Brasilia, UNDP, IPEA, FJP, 2016).

5 For a good study of the practices of traditional popular Catholicism, see Brandão (1980).

6 Ministry of Tourism (2016). At this point, it is hard to assess the impact of widespread Covid-19 infections on this travel and circulation.

7 On the folia, see Castro and Couto (1961) and Tremura (2004).

8 Pinheiro (2004).

9 It is interesting to note that, although Bahia has a very high percentage of Afro-Brazilians, only 0.34 percent of its population declare themselves as practitioners of Umbanda and Candomblé. The state of Rio de Janeiro has the largest population of self-declared practitioners of these traditions. Nevertheless, African-based religions and cultures permeate everything in Bahia, especially in Salvador, from music to food and from architecture to clothing.

10 Ayahuasca is a Quechua (the lingua franca of the Inca empire that comprised part of the Amazonian lowlands) word meaning "vine of souls" or "vine of dead," referring to *cipó*, a woody vine that is one of the key components of the brew. See Labate and MacRae (2010).

11 Santo Daime was founded in Acre in 1930 by Afro-Brazilian Raimundo Irineu Serra who had migrated from the northeastern state of Maranhão to tap rubber. One of the most vivid visions Mestre Irineu, as he is known among followers, experienced upon imbibing ayahuasca was that of a woman who revealed to him how to use the sacred brew to heal. Initially, he thought the woman was a forest spirit, but later he came to associate her with Our Lady of Conception, whom he called the "Queen of the Forest." Since Irineu's death in 1971, the religion has fragmented and spread not only to urban centers in Brazil, but now throughout the world.

12 Santo Daime also blends indigenous and Christian beliefs and practices with Umbanda and Kardecist Spiritism.

13 Aleijadinho (literally "the little cripple," for a disease that disfigured and debilitated him), whose real name was Antônio Francisco Lisboa, designed and constructed in rococo style the Church of St. Francis of Assisi, one of Ouro Preto's main architectural landmarks.

14 This section draws from Fernandes (2013).

15 Sociologists of religion define "detraditionalization" as the rupture of taken-for-granted and authoritative religious "chains of memories" that have held collective and individual identities relatively coherent and stable (Hervieu-Léger 2000). This process of detraditionalization may be paradoxically accompanied by a re-traditionalization, as the social actors (re)draw hard and fast boundaries, as with Pentecostal asceticism, to protect themselves from an anti-structural situation, when the old structures no longer hold but there are no new overarching ones to direct and organize action (Heelas, Lash, and Morris 1996).

200   *Notes*

16 I am grateful to Marcelo Pitta for his help in the preparation of graphs and his critical reading.

17 My gratitude to Bruno Souza Nascimento and Paulo Limongi for helping me with this graph.

Chapter 5

1 For an incisive analysis of the Protestant "semiotic ideology" and its production of particular forms of subjectivity and conceptions of material reality, see Keane (2007).

2 For more on the contributions of the Dutch in Brazil, see Silva (2005).

3 Borrowing the notion of karma from Hindu traditions, Spiritism holds that the actions of an individual generate effects over his/her many lives, effects which depending on their value, determine the place of the self in the path toward becoming an enlightened spirit. The task is to engage in positive actions, particularly charity and education, to disentangle spirits from the negative karmic effects that trap them in the material world where they can interfere with the living. In its stress on education, particularly reading, and on ethics, Spiritism resonates with mainline Protestantism.

4 See the *Political Constitution of the Empire of Brazil—Law Letter of March 25, 1824*. Available online: http://www.planalto.gov.br/ccivil_03/Constituicao/Constituic ao24.htm (accessed August 23, 2020).

5 This distinction which was used early in the production of official statistics was eventually abandoned, replaced by the categories "Mission Evangelicals" and "Pentecostal Evangelicals."

6 According to the IBGE, these numbers are approximate because it includes groups who spoke dialects derived from German but who were not from Germany, which had been recently unified (1870).

7 For more details, see the Lutheran Church's official website ("Portal Luteranos"): https://www.luteranos.com.br/paroquia/arquivo-historico-da-ieclb (accessed August 23, 2020).

8 I am grateful to Clemir Fernandes, Baptist pastor and PhD in the social sciences at the State University of Rio de Janeiro, for the bibliographic source.

9 See also *Provai e Vede* (2014).

10 On diversity within Brazilian Presbyterianism, see Matos (2011). Regarding the Renewed Presbyterian Church, see Gini (2010).

11 See https://novo.igrejabrasileira.com.br/ (accessed August 23, 2020).

12 For a breakdown of the numbers and percentages of Catholics, Protestants, Spiritists (including practitioners of African-based religions), and "without religion"

in Brazil from 1872 to 2010, see: https://seriesestatisticas.ibge.gov.br/series.aspx ?vcodigo=POP60&t=populacao-religiao-populacao-presente-residente (accessed August 23, 2020).

13 The LDS Church claims to have 1,326,738 members in Brazil served by 2,038 congregations and six temples. See http://www.mormonnewsroom.org/facts-and-statistics/country/brazil. While the census in all likelihood undercounted Brazilian Mormons, the church, which prides itself on carefully recording family histories, tends to inflate membership numbers. See Phillips (2006). Still, it is clear that the church is growing at a faster rate in Latin America than in the United States.

14 In the 2010 census, only 0.3 percent of the Brazilian population (588,797) declared themselves affiliated to African-based religions. As we saw in Chapter 2, the structures of feeling and experiences that inform these religions dovetail with those of traditional Luso-Catholicism, facilitating the circulation of followers among these traditions and/or "multiple affiliation," with the faithful practicing Catholicism or Umbanda in different settings or periods in the life cycle or in response to different existential needs. Nevertheless, in the postcolonial context, the quest to recover racial-ethnic identities has intensified, particularly in the face of persistent prejudices, exclusion, and inequalities that affect Brazilians of African descent. Part of this quest involves calls to "decolonize" African-based religions, to rid them of European influences. According to Duccini and Rabelo (2013: 232), the fact that the fastest-growing African-based religion in Brazil is Candomblé, and not the more hybrid Umbanda, could be related to this struggle to rescue and affirm a subaltern religious and ethnic-racial identity. The Brazilian Catholic Church, for its part, has sought to be more welcoming to Brazilians of African descent through a *pastoral do negro*, which among other things includes African drums and other musical instruments, as well as symbols and foods, in liturgical celebrations. While these efforts have made a positive difference, they have not been free of contradictions. See Burdick (1998) and Selka (2007).

15 As an example of these innovations, Deus é Amor sees its founder (now deceased) as a prophet directly inspired by God and asks their faithful to make pilgrimages (*caravanas*) to the church's headquarters in São Paulo, the Temple of God's Glory, incorporating a long-standing Catholic practice. The followers also cannot watch TV, making radio the church's main outreach vehicle.

16 On the UCKG's transnational ministries, see Freston (2001b), Mafra et al. (2013), Van de Kamp (2011), and Van Wyk (2014).

17 Since 2014, when he moved to Orlando, Florida, a city that has a large Brazilian immigrant community, to play professional soccer, Kaká has been associated with the First Baptist Church, where he participates in multicultural camps.

18 Another interesting "fourth-wave" church is the "informal," "trendy," "cool," "rock-concert-style" Australian Hillsong, which is the church of Justin Bieber and basketball superstar Kevin Durant. Starting as a successful worship band, Hillsong

202 Notes

has "released over 120 albums and sold more than 16 million records across the globe" (Roark 2016). Currently, the church has temples in twenty-one countries, in places as diverse as London, Moscow, Los Angeles, Toronto, Bali, Tel Aviv, and Cape Town, where an estimated 130,000 people attend weekly services, with over ten million followers on social media. Hillsong now has a temple in São Paulo and a congregation that ministers to Brazilians in Sydney. Many middle-class young Brazilians travel to Hillsong's International Leadership College in Australia to train for the ministry and in search of cosmopolitanism. See Rocha (2013). Hillsong is good example of the thickening of south-to-south Christian networks that are part of the new global religious cartography (Vásquez and Rocha 2013).

19 "Ex Funkeiro Vira Crente e Promove o Passinho do Abençoado em Igreja." Available online: https://www.youtube.com/watch?v=BWZw0PRvkXI (accessed August 23, 2020). In this video, Tonhão, who belongs to a group of secular funk music, converts and performs in a Pentecostal Church the "little step of the blessed," teaching its choreography to the participants while yelling phrases that are common among Brazilian Pentecostals, such as "palms for Jesus."

20 Favelas are urban shantytowns that suffer from high rates of unemployment and crime and generally have a very precarious infrastructure. They are often located in the middle of large cities, side by side to affluent neighborhoods, or at their periphery.

21 "*Cracudo*" is a slang term for crack users. Close to 1 percent of the population in Brazilian urban centers consume crack. Although the media in Brazil has tended to stereotype the southeast of the region of the country, which includes Rio de Janeiro and São Paulo, as crack infested, research conducted in 2014 shows that the northeast (1.29 percent) and south (1.05 percent) have a higher proportion of users. In comparison, only 0.56 percent of the population in the southeast reported using crack. See Portela (2014).

22 Sociologist Luiz Alberto Gómez de Souza (2000) has challenged the assertion that CEBs have collapsed, estimating that "at a minimum between 60,000 and 80,000 communities" continue to be active.

23 Prezzi (2017). The estimate of 800 communities should be taken with a grain of salt, since these communities tend to have a short lifespan, with new ones emerging all the time. This is part of the mobility and circulation in the Brazilian religious field that I will take up in the conclusion.

24 Fernandes (2019). Also see Guerra (2003).

Chapter 6

1 As evidence, they cite the examples of the states of Amapá, Pará, and Acre in the northern region of Brazil, a region that as we saw in the previous chapter is

the fastest growing in the country in terms of population. The percentages of Pentecostals in those states—all at 20 percent—are well above the percentage for Brazil as a whole (which is 13 percent).

2 In contrast, only 56 percent of Catholics earn no more than one minimum wage per capita. In 2017, the monthly minimum wage in Brazil stood at 937 reais, about $288.

3 Mariano takes Martin to task for the "idealization and super-valorization of certain characteristics of Pentecostalism such as voluntarism, self-governance, and personal initiative. In reality, the Pentecostal religion does not stimulate these traits to such a great extent, or at least, does not stimulate them more than other popular religions, like Umbanda, Candomblé, Kardecism, or even the Catholic Base Communities or the Charismatic Renewal" (1996: 44).

4 Chesnut (2003: 60) found in many congregations of the Assemblies of God in Belém—(in the state of Pará) a "participatory authoritarianism" that involved intensive engagement of the faithful in multiple church activities and offices, but that centralized power in the hands of the *pastor-presidente*, the head pastor. "The most important decisions on church policy were made by the head pastor, often in consultation with a cabal of loyal salaried pastors."

5 For a comparative view of race in Brazil, see Winant (2001).

6 Traditionally, the AG, the Universal Church of the Kingdom of God, and the Four-Square Gospel Church have been the main contributors of candidates for congress, with God Is Love, the Christian Congregations, and to some extent Brazil for Christ remaining ambivalent toward politics. In early 2019, the *bancada evangélica* (Evangelical caucus) had eighty-four deputies and seven senators.

7 As Freston (2017) puts it, for Brazilian Evangelicals "party affiliation is secondary. The important affiliation is with the church."

8 Even regarding these issues, there is diversity in the *bancada evangélica*. The UCKG is not explicitly opposed to abortion, for example. Perhaps we can say that the members of the caucus share a common concern with the "moralization of the family," that is, their opposition to the transformation of traditional gender roles. A good example is Marcelo Crivella, a bishop in the UCKG who was elected as mayor of Rio de Janeiro in 2016. Although he assured voters that he would not impose his religious views, he has taken actions like cutting municipal funds for the carnival by half, leading to accusations that this lack of support is due to his moral conservatism. As a leader in one of the most prestigious samba schools puts it: "according to Evangelical doctrine, carnival is the devil's party." Crivella claims that he made the cuts for purely financial reasons. See "A Um Mês do Carnaval, o Rio Fica à Sombra de Marcelo Crivella," *Isto É*, June 9, 2018. Available online: https ://istoe.com.br/a-um-mes-do-carnaval-rio-fica-a-sombra-de-marcelo-crivella/ (accessed August 23, 2020).

9 For example, in April 2019, Rio de Janeiro's City Council (*câmara de vereadores*) opened impeachment proceedings against Mayor Marcello Crivella, who as I noted,

204 *Notes*

is a prominent bishop in the Universal Church. He was charged with administrative improprieties.

10 However, there are countervailing currents within Brazilian Pentecostalism. Entre Nós (Between Us), an electronic platform-network of socially-conscious Evangelicals, emerged in 2014, to demonstrate "within the Protestant religious universe there is much more than the participation of the so-called Evangelical Caucus in Brazilian public life. Most churches are made up of men and women who want to use their talents and faith to promote the common good." See http://www .entrenos.co/#/ (accessed August 23, 2020).

11 This *cartilha para educadores* (booklet for educators) was just part of a larger program Brasil Sem Homofobia, created in 2004 by the federal Special Secretariat for Human Rights.

12 For an in-depth analysis of the profiles and opinions of the various groups that voted for Bolsonaro, see Kalil (2018). As the proverbial voice crying out in the wilderness and the leader of a poor settlement in the hinterlands of the northeast, Antônio Conselheiro's Sebastianism had a different valence than Bolsonaro's messianism. Yet, it is interesting to observe both a re-assertion of masculinity in the face of change (whether the secular republic or the pluralism of a Brazil deeply connected to global flows) and a perceived crisis. Conselheiro's exhortation that "it is in this crisis that your responsibilities grow as guardians of your families, as if at this moment a voice tells you: fathers, defend the morality of your families" (see Chapter 3) would fit well in Bolsonaro's discourse.

13 Fishman et al. (2019).

14 See BBC News (2018).

15 Bolsonaro's not-so-veiled endorsement of vigilantism lends legitimacy the activities of *milícias* (paramilitary gangs, many of which are led by current and former police officers), which might have originally emerged as local mechanisms for self-defense against drug traffickers and criminals, but have now become part of the problem, as syndicates that represent the underside of the state and are engaging in torture, executions, and illegal activities like extortion. On milícias, see "José Claúdio Souza Alves Fala Sobre o Poder das Milícias," April 15, 2019. Available online: https:// globoplay.globo.com/v/7546172/ (accessed August 23, 2020).

16 Despite #EleNão (#NotHim), a vibrant social media campaign targeting him, Bolsonaro won 52 percent of the women's votes (with a 2 percent margin of error) and 61 percent of the men's votes (Bramatti 2018).

17 Weber used the concept of elective affinity (*Wahlverwandtschaft*) to characterize the close kinship in terms of meaning and experience and the relations of reciprocal influence between two cultural forms, particularly between "ideational" and "material" dynamics (Löwy 2004). Here, Weber was trying to advance a notion of complex co-determination against mono-causal explanations and

reductive readings of social phenomena. Whereas Weber focused on the mutual reinforcement (but also the unintended consequences—such as the iron cage—emerging) between, on the one hand, Calvinist notions of predestination and its this-worldly asceticism and, on the other hand, the calculative, means-ends rationality of early capitalism, Jean and John Comaroff (2001) have hypothesized that there is an elective affinity between late, "turbo" neoliberal capitalism and "economies of the occult," spirit-infused prosperity theologies advocated by Neo-Pentecostal churches in Africa. We can bring Michel Foucault (2009) into this conversation, especially his notion of governmentality ("the conduct of conduct") to highlight links between these theologies and economic logics and panoptical and disciplinary politics. For an in-depth analysis along these lines, focusing on the entanglement of governmental policies to restore law and order and a Christian piety aimed at "securing" and saving the soul in post–civil war Guatemala, see O'Neill (2015).

18 Bolsonaro also won twenty-one of the state capitals (versus only six for Haddad), raising the question of the urban-rural split.

19 They are also correct on their emphasis on the important role of economic disparities; Bolsonaro won 67 percent of the vote of those with earning above two minimum wages. In fact, he won the votes of "less poor" Brazilians regardless of gender, and in all age groups, levels of schooling, and regions of the country, except for the northeast.

20 Here the mythical analogies are almost uncanny. Dovetailing with the mythology around King Sebastian, Bolsonaro is a man of arms, a warrior who has come back from death to save the motherland—Bolsonaro was stabbed during his campaign and had to spend time in the hospital recovering. Here, he seems to have endured a certain kind of martyrdom and, in the end, overcome the senseless violence that threatens Brazilians' daily lives. Bolsonaro, himself, has encouraged this mythologization. When speaking or tweeting about how he survived the attack against him to be elected president, he often points out that his middle name is Messias (as in Messiah). Bolsonaro might not be *o desejado*, as King Sebastian was called (see Chapter 1), but he is certainly *o escolhido*, chosen by God to save the nation.

21 In fact, there were several evangelical groups, such as Frente de Evangélicos pelo Estado de Direito (Evangelical from for the State of Rights), O Amor Vence o Ódio (Love Defeats Hate), and Evangélicos Contra Bolsonaro (Evangelicals against Bolsonaro), which publicly expressed their support for Haddad. In the words of a member of a progressive Baptist Church who participated in a march of Love Defeats Hate: "Our goal is to show that we as Christians are against the blind religious fundamentalism in Bolsonaro's speech [*fala*]." She continues: "We do not see this as consonant with our faith in Jesus. We are on the side of the poor, of

compassion, of love, of rights for all people, of equal rights for men and women. This makes a lot of sense with our faith, because for us, this has to do with what Jesus came to teach us: that the most important thing is love" (Deister 2018).

22 According to the World Bank, when Lula took office in 2002, 12.3 percent of Brazil's population (22 million) were below the poverty line. By 2013, that percentage had gone down to 4.8 (9.7 million Brazilians) (Rapoza 2016).

23 Shalders (2019).

24 In fact, Bolsonaro traveled to Washington, DC, to meet Trump. Expressing admiration for each other, they pledged to forge a new American-Brazilian relationship to fight the scourge of socialism in Venezuela, Cuba, and Nicaragua and Chinese influence in the region. During his visit he declared: "Brazil and the United States stand side-by-side in their efforts to ensure liberties and respect to traditional family lifestyles, respect to God our creator, and stand against gender ideologies and politically correct attitudes and against fake news" (Harris 2019).

25 Olavo de Carvalho, one of Bolsonaro's closest intellectual advisers, characterizes this progressive agenda with the term "socio-constructivism," in his view, a dogmatic Marxist ideology imposed by an entrenched leftist elite (disciples of Paulo Freire, an influential thinker for progressive Catholics—see Chapter 2) on Brazil's public education that is indoctrinating children. On Carvalho, see Winter (2018).

26 Although Bolsonaro traveled to Israel to visit the Western Wall accompanied by Prime Minister Benjamin Netanyahu, he backtracked from his decision to move Brazil's embassy to Jerusalem, only setting up a business interests office. This move angered many of his Evangelical supports, exposing some fractures in his religious coalition. See Osborn (2019).

27 Bolsonaro, his advisers, and his cabinet ministers see professors at public universities as the main promoters of this "cultural Marxism." By teaching humanities and social sciences, they are disseminating "ideologies," or "*balbúrdia*" (bedlam or confusion) in the word of Bolsonaro's minister of Education, rather than producing science. Thus, his administration has sought to drastically cut funding for and scholarships at public universities, leading to widespread protests by professors, students, and their supporters. Bolsonaro's critics see this move as yet another to effort to weaken civil society and curtail informed public debate about his policies (Mori 2019).

28 See his webpage: https://www.metapoliticabrasil.com/about (accessed August 23, 2020). Araújo has complained about the "criminalization" of heterosexual sex (as rape), red meat, oil, and air conditioners. In his article "Trump e o Ocidente," Araújo celebrated the election of Trump as the expression of the "expansionism" of "pan-nationalism," which seeks to rescue Western civilization from the ravages of rootless postmodern cosmopolitanism and reinvigorate it from within. Araújo concluded his essay by borrowing from Martin Heidegger's interview in *Der Spiegel*

in 1966, where the German philosopher tried to explain the rise of Nazism and his support for it as an ontological crisis of modernity from which "only a god can save us." Araújo went on to assert that "Only one God could still save the West, a God operating through the nation—including, and perhaps most importantly, the American nation . . . only Trump can still save the West" (Araújo 2017).

29 As he completed his first 100 days in office, Bolsonaro had the lowest popularity of any first-term president during this period (Londoño and Casado 2019), failing to reactivate the Brazilian economy and unable to advance his bills in congress due to his pugnacious style and penchant for controversies. Francisco Borba Ribeira Neto, a professor at the Pontifical Catholic University of São Paulo, thinks that "Bolsonaro's position on human rights will depend on his success on the economic and social front . . . . If he is able to reverse the path of deepening economic crisis, he will gain political support and will not resort to controversial measures in the socio-cultural field, including [repressing] democratic freedoms. If he fails, he will have to create an enemy that unifies his political and social base" (Domingues 2018a).

30 In fact, the MST emerged in 1984 in southern Brazil out of the efforts of the Catholic Pastoral Land Commission (CPT) (Poletto 2015). One of the most powerful religious tropes MST activists use is that of the Exodus, which involves liberation from bondage and finding the Promised Land.

31 See Renovação Carismática Católica, "Ministério Fé e Política." http://rccbrasil.org /br/institucional/fe-e-politica.html (accessed August 23, 2020).

32 A good example of interdenominational collaboration between Charismatic Catholics and Evangelicals is ENCRISTUS (Encontro Nacional de Cristãos em Busca da Unidade e Santidade—National Encounter of Christians in Search of Unity and Sanctity) created in 2008 with support from the CNBB (Machado 2015). See also: https://www.encristus.org/ (accessed August 23, 2020).

33 Compare this with: "Liberation theology and ecological discourse have something in common: they start from two bleeding wounds. The wound of poverty breaks the social fabric of millions and millions of poor people around the world. The other wound, systematic assault on the Earth, breaks down the balance of the planet, which is under threat from the plundering of development as practiced by contemporary global societies. Both lines of reflection and practice have as their starting point a cry: the cry of the poor for life, freedom, and beauty . . . and the cry of the Earth groaning under oppression" (Boff 1997: 104).

34 Francis has declared, for example, that "we have created new idols. The worship of the golden calf of old has found a new and heartless image in the cult of money and the dictatorship of an economy which is faceless and lacking any truly humane goal" (Donadio 2013).

35 Gauchazh (2013).

36 See *O Globo* (2013) and Folha de São Paulo (2013).

37 Manuela Davila, Haddad's running mate who is a member of the Brazilian Communist Party, also took communion, a fact that upset conservative Catholics even more. They railed against liberationists who enabled her. See "Comunistas Brasileiros Recebem de Forma Indigna Santíssima Eucaristia, das Mãos de Padre da Nefasta Teologia da Libertação, em Igreja de São Paulo," *Rainha Maria*, October 12, 2018. https://www.rainhamaria.com.br/Pagina/22996/Comunistas-brasileiros-rec ebem-de-forma-indigna-a-Santissima-Eucaristia-das-maos-de-padre-da-nefasta-Teologia-da-Libertacao-em-Igreja-de-Sao-Paulo (accessed August 25, 2020).

38 The Marian apparitions at Fatima have consistently been central in the conservative Catholic imaginaire from Pius XII to John Paul II. Manuel (2000) argues that they were used by conservatives in Lisbon to discredit Portugal's anti-clerical First Republic (1910–26), galvanizing rural resistance to urban-based secular elites and laying the foundation for the anti-modernist, authoritarian Salazar regime (1932–68), which had as its motto *Deus, Pátria e Familia* (God, Fatherland, and Family). In the Constitution of 1933, Salazar recognized Catholicism as the "religion of the Portuguese Nation."

39 Uribe and Carvalho (2020).

40 "Bolsonaro pede na TV 'volta `a normalidade' e fim do 'confinamento em massa' e diz que meios de comunicação espalharam 'pavor,'" *O Globo*, March 24, 2020. https://g1.globo.com/politica/noticia/2020/03/24/bolsonaro-pede-na-tv-volta-a-normali dade-e-fim-do-confinamento-em-massa.ghtml (accessed August 25, 2020).

41 Benites and Gortázar (2020).

42 Ramos (2020).

43 Souza et al. (2020).

44 It is important to highlight that the dismissal of Covid-19's infectiousness and lethality was shared by other heads of state, including Boris Johnson (in the UK, before he himself became infected), Alexander Lukashenko (Belarus), Gurbanguly Berdymukhamedov (Turkmenistan), Daniel Ortega (Nicaragua), Manuel Lopez Obrador (Mexico), and initially and inconsistently by Donald Trump. Given the diversity of these leaders, it would be interesting to study comparatively the confluence of political, economic, cultural, and religious dynamics that informed this attitude.

45 Cancian and Onofre (2020).

46 Calcagno (2020).

47 "Silas Malafaia Afirma que sua Igreja não Sera Fechada Durante Quarentena do Coronavírus." *BlastingNews*, March 3. https://br.blastingnews.com/brasil/2020/03/silas-malafaia-afirma-que-sua-igreja-nao-sera-fechada-durante-quarentena-do-c oronavirus-003092419.html (accessed August 25, 2020).

48 Pires (2020).

Notes 209

49 Behs (2020). Another Evangelical leader, Pastor Romi Marcia Bencke, General Secretary of the National Council of Christian Churches (CONIC), also declared in no uncertain terms that it is not the role of the president to make this type of convocation, especially in a secular state. See: Santos (2020).

50 "Veja e Leia a Íntegra do Pronunciamento em que Moro Anunciou Saída do Governo." *O Globo*, April 24. https://g1.globo.com/politica/noticia/2020/04/24/veja -e-leia-a-integra-do-pronunciamento-em-que-moro-anunciou-saida-do-governo .ghtml (accessed August 25, 2020).

Conclusion

1 Glocalization may be defined as the globalization of local discourses and practices which have become detached from their original moorings, are circulating worldwide, and have become re-localized, creatively incorporated into different local contexts. See Vásquez and Marquardt (2003).

2 As anthropologist Webb Keane (2008: 230) puts it: "Materiality is a precondition for the social circulation and temporal persistence of experiences and ideas."

3 Dieguez (2013).

4 Fundação Getúlio Vargas (2016).

5 Cited in Dolce (2017).

6 It is important to note here that even though Bishop Steiner spoke for the CNBB, there is disagreement among the bishops as to how to respond to Temer's government and the reforms it has proposed. In 2019, Joel Portella Amado, Auxiliary Bishop of Rio de Janeiro, once considered a progressive but who has increasingly taken a more conservative stance, was elected as the new Secretary-General of the CNBB.

7 Modino (2018).

8 Campos Lima (2020).

9 See Datafolha (2016) and Balloussier (2018). Demographer José Eustáquio Diniz Alves has constructed a model in which the percentage of Catholics drops below 50 percent as early as 2022 and they become a minority within Christianity (38.6 percent versus 39.8 percent for *evangélicos*) by 2032. See Alves (2018).

10 In contrast, CERIS also reported a decline in the number of nuns, who often do the brunt of the door-to-door pastoral work.

11 In 2012, 45 percent of the priests were in the southeast, 25 percent in the south, 16 percent in the northeast, and only 9 percent in the Midwest and 3 percent in the north. See CNBB (2012).

12 "Número de Diáconos na Igreja Católica Cresce Mais do que o de Padres no Brasil, Segundo um Novo Censo," *Catholicus*, March 24, 2015. https://catholicus.org.br

/numero-de-diaconos-na-igreja-catolica-cresce-mais-que-o-de-padres-brasil/ (accessed August 26, 2020).

13 Beck introduced the notion of risk society (*Risikogesellschaft*) to highlight the unintended consequences of what he called a "reflexive modernity," a modernity that despite its claim to be emancipatory of all forms of heteronomy (forces external to the rational, free-willed individual), introduces in a boomerang effect contradictions, dangers, and uncertainties of its own. Beck highlighted environmental crises, but we can extend his notion to include (trans)national uncivil society (e.g., gangs, terrorist networks, arms and drug traffickers, and crime syndicates).

14 In a book that ignited the interest in Latin American Pentecostalism among American and European scholars, anthropologist David Stoll asked: is Latin America turning Protestant? See Stoll (1990). Interestingly, 48 percent of Protestants indicated that they did not have a religion before. So, we have simultaneous processes of de-affiliation (with the no religion category growing) and re-affiliation (with both Catholics and Protestants capturing new followers from the no religion category).

15 Freston (2009) hypothesizes that, even under the most propitious conditions, Evangelicals will not go above 35 percent of the population in Brazil. The intense circulation within Evangelical Protestantism is well known. The 2015 Datafolha survey found that average affiliation to a particular Protestant Church was twelve years, in contrast to thirty-two years for Catholics.

16 Francis has had a change of heart, declaring in a letter celebrating the fiftieth anniversary of the CCR (part of a series of events in Rome to which he has invited Pentecostals and other Evangelical Protestants to participate) that the "Charismatic Renewal is a great force at the service of the proclamation of the Gospel, in the joy of the Holy Spirit. You received the Holy Spirit that made you discover the love of God for all his children and love of the Word." See "Pope Francis' Comments and Address at the Charismatic Renewal Convention," *Zenit*, June 3, 2014. https://zenit .org/articles/pope-francis-comments-and-address-at-charismatic-renewal-conven tion/ (accessed August 26, 2020).

17 Prezzi.

18 Tornielle (2017).
Dedicated to the promotion of a Catholic civilization, TFP combats communism, liberation theology, abortion, divorce, the use of contraceptives, and land reform. See Zanotto (2010).

19 For example, the leader of the spirits of light who came to earth to guide human spiritual and intellectual development, Pai Seta Branca (Father White Spear), is thought to have incarnated himself throughout history as an Inca chief, the African *orixa* Oxalá, Jesus's closest disciple John, and Francis of Assisi.

20 See also Teixeira (2013: 23–6).

21 Center for the Study of Global Christianity (2016), https://twitter.com/CSGC/statu s/755066880038084608, *CSGC*, July 18 (accessed August 26, 2020). Particularly active is JOCUM Brasil, *Jovens Com Uma Missão* (Youth with A Mission), the Brazilian branch of the interdenominational missionary movement founded in the United States by Loren and Darlene Cunningham in 1960. See http://www.jocum .org.br/quem-somos/ (accessed August 26, 2020).

22 See here, for example, Mafra, Swatowiski, and Sampaio (2013), Van de Kamp (2011), and Van Wyk (2014). This expansion has not been without some setbacks. In 2013, following the death of sixteen people at a massive UCKG event in Luanda, the government of Angola temporarily banned the largest Brazilian Neo-Pentecostal churches (including the Igreja Mundial do Poder de Deus). According to a government official, these churches "play with the fragilities of the Angolan people and [engage in] deceiving propaganda . . . . They are a business, that is more than obvious; they [are here] to sell miracles" (Mello 2013).

23 A battle for one-upmanship within world Pentecostalism is underway. The Lighthouse Chapel International planted two churches in Brazil (in Rio de Janeiro and São Paulo), while the RCCG also came to Brazil to great fanfare in 2009, with plans to build temples in eight cities, including Brasília, the capital. In the words of Enoch Adeboye, leader of the Redeemed Church, "I know that we are going to cover the nation of Brazil with temples" (Dweck 2011). In turn, the Universal Church inaugurated a new cathedral in Lagos in 2011. While the UCKG and the Redeemed Christian Church of God seem to willfully ignore each other, they share not only an unabashed prosperity theology but also the tendency to inflate their international impact and the geo-spiritual vision of becoming the cornerstone of the new global Pentecostal architecture (Premack 2016).

24 A similar dynamic might be at work in Haiti, in which Brazilian Pentecostals accompanying the large group of Brazilians in the United Nations Stabilization Mission confront Vodou (Bazzo 2016). In Peru, God Is Love has taken advantage of Portunhol (a mixture of Spanish and Portuguese) and structural parallels between shamanism and Pentecostal charism to appeal to Indigenous people from the Andean highlands, who finds themselves displaced in Lima and ridiculed for their accented Spanish, appearance, and worldview (Rivera 2013).

25 O'Connell (2020).

Bibliography

Abreu, C. de (2000), *Capítulos de história colonial—1500–1800*, 7th ed., edited and prefaced by J. H. Rodrigues, Belo Horizonte and Itatiaia, São Paulo: Publifolha.

Alcântara, P. (2012), *O missionário e intelectual da educação: Robert Reid Kalley (1855–1876)*, Master's Thesis, Tiradentes University, Aracaju, Sergipe.

Almeida, R. de (2013), "A visita do Francisco e abertura do compasso," *Le Monde Diplomatique—Brasil*. http://www.diplomatique.org.br/artigo.php?id=1518 (accessed November 5, 2016).

Almond, G. A., Appleby, S., and Sivan, E. (2003), *Strong Religion: The Rise of Fundamentalisms around the World*, Chicago: University of Chicago Press.

Alves, J. E. D. (2018), "Transição Religiosa—Católicos Abaixo de 50% até 2022 e Abaixo do Porcentual de Evangélico em 2032," *Instituto Humanitas Unisinos*, December 6. Available online: http://www.ihu.unisinos.br/78-noticias/585245-transicao-religiosa -catolicos-abaixo-de-50-ate-2022-e-abaixo-do-percentual-de-evangelicos-ate-2032 (accessed August 26, 2020).

Alves, J. E. D., Barros, L. F. W., and Cavenaghi, S. (2012), "A dinâmica das filiações religiosas no Brasil entre 2000 e 2010: diversificação e processo de mudança de hegemonia," Paper presented at the XVIII Encontro Nacional de Estudos Populacionais, ABEP, realizado em Águas de Lindóia, São Paulo, November 19–23.

Alves, J. E. D., Cavenaghi, S., Barros, L. F., and de Carvalho, A. A. (2017), "Distribuição espacial da transição religiosa no Brasil," *Tempo Social, Revista de Sociologia da USP* 29 (2): 215–42.

Amaral, R. (2003), "Festas católicas brasileiras e os milagres do povo," *Civitas (Porto Alegre)* 3 (1): 187–205.

Anchieta, J. de (1933), *Cartas, informações, fragmentos históricos, e sermões (1554–1594)*, Rio de Janeiro: Civilização Brasileira.

Anderson, B. (1983), *Imagined Communities: Reflections on the Origins and Spread of Nationalism*, London: Verso.

Antunes, A. (2013), "The Richest Pastors in Brazil," *Forbes*, January 17. Available online: https://www.forbes.com/sites/andersonantunes/2013/01/17/the-richest-pastors-in-b razil/#180589195b1e (accessed March 2, 2017).

Antunes, A. (2014), "The Complete List of the 150 Richest People in Brazil," *Forbes*, September 18. Available online: https://www.forbes.com/sites/andersonantunes/ 2014/09/18/the-complete-list-with-the-150-richest-people-in-brazil/#3b7db3333da8 (accessed March 2, 2017).

Aquino, M. de (2014), "A diáspora das congregações femininas portuguesas para o Brasil no início do século XX: política, religião, gênero," *Cadernos do Pagu (Campinas)* 42: 393–415.

Bibliography

Araújo, E. H. F. (2017), "Trump e o Ocidente," *Cadernos de Política Exterior* ano III, número 6: 324–56. Available online: http://segundasfilosoficas.org/trump-e-o-ocidente/ (accessed April 26, 2019).

Araújo, I. de (2016), *História do movimento pentecostal no Brasil—o caminho do Pentecostalismo Brasileiro até os dias de hoje*, Rio de Janeiro: CPAD.

Arêas, G. F. (2007), *Momento de fé: um fenômeno no rádio brasileiro*, Bachelor's in social communication thesis, Federal University of Juiz de Fora, Minas Gerais.

Azzi, R. (1974), "O movimento brasileiro de reforma católica durante o século 19," *Revista Eclesiástica Brasileira* 135: 646–62.

Azzi, R. (1983), "A vida religiosa feminina no Brasil colonial," in R. Azzi (ed.), *A Vida Religiosa no Brasil: Enfoques Históricos*, 24–60, São Paulo: Edições Paulinas.

Bailey, S. P. (2017), "A Trump-Like Politician in Brazil Could Snag the Support of a Powerful Religious Group: Evangelicals," *The Washington Post*, November 28. Available online: https://www.washingtonpost.com/news/acts-of-faith/wp/2017/11/28/a-trump-like-politician-in-brazil-could-snag-the-support-of-a-powerful-religious-group-evangelicals/?utm_term=.145222bf7cee (accessed January 1, 2018).

Balloussier, V. (2018), "Padres mais velhos puxam o aumento de clérigos no Brasil," *Folha de São Paulo*, May 7.

Baptista, P. A. N. (2007), *Libertação e diálogo: a articulação entre teologia da libertação e teologia do pluralismo religioso em Leonardo Boff*, PhD Thesis, Graduate Program in Science of Religion, Universidade Federal de Juiz de Fora. Minas Gerais. Available online: http://www.dominiopublico.gov.br/download/texto/cp050187.pdf (accessed May 20, 2017).

Barbosa, M. de F. M. (2006), *As Letras e a Cruz—pedagogia da fé e estética religiosa na experiência missionária de José de Anchieta, S.I. (1534–1597)*, Roma: Ed. Pontifícia Universitá Gregoriana.

Barros, A. de (2008), *Vida do apóstolo padre Antonio Vieira—pensador, estrategista e educador. Humanista, missionário e orador. Primeira biografia do grande Mestre*, Edição preparada por José Jorge Peralta, São Paulo: Eurobrás.

Barros, M. (n.d), "Daniel Berg." http://www.sepoangol.org/berg.htm (accessed March 10, 2017).

Bastide, R. (1978), *The African Religions of Brazil: Toward a Sociology of the Interpretation of Civilizations*, Baltimore: Johns Hopkins University Press.

Batista, C. R. (2008), "The Testament of Cícero Romão Batista," in A. L. Peterson and M. A. Vásquez (eds.), *Latin American Religions: Histories and Documents in Context*, 152–5, New York: New York University Press.

Bauman, Z. (2000), *Liquid Modernity*, London: Polity.

Bauman, Z. (2006), *Liquid Fear*, Cambridge: Polity.

Bazzo, G. (2016), "Haitian Immigrants Pouring into Brazil Don't Find a Warm Welcome," *HuffPost Brazil*, August 22. http://www.huffingtonpost.com/entry/haitians-migrants-brazil_us_56b4ca40e4b08069c7a6efe7 (accessed June 16, 2017).

BBC News. (2018), "Brazil Elections: Why Are There So Many Murders," October 6. Available online: https://www.bbc.com/news/world-latin-america-45732 801(accessed April 29, 2021).

Beck, U. (1992), *Risk Society: Towards a New Modernity*, New Delhi: Sage.

Behs, E. (2020), "Bolsonaro, de Presidente a Sumo Sacerdote," *Instituto Humanitas Unisinos*, April 7. Available online: www.ihu.unisinos.br/78-noticias/597867-bolson aro-de-presidente-a-sumo-sacerdote (accessed August 25, 2020)

Benedict XVI. (2007a), "Entrevista concedida pelo santo padre aos jornalistas durante o voo para o Brasil," May 9. http://w2.vatican.va/content/benedict-xvi/pt/speeches /2007/may/documents/hf_ben-xvi_spe_20070509_interview-brazil.html (accessed September 11, 2020).

Benedict XVI. (2007b), "Discurso do Papa Bento XVI. Sessão inaugural dos trabalhos da V conferência geral do episcopado da América Latina e do Caribe," May 13. https://w2.vatican.va/content/benedict-xvi/pt/speeches/2007/may/documents/h f_ben-xvi_spe_20070513_conference-aparecida.html (accessed September 11, 2020).

Benites, A. and Gortázar, N. G. (2020), "Mandetta, o Conservador que Vestiu o Colete do SUS e Entrincherou o Bolsonaro," *El País*, April 5. Available online: https://brasil. elpais.com/brasil/2020-04-04/mandetta-o-conservador-que-vestiu-o-colete-do-sus-e -entrincheirou-bolsonaro.html (accessed August 25, 2020).

Beozzo, J. O. (1986), "A Igreja entre a Revolução de 1930, o Estado Novo e a redemocratização," in B. Fausto (ed.), *História Geral da Civilização Brasileira III*, 271–341, São Paulo: DIFEL.

Besselaar, J. v. d. (1981), *Antônio Vieira: o homem, a obra, as ideias*, Lisboa: ICALP (Colecção Biblioteca Breve - Volume 58).

Biehl, J. (2008), "The Mucker War: A History of Violence and Silence," in M. Del Vecchio (ed.), *Postcolonial Disorders*, 279–308, Berkeley: University of California Press.

Bittencourt Filho, J. (2003), *Matriz religiosa brasileira: religiosidade e mudança social*, Petrópolis: Vozes/Koinonia.

Boff, C. (2008), *Feet-on-the-Ground Theology: A Brazilian Journey*, Eugene: Wipf & Stock Pub.

Boff, L. (1978), *Jesus Christ Liberator: A Critical Christology for our Time*, Maryknoll: Orbis Books.

Boff, L. (1985), *Church: Charism and Power: Liberation Theology and the Institutional Church*, New York: Crossroad.

Boff, L. (1986), *Ecclesiogenesis: The Base Communities Reinvent the Church*, Maryknoll: Orbis.

Boff, L. (1990), "Defense of His Book, *Church: Charism and Power*," in A. Hennelly (ed.), *Liberation Theology: A Documentary History*, 431–4, Maryknoll: Orbis.

Boff, L. (1997), *Cry of the Earth, Cry of the Poor*, Maryknoll: Orbis Books.

Boff, L. (2013), "Roma e a Teologia da Libertação: o fim da guerra." https://leonard oboff.wordpress.com/2013/07/04/roma-e-a-teologia-da-libertacao-fim-da-guerra/ (accessed November 1, 2016).

Bibliography

Boff, L. and Boff, C. (1987), *Introducing Liberation Theology*, Maryknoll: Orbis.

Bourdieu, P. (1991), "Genesis and Structure of the Religious Field," *Comparative Social Research* 13: 1–44.

Bourne, R. (2008), *Lula of Brazil: The Story So Far*, Berkeley: University of California Press.

Braga, A. (2008), *Padre Cícero. Sociologia de um padre, antropologia de um santo*, Bauru: Edusc.

Bramatti, D. (2018), "Bolsonaro também ganhou entre as mulher, diz o Ibope," *O Estado de São Paulo*. November 6. Available online: https://politica.estadao.com.br/noticias/eleicoes,bolsonaro-tambem-ganhou-entre-as-mulheres-diz-ibope,70002588225 (accessed April 30, 2019).

Brandão, C. R. (1980), *Os deuses do povo: Um estudo sobre a religião popular*, Rio de Janeiro: Livraria Brasiliense Editora.

Bruneau, T. (1974), *The Political Transformation of the Brazilian Catholic Church*, Cambridge: Cambridge University Press.

Bruneau, T. (1982), *The Church in Brazil: The Politics of Religion*, Austin: University of Texas Press.

Burdick, J. (1993), *Looking for God in Brazil: The Progressive Catholic Church in Brazil's Urban Religious Arena*, Berkeley: University of California Press.

Burdick, J. (1998), *Blessed Anastácia: Women, Race, and Popular Christianity in Brazil*, New York: Routledge.

Burdick, J. (2004), *Legacies of Liberation: The Progressive Catholic Church in Brazil*, Aldershot: Ashgate Publishing Company.

Bynum, C. W. (2011), *Christian Materiality: An Essay on Religion in Late Medieval Europe*, New York: Zone Books.

Cagle, H. (2018), "Review Essay: Fluvial Communities and Amazonian Itineraries," *Ethnohistory* 61 (1): 157–60.

Caicedo, F. V. (2014), "*The Mission*: Economic Persistence, Human Capital Transmission and Culture in South America." http://sites.bu.edu/neudc/files/2014/10/paper_320.pdf (accessed January 1, 2018).

Calcagno, L. (2020), "Em Conversa 'Vazada,' Onyx e Osmar Terra Discutem Saída de Mandetta," *Correio Braziliense*, April 9. Available online: https://www.correiobraziliense.com.br/app/noticia/politica/2020/04/09/interna_politica,843505/em-conversa-vazada-onyx-e-osmar-terra-discutem-saida-de-mandetta.shtml (accessed August 25, 2020).

Campanha, D. (2012), "Padre Marcelo inaugura hoje o santuário Mãe de Deus," *Folha de São Paulo*, November 11. Available online: http://www1.folha.uol.com.br/poder/1179253-padre-marcelo-inaugura-hoje-o-santuario-mae-de-deus.shtml (accessed March 10, 2017).

Camporez, P. (2019), "Membros da CNBB criticam medidas do governo Bolsonaro," *O Globo*, March 6. Available online: https://oglobo.globo.com/brasil/membros-da-cnbb-criticam-medidas-do-governo-bolsonaro-23502850 (accessed April 27, 2019).

Campos, L. (1997), *Teatro, Templo e Mercado—organização e Marketing de um empreendimento neopentecostal*, Petrópolis: Vozes.

Campos, L. (2005), "As origens norte-americanas do pentecostalismo brasileiro: observações sobre uma relação ainda pouco avaliada," *Revista USP* 67: 100–15. Available online: http://www.revistas.usp.br/revusp/article/viewFile/13458/15276 (accessed on 10 March 2017).

Campos, R. B. (2000), *When Sadness is Beautiful: A Study of the Place of Rationality and Emotion within the Social Life of the Ave de Jesus*, Doctoral Thesis, University of St. Andrews, UK.

Campos, R. B. (2009), "Interpretações do catolicismo: do sincretismo e antissincretismo na/da cultura brasileira," in F. Teixeira and R. Menezes (eds.), *Catolicismo plural—dinâmicas contemporâneas*, 135–50, Petropolis: Vozes.

Campos, R. B. and Reesink, M. L. (2011), "Mudando o eixo e invirtendo o mapa: para uma antropologia da religião plural," *Religião e Sociedade* 31 (1). Available online: http://www.scielo.br/scielo.php?script=sci_arttext&pid=S0100-85872011000100009&lng=en&nrm=iso&tlng=pt (accessed August 15, 2017).

Campos Lima, E. (2020), "Over 1,500 Brazilian Priests Support Bishops' Attack on Bolsonaro," *Crux*, August 5. Available online: https://cruxnow.com/church-in-the-americas/2020/08/over-1500-brazilian-priests-support-bishops-attack-on-bolsonaro/ (accessed August 26, 2020).

Camurça, M. (2009), "Entre sincretismos e 'guerras santas': dinâmicas e linhas de força do campo religioso brasileiro," *Revista USP* 81: 173–85.

Camurça, M. (2013), "O Brasil religioso que emerge do Censo de 2010: consolidações, tendências e perplexidades," in F. Teixeira and R. Menezes (eds.), *Religiões em movimento—o censo de 2010*, 63–88, Petrópolis: Vozes.

Cancian, N. and Onofre, R. (2020), "Em Despedida Privada com Auxiliares Mandeta Fala em Ingratidao e Risco de Colapso na Saude," *Folha de São Paulo*, April 16. Available online: https://www1.folha.uol.com.br/poder/2020/04/em-despedida-privada-com-auxiliares-mandeta-fala-em-ingratidao-e-risco-de-colapso-na-saude.shtml (accessed August 25, 2020).

Capone, S. (2010), *Searching for Africa in Brazil: Power and Tradition in Candomblé*, Durham: Duke University Press.

Cardoso, F. H. and Faletto, E. (1979), *Dependency and Development in Latin America*, Berkeley: University of California Press.

Cardoso, R. (2011), "O novo retrato da fé no Brasil," *Isto é*, August 24. Available online: http://istoe.com.br/152980_O+NOVO+RETRATO+DA+FE+NO+BRASIL/ (accessed May 28, 2017).

Cardoso, R. (n.d.), "Pr. Marco Feliciano Pede a Senha do Cartão." https://goo.gl/MUVNQq (accessed August 22, 2020).

Carranza, B. (2000), *Renovação Carismática Católica*, Aparecida: Santuário.

Carranza, B. (2009), "Uma novidade na estrutura de vida consagrada na igreja," Interview with Graziela Wolfart and Márcia Junges. *IHU On-line*, September 8. http://www.ihuonline.unisinos.br/index.php?option=com_content&view=article&id=2792&secao=307 (accessed June 22, 2017).

Carranza, B. and Mariz, C. (2013), "Catholicism for Export: The Case of Canção Nova," in C. Rocha and M. A. Vásquez (eds.), *The Diaspora of Brazilian Religions*, 137–62. Leiden: Brill.

Carranza, B., Mariz, C., and Camurça, M. (organizers). (2009), *Novas comunidades católicas: em busca do espaço pós-moderno*, Aparecida: Idéias e Letras.

Carter, M. (2015), "Conclusion. Challenging Social Inequality: Contention, Context, and Consequences," in M. Carter (ed.), *Challenging Social Inequality: The Landless Rural Worker's Movement and Agrarian Reform in Brazil*, 391–412, Durham: Duke University Press.

Carvalho, N. R. de and Santos Junior, O. A. dos (2019), "Bolsonaro and the Inequalities of Geographical Development in Brazil," *Journal of Latin American Geography* 18 (1): 198–202.

Casado, L. and Andreoni, M. (2019), "Decisions by Brazil's Top Court Have Public Questioning its Credibility," *The New York Times*, April 28, A11.

Castro, Z. M. de and Couto, A do P. (1961), *Folias de Reis*, Rio de Janeiro: Ministério da Educação e Cultura, Departamento de Assuntos Culturais.

Cavassa, E. (2013), "On the Trail of Aparecida: Jorge Bergoglio and the Latin American Ecclesial Tradition," *America: A Jesuit Review*, October 30. Available online: http://www.americamagazine.org/trail-aparecida (accessed May 28, 2017).

Chakrabarty, D. (2000), *Provincializing Europe: Postcolonial Thought and Historical Difference*, Princeton: Princeton University Press.

Chesnut, R. A. (1997), *Born Again in Brazil: The Pentecostal Boom and the Pathogens of Poverty*, New Brunswick: Rutgers University Press.

Chesnut, R. A. (2003), *Competitive Spirits: Latin America's New Religious Economy*, New York: Oxford University Press.

Clark, P. (1999), "'Top-star' Priests and the Catholic Response to the 'Explosion' of Evangelical Protestantism in Brazil: The Beginning of the End of the 'Walkout'?" *Journal of Contemporary Religion* 14 (2): 189–202.

Clossey, L. (2008), *Salvation and Globalization in the Early Jesuit Missions*, Cambridge: Cambridge University Press.

Clossey, L. (2015), "The Early-Modern Jesuit Missions as a Global Movement." A working paper presented at the "Global Social Movements in World Historical Perspective," A Conference of the World History Multi-Campus Research Group. University of California, Santa Cruz, October 31. Available online at: https://eschola rship.org/uc/item/0h45m0jw (accessed April 25, 2021).

CNBB. (2012), "IBGE Divulga Dados, CERIS Mostra 'Igreja Viva.'" June 29. Available online: http://www.cnbb.org.br/ibge-divulga-dados-ceris-mostra-qigreja-vivaq/ (accessed 26 August 2020).

Coleman, S. and Vásquez, M. A. (2017), "On the Road. Pentecostal Pathways Through the Mega-City," in D. Garbin and A. Strhan (eds.), *Religion and the Global City*, 27–46, London: Bloomsbury.

218   *Bibliography*

Comaroff, J. and Comaroff, J. L. (2001), "Millennial Capitalism: First Thoughts on a Second Coming," in J. L. Comaroff (ed.), *Millennial Capitalism and the Culture of Neoliberalism*, 1–56, Durham: Duke University Press.

Conference of Latin American and Caribbean Bishops (CELAM) (1968), *Documento de Medellín*. https://web.archive.org/web/20090502162024/http://www.documentode medellin.com.ar/ (accessed January 1, 2018).

Conference of Latin American and Caribbean Bishops (CELAM) (2007), *Documento de Aparecida*, Santa Fe de Bogota, Colombia: CELAM. Available online: http://www .caritas.org.pe/documentos/documento_conclusivo_aparecida.pdf (accessed May 28, 2017).

Conselheiro, A. (2008), "'About the Republic' and 'Farewell,'" in A. L. Peterson and M. A. Vásquez (eds.), *Latin American Religions: Histories and Documents in Context*, 148–52, New York: New York University Press.

COSTA, O. B. R. da. (2016), *O dinheiro: o novo deus da humanidade: Uma análise da cultura do consumismo selvagem e de como ele se tornou a nova religião da humanidade*, Lisboa: Novas Edições Acadêmicas.

Cox, H. (1988), *The Silencing of Leonardo Boff: The Vatican and the Future of World Christianity*, Oak Park: Meyer-Stone Books.

Cunha, E. da. (1902), *Os sertões: Campanha de Canudos*, São Paulo: Brasiliense.

Cunha, M. do N. (2016), "Religião e política: ressonâncias do neoconservadorismo evangélico nas mídias brasileiras," *Perseu* 11: 147–66.

Datafolha. (2016), "44% dos evangélicos são ex-católicos," December 18. http://datafolh a.folha.uol.com.br/opiniaopublica/2016/12/1845231-44-dos-evangelicos-sao-ex-cato licos.shtml (accessed June 10, 2017).

Daudelin, J. (1992), "L'Eglise progressiste au Brésil: la fin d'un mythe?" in J. Zylberberg (ed.), *L'Amérique et les Amériques*, 673–92, Québec: Presses de l'Université Laval.

Dawsey, C. and Dawsey, J., eds. (1995), *The Conferados: Old South Immigrants in Brazil*, Tuscaloosa: University of Alabama Press.

Deister, J. (2018), "Setores evangélicos denunciam Jair Bolsonaro como uma ameaça aos valores cristãos," *Brasil de Fato*, October 24. https://www.brasildefato.com.br/2018 /10/24/setores-evangelicos-denunciam-jair-bolsonaro-como-uma-ameaca-aos-va lores-cristaos/ (accessed April 26, 2019).

Della Cava, R. (1970), *Miracle in Juazeiro*, New York: Columbia University Press.

Della Cava, R. (1988), "The Church and the *Abertura* in Brazil, 1974–1985," Working paper, Notre Dame: Helen Kellogg Institute for International Studies, University of Notre Dame.

Denevan, W., ed. (1992), *The Native Population of the Americas in 1492*, 2nd ed., Madison: University of Wisconsin Press.

Descola, P. (2013), *Beyond Nature and Culture*, Chicago: University of Chicago Press.

De Theije, M. (1990), "'Brotherhoods Throw More Weight Around than the Pope': Catholic Traditionalism and Lay Brotherhoods in Brazil," *Sociological Analysis* 51 (2): 189–204.

De Theije, M. (1999), "CEBs and Catholic Charismatics in Brazil," in C. Smith and J. Prokopy (eds.), *Latin American Religion in Motion*, 111–24, New York: Routledge.

Diacon, T. (1991), *Millenarian Vision, Capitalist Reality: Brazil's Contestado Rebellion, 1912–1916*, Durham: Duke University Press.

Dieguez, M. (2013), "Papa Francisco Rezou com Cristãos Evangélicos da Assembléia de Deus, em Manguinhos," *Folha1*, July 26. Available online: https://www.folha1.com.br /_conteudo/2013/07/blogs/blogdacoluna/1152133-papa-francisco-rezou-com-cris taos-evangelicos-da-assembleia-de-deus-em-manguinhos.html (accessed August 26, 2020).

Dolce, J. (2017), "CNBB e paróquias mobilizam fieis contra o desmonte da Previdência de Temer," *Radioagência Brasil de Fato*, April 12. https://www.brasildefato.com.br /2017/04/12/cnbb-e-paroquias-mobilizam-fieis-contra-o-desmonte-da-previdencia -de-temer/ (accessed June 10, 2017).

Domingues, F. (2018a), "Brazil Turns Far Right: What Role Did Religion Play in Bolsonaro's Election?" *America: The Jesuit Review*, December 10. https://www.ame ricamagazine.org/politics-society/2018/11/19/brazil-turns-far-right-what-role-did -religion-play-bolsonaros-election (accessed April 27, 2019).

Domingues, F. (2018b), "In Election Shaped by Fake News Brazil's Bishops are Divided," *Crux*, October 22. https://cruxnow.com/global-church/2018/10/22/in-election-sha ped-by-fake-news-brazils-bishops-are-divided/ (accessed April 27, 2019).

Donadio, R. (2013), "Francis' Humility and Emphasis on the Poor Strike a New Tone in the Vatican," *The New York Times*, May 25. Available online: http://www.nytimes .com/2013/05/26/world/europe/pope-francis-changes-tone-at-the-vatican.html (accessed November 4, 2016).

Drogus, C. and Stewart-Gambino, H. (2005), *Activist Faith: Grassroots Women in Democratic Brazil and Chile*, University Park: Penn State University Press.

Drooger, A. (1987), "Religiosidade mímima brasileira," *Religião e Sociedade* 14 (2): 62–86.

Duccini, L. and Rabelo, M. (2013), "As religiões afro-brasileiras no Censo de 2010," in F. Teixeira and R. Menezes (eds.), *Religiões em movimento: o censo de 2010*, 219–34, Petrópolis: Vozes.

Durkheim, É. (2001 [1918]), *The Elementary Forms of Religious Life*, New York: Oxford University Press.

Dweck, D. (2011), "O pastor nigeriano que quer salvar a alma dos brasileiros," *Super interesante*, February 18. http://super.abril.com.br/saude/o-pastor-coca-cola/ (accessed June 17, 2017).

Eltis, D. (2001), "Volume and Structure of the Transatlantic Slave Trade: A Reassessment," *William and Mary Quarterly* 58 (1): 17–31.

Engler, S. (2011), "Other Religions as Social Problems: The Universal Church of the Kingdom of God and Afro-Brazilian Traditions," in Titus Hjelm (ed.), *Religion and Social Problems*, 213–28, New York: Routledge,

Every-Clayton, J. E. W. (2002), "The Legacy of Robert Reid Kalley," *International Bulletin of Missionary Research* 26 (3): 123–7.

Fellet, J. (2017), "Não há condições éticas de Temer seguir no cargo, diz secretário-geral da CNBB," *BBC Brasil*, May 24. http://www.bbc.com/portuguese/brasil-40024325 (accessed May 27, 2019).

Fernandes, S. (2019), "The Catholic Charismatic Renewal and the Catholicism that Remains: A Study of the CCR Movement in Rio de Janeiro," *Religions* 10 (6): 397. Available online: https://www.mdpi.com/2077-1444/10/6/397/htm# (accessed February 12, 2021).

Fernandes, S. and Vásquez, M. A. (2013), "This Pope is a Brazilian," *Religion Dispatches*. http://religiondispatches.org/this-pope-is-a-brazilian/ (accessed February 2, 2016).

Fernandes, S. R. A. (1996), "Movimento de Renovação Carismática Católica—ethos comum e antagônico em camadas populares no Rio de Janeiro," *Revista de Ciências Humanas e Sociais* 18: 109–24.

Fernandes, S. R. A. (2003), "Catolicismo, massa e revival: padre Marcelo Rossi e o modelo kitsch," *Cadernos de Campo*, USP 11(11): 87–98. Available online: https://goo.gl/J8GilE, (accessed March 10, 2019).

Fernandes, S. R. A. (2005a), "Padres cantores e a mídia—representações da identidade sacerdotal," *Ciencias Sociales y Religión/Ciências Sociais e Religião* 7 (7): 131–55.

Fernandes, S. R. A. (2005b), "A não ordenação feminina: delimitando as assimetrias de gênero na igreja católica a partir de rapazes e moças vocacionados/as," *Revista Estudos Feministas* 13 (2): 425–36.

Fernandes, S. R. A. (2006), *Mudança de Religião no Brasil – desvendando sentidos e motivações*, São Paulo/Rio de Janeiro: Palavra & Prece e CERIS.

Fernandes, S. R. A. (2010), "Teologia da Libertação e CCR—conciliações, antagonismo e ponderações. Que influências na construção social da vocação?" in *Jovens católicos e o catolicismo (ed.), escolhas, desafios e subjetividades,* Rio de Janeiro: FAPERJ/Quartet.

Fernandes, S. R. A. (2012), "A (re)construção religiosa inclui dupla ou tripla pertença," *Revista IHU On-Line.* https://goo.gl/ow8q4r (accessed March 10, 2019).

Fernandes, S. R. A. (2013), "Os números de católicos no Brasil—Mobilidades, experimentação e propostas nao reductivistas na análise do Censo," in F. Teixeira and R. Menezes (eds.), *Religiões em movimento: o censo de 2010*, 111–26, Petrópolis: Vozes.

Fernandes, S. R. A. (2015), "Catolicismo estrutural—interpretações sobre o censo da igreja católica e a mudança sociocultural do catolicismo brasileiro," *Revista Interdisciplinar em Cultura e Sociedade* 1 (1): 185–202.

Fernandes, S. R. A. (2017),"Desvinculação religiosa entre os jovens é maior do que a adesão ao pentecostalismo," Entrevista com Sílvia Fernandes. *Instituto Humanitas Unisinos.* http://www.ihu.unisinos.br/566902-desvinculacao-religiosa-entre-os-jov ens-e-maior-do-que-a-adesao-ao-pentecostalismo-entrevista-especial-com-silvia-fe rnandes (accessed August 19, 2017).

Fernandes, S. R. A. and Santos de Souza, E. (2014), "As moças e os pobres: considerações sobre a comunidade feminina 'Toca de Assis." *Religião e Sociedade* 34 (2): 86–113.

Ferraz, J. (2009), "Carta ao fiéis de Olinda e Recife—Dom Leme." http://www.deuslovult .org/2009/11/18/carta-aos-fies-de-olinda-e-recife-dom-leme/ (posted November 18, 2009 and accessed March 5, 2019).

Filho, J. J. de O. (2004), "Formação histórica do movimento adventista," *Estudos Avançados* 18 (52): 157–79. Available online: http://www.scielo.br/pdf/ea/v18n52/a12v1852.pdf (accessed July 6, 2019).

Filho, P. C. (2012), "Truth Commission in Brazil: Individualizing Amnesty, Revealing the Truth," *Yale Review of International Studies*. Available online: http://yris.yira.org/essays/440#_ftn7 (accessed August 15, 2017).

Fishman, A., Martins, R. M., Demori, L., Greenwald, G., and Audi, A. (2019), "Their Little Show," *The Intercept*, June 17. Available at: https://theintercept.com/2019/06/17/brazil-sergio-moro-lula-operation-car-wash/ (accessed April 29, 2021).

Folha de São Paulo. (2013), "Leia à Íntegra do Discurso do Papa na Missa de Encerramento da Jornada," July 28. Available online: http://www1.folha.uol.com.br/poder/2013/07/1318012-leia-integra-do-discurso-do-papa-na-missa-de-encerramento-da-jornada.shtml (accessed August 23, 2020).

Foucault, M. (1978), *The History of Sexuality, Volume 1, An Introduction*, New York: Pantheon Books.

Foucault, M. (2009), *Security, Territory, Population*, New York: Picador.

Francis. (2013), *Lumen Fidei*. http://w2.vatican.va/content/francesco/en/encyclicals/documents/papa-francesco_20130629_enciclica-lumen-fidei.html (accessed November 4, 2016).

Francis. (2015), *Laudato Si': On Care for Our Common Home*, Vatican City: Libreria Editrice Vaticana.

Franco, A. (1898), *José de Anchieta—Thaumaturgo do novo mundo*, Rio de Janeiro: João Lopes da Cunha Editor.

Freire, P. (1970), *The Pedagogy of the Oppressed*, New York: Herder and Herder.

Freston, P. (1995), "Pentecostalism in Brazil: A Brief History," *Religion* 25 (2): 119–33.

Freston, P. (2001a), *Evangelicals and Politics in Africa, Asia, and Latin America*, Cambridge: Cambridge University Press.

Freston, P. (2001b), "The Transnationalisation of Brazilian Pentecostalism. The Universal Church of the Kingdom of God," in A. Corten and R. Marshall-Fratani (eds.), *Between Babel and Pentecost: Transnational Pentecostalism in Africa and Latin America*, Bloomington: Indiana University Press.

Freston, P. (2009), "Presente e futuro da igreja evangélica no Brasil (parte 2)," *Ultimato*. Available online: http://www.ultimato.com.br/revista/artigos/316/presente-e-futuro-da-igreja-evangelica-no-brasil-parte-2 (accessed May 28, 2017).

Freston, P. (2017), *Protestant Political Parties: A Global Survey*, New York: Routledge.

Bibliography

Freyre, G. (1987), *Slaves and Masters: A Study in the Development of Brazilian Civilization*, Berkeley: University of California Press.

Frigerio, A. (2013), "Umbanda and Batuque in the Southern Cone: Transnationalization as Cross-Border Religious Flow and as Social Field," in C. Rocha and M. A. Vásquez (eds.), *The Diaspora of Brazilian Religions*, 165–95, Leiden: Brill.

Fundação Getúlio Vargas. (2016), *Relatória ICJBrasil. Primeiro Semester*. Available online: http://bibliotecadigital.fgv.br/dspace/bitstream/handle/10438/17204/Re latorio-ICJBrasil_1_sem_2016.pdf?sequence=1&isAllowed=y (accessed August 26, 2020).

Gauchazh (2013), "Leia à Íntegra do Discurso do Papa na Favela Varginha," July 17. Available at: http://zh.clicrbs.com.br/rs/noticias/noticia/2013/07/leia-a-integra-do -discurso-do-papa-na-favela-de-varginha-4213152.html (accessed August 23, 2020).

Gebara, I. (1993), "O aborto não é pecado," *Veja*, October 6, 7–10.

Gebara, I. (1994), *Trindade, palavra sobre coisas velhas e novas. Uma perspectiva ecofeminista*. São Paulo: Paulinas.

Gebara, I. and Bingemer, M. C. (1989), *Mary, Mother of God, Mother of the Poor*, Maryknoll: Orbis.

Gini, S. (2010), "Conflitos no campo protestante: O movimento carismático e o surgimento da Igreja Presbiteriana Renovada (1965–1975)," *Revista Brasileira de História das Religiões* 2 (8): 121–64.

Glick-Schiller, N. (2005), "Transnational Social Fields and Imperialism: Bringing a Theory of Power to Transnational Studies," *Anthropological Theory* 5 (4): 431–69.

Globo. (2013), "Veja a íntegra da homilia de Francisco na missa para jovens em Copacabana." Available online: http://g1.globo.com/jornada-mundial-da-juventude /2013/noticia/2013/07/veja-integra-da-homilia-de-francisco-na-missa-para-jovens -em-copacabana.html (accessed April 29, 2021).

Gomes, L. M. da S. (2010), *Irmandades negras: Educação, música e resistencia nas Minas Gerais no século XVIII*, São Paulo: Master's Thesis Universidade Salesiana (UNISAL).

Grover, M. L. (1984), "Religious Accommodation in the Land of Racial Democracy: Mormon Priesthood and Black Brazilians," *Dialogue: A Journal of Mormon Thought* 17 (3): 23–34.

Guerra, L. (2003), "As influências da lógica mercadológica sobre as recentes transformações na Igreja Católica," *Revista de Estudos da Religião* 1 (2): 1–23.

Hall, D., ed. (1997), *Lived Religion in America: Toward a History of Practice*, Princeton: Princeton University.

Harris, M. and Espelt-Bombin, S. (2018), "Rethinking Amerindian Spaces in Brazilian History," *Ethnohistory* 65 (4): 537–47.

Harris, T. (2019), "Jair Bolsonaro: U.S. and Brazil Stand Together against 'Gender Ideology, Politically Correct Attitudes, and Fake News," *Real Clear Politics*, March 19. https://www.realclearpolitics.com/video/2019/03/19/jair_bolsonaro_us_and_br azil_stand_together_against_gender_ideology_politically_correct_attitudes_and_fa ke_news.html (accessed April 26, 2019).

Heelas, P., Lash, S., and Morris, P., eds. (1996), *Detraditionalization: Critical Reflections on Authority and Identity at a Time of Uncertainty*, London: Wiley Blackwell.

Hemming, J. (1978), *Red Gold: The Conquest of Brazilian Indians 1500–1760*, Cambridge, MA: Harvard University Press.

Hervieu-Léger, D. (2000), *Religion as Chain of Memory*, New Brunswick: Rutgers University Press.

Hewitt, W. E. (1991), *Base Christian Communities and Social Change in Brazil*, Lincoln: University of Nebraska Press.

Hobsbawm, E. (1965), *Primitive Rebels: Studies in Archaic Forms of Social Movement in the 19th and 20th Centuries*, New York: WW Norton.

Hoornaert, E. (1977), *A Evangelização e Cristandade durante o Primeiro Período Colonial*, Petrópolis: Vozes.

Hoornaert, E. (1979), *História geral da igreja na América Latina, história da igreja no Brasil, vol. 2*, Petróplis: Vozes.

Hoornaert, E. (1982), *A Igreja no Brasil—Colônia (1500–1800)*, São Paulo: Brasiliense.

Hoornaert, E. (1991), *Catolicismo Moreno do Brasil*, Petrópolis: Vozes.

Hoornaert, E., Azzi, R., Van der Grijp, K., and Brod, B. (2008), *História da Igreja no Brasil: ensaio de interpretação a partir do povo: primeira época—período colonial*, 5th ed., Petrópolis: Vozes.

Ikeuchi, S. (2017), "From Ethnic Religion to Generative Selves: Pentecostalism among Nikkei Brazilian Migrants in Japan," *Contemporary Japan* 29 (2): 214–29.

Ingold, T. (2011), *Being Alive: Essays on Movement, Knowledge and Description*, New York: Routledge.

Ireland, R. (1992), *Kingdoms Come: Religion and Politics in Brazil*, Pittsburgh: University of Pittsburgh Press.

Ireland, R. (1993), "The *Crentes* of Campo Alegre and the Religious Construction of Brazilian Politics," in V. Garrard-Burnett and D. Stoll (eds.), *Rethinking Protestantism in Latin America*, 45–65, Philadelphia: Temple University Press.

Jenkins, P. (2008), *The New Faces of Christianity: Believing the Bible in the Global South*, New York: Oxford University Press.

Jenkins, P. (2011), *The Next Christendom: The Coming of Global Christianity*, New York: Oxford University Press.

John Paul II. (1983), "Discurso del Santo Padre Juan Pablo II a la Asamblea de CELAM." http://w2.vatican.va/content/john-paul-ii/es/speeches/1983/march/documents/hf_jp -ii_spe_19830309_assemblea-celam.html (accessed October 31, 2016).

Johnson, S. (2012), "The Rise of the Nacirema and the Descent of European Man: A Response to Manuel Vásquez's *More than Belief*," *Method & Theory in the Study of Religion* 24 (4–5): 464–81.

Johnson, T. (2009), "The Global Demographics of the Pentecostal and Charismatic Renewal," *Society* 46 (6): 479–86.

Júnior, P. G. (2008), "Minas são muitas, mas convém não exagerar—identidade local e resistência ao pentecostalismo em Minas Gerais," *Cadernos CRH* 21 (52): 145–62.

Bibliography

Kalil, I. O., coordinator. (2018), *Quem são e no que acreditam os eleitores do Jair Bolsonaro*, São Paulo: Fundação Escola de Sociologia e Política de São Paulo.

Karash, M. (2002), "Zumbi of Palmares: Challenging the Colonial Portuguese Order," in K. J. Adrien (ed.), *The Human Tradition in Colonial Latin America*, 104–20, Wilmington: SR Books.

Keane, W. (2007), *Christian Moderns: Freedom and Fetish in the Mission Encounter*, Berkeley: University of California Press.

Keane, W. (2008), "On the Materiality of Religion," *Material Religion* 4 (2): 230–31.

Kiddy, E. (2005), *Black of the Rosary: Memory and History in Minas Gerais, Brazil*, University Park: Penn State University Press.

Kirschke, P. J. (2001), *The Learning of Democracy in Latin America: Social Actors and Cultural Change*, New York: Nova Science Publishers.

Koschorke, K. (2016), "Transcontinental Links, Enlarged Maps, and Polycentric Structures in the History of World Christianity," *Journal of World Christianity* 6 (1): 28–56.

Kramer, E. (2001), "Possessing Faith: Commodification, Religious Subjectivity, and Collectivity in a Brazilian neo-Pentecostal Church," Doctoral Dissertation, The University of Chicago.

Labate, B. C. and Cavnar, C., eds. (2014), *Ayahuasca Shamanism in the Amazon and Beyond*, New York: Oxford University Press.

Labate, B. C. and MacRae, E., eds. (2010), *Ayahuasca, Ritual and Religion in Brazil*, London: Equinox.

Lalive D'Epinay, C. (1968), *El refugio de las masas: estudio sociológico del protestantismo chileno*, Santiago: Editorial del Pacífico.

Langfur, H. (2006), *Forbidden Lands: Colonial Identity, Frontier Violence, and the Persistance of Brazil's Eastern Indians 1750–1830*, Stanford: Stanford University Press.

Langfur, H. (2014), "Introduction: Recovering Brazil's Indigenous Past," in H. Langfur (ed.), *Native Brazil: Beyond the Convert and the Cannibal, 1500–1900*, 1–28, Albuquerque: University of New Mexico Press.

Leal, V. N. (2012 [1975]), *Coronelismo, enxada, e voto: O município e o regime representative no Brasil*, 4th ed., São Paulo: Companhia das Letras.

Leitão, H. and Romeiras, F. M. (2015), "The Role of Science in the History of Portuguese Anti-Jesuitism," *Journal of Jesuit Studies* 2: 77–99.

Leite, S. (1940), *Novas Cartas Jesuíticas (de Nóbrega a Vieira)—Série 5ª Brasiliana—vol. 194, Biblioteca Pedagógica Brasileira*. São Paulo: Companhia Editorial Nacional.

Lemos, C. and Tavolaro, D. (2007), *O bispo: A história revelada de Edir Macedo*, Rio de Janeiro: Larousse do Brasil.

Léonard, É.-G. (2002), *O protestantismo brasileiro: estudo de eclesiologia e história social*, Tradução de Linneu de Camargo Schützer, São Paulo: ASTE.

Léry, J. de (1961), *Viagem à terra do Brasil*, Tradução integral e notas de Sergio Milliet, São Paulo: Biblioteca do Exército.

Levine, D. (1989), "Popular Groups, Popular Culture, and Popular Religion," Working paper number 127, Notre Dame: Helen Kellogg Institute for International Studies, University of Notre Dame.

Levine, D. (1992), *Popular Voices in Latin American Catholicism*, Princeton: Princeton University Press.

Levine, R. (1995), *Vale of Tears: Revisiting the Canudos Massacre in Northeastern Brazil, 1893-1897*, Berkeley: University of California Press.

Londoño, E. and Casado, L. (2019), "Bolsonaro, a Combative 'Soldier,' Gets off to a Turbulent Start in Brazil," *The New York Times*, A10.

Löwy, M. (2004), "Le concept d'affinité élective chez Max Weber," *Archives des Science Sociales de Religion* 127: 93–103.

Macca, M. (2003), *Nossa Senhora Aparecida: Padroeira do Brasil*, São Paulo: Planeta.

Machado, M. das D. C. (2005), "Representações e relações de gênero nos grupos pentecostais," *Estudos Feministas* 13 (2): 387–96.

Machado, M. das D. C. (2015), "Religião e política no Brasil contemporâneo: uma análise dos pentecostais e carismáticos católicos," *Religião & Sociedade* 35 (2). Available online: http://www.scielo.br/scielo.php?script=sci_arttext&pid=S0100-85 872015000200045 (accessed November 5, 2016).

Mafra, C. (2007), "Casa dos homens, casa de Deus," *Análise Social* 42 (182): 145–61.

Mafra, C., Swatowiski, C., and Sampaio, C. (2013), "Edir Macedo's Pastoral Project: A Globally Integrated Pentecostal Network," in C. Rocha and M. A. Vásquez (eds.), *The Diaspora of Brazilian Religions*, 45–67, Leiden: Brill.

Mainwaring, S. (1986), *The Catholic Church and Politics in Brazil, 1916–1985*, Stanford: Stanford University Press.

Manuel, P. C. (2000), "The Marian Apparitions in Fátima as Political Reality: Religion and Politics in Twentieth-Century Portugal," Working Paper #88. Center for European Studies, Harvard University. http://www.people.fas.harvard.edu/~ces/p ublications/docs/pdfs/manuel.pdf (accessed 16 July 2019).

Mariano, R. (2003), "A Igreja Universal no Brasil," in A. Oro, A. Corten, and J.-P. Dozon, Organizers (eds.), *Igreja Universal do Reino de Deus—os novos conquistadores da fé*, São Paulo: Paulinas.

Mariano, R. (2004). "Os neo-pentecostais e a teologia da prosperidade," *Novos Estudos CEBRAP* 44: 24–44.

Mariano, R. (2005). *Pentecostais—sociologia do novo pentecostalismo no Brasilm*, 2nd ed., São Paulo: Loyola.

Mariano, R. (2011). "Sociologia do crescimento pentecostal no Brasil: um balanço," *Perspectiva Teológica* 43 (119): 11–36.

Mariano, R. (2013), "Mudanças no campo religioso brasileiro no censo 2010," *Debates do NER* 14(24): 119–37.

Mariz, C. (1994), *Coping with Poverty: Pentecostals and Base Communities in Brazil*, Philadelphia: Temple University Press.

Mariz, C. and Gracino, P. (2013), "As igrejas pentecostais no Censo de 2010," in F. Teixeira and R. Menezes (eds.), *Religiões em movimento: o censo de 2010*, 161–90, Petrópolis: Vozes.

Mariz, C. and Medeiros, K. M. C. (2013), "Toca de Assis em crise: uma análise dos discursos dos membros que permaneceram na comunidade," *Religião e Sociedade* 33 (2): 141–73.

Mariz, C. and Souza, C. H. (2015), "Carismáticos e pentecostais: os limites das trocas ecumênicas," *Comtemporânea* 5 (2): 381–408.

Mariz, C. L., Machado, M., and Das D. C. (1997), "Pentecostalism and Women in Brazil," in E. Cleary and H. Stewart-Gambino (eds.), *Power, Politics, and Pentecostals in Latin America*, 41–54, Boulder: Westview.

Mariz, V. and Provençal, L. (2015), *Os franceses na Guanabara—Villegagnon e a França Antártica (1555–1567)*, Rio de Janeiro: Editora Nova Fronteira.

Marra, H. (2015), *Padre Marcelo Rossi—uma vida dedicada a Deus*, Rio de Janeiro: Best Seller.

Martin, D. (1990), *Tongues of Fire: The Explosion of Protestantism in Latin America*, Oxford: Blackwell.

Marx, K. (1978), "Contribution to the Critique of Hegel's *Philosophy of Right*," in Robert Tucker (ed.), *Marx-Engels Reader*, New York: Norton.

Matos, A. de Souza. (2011), *Presbyteral Names in Brazil*. Available online: http://www.mackenzie.br/15616.html (accessed December 12, 2015).

Matos, A. de Souza. (n.d.), *"Robert Reid Kalley: o pioneiro do protestantismo missionário na Europa e nas Américas,"* Instituto Presbiteriano Mackenzie, s/d. *Portal Mackenzie*—Centro Presbiteriano de Pós-Graduação Andrew Jumper. http://cpaj.mackenzie.br/historiadaigreja/pagina.php?id=290 (accessed March 10, 2017).

McCutcheon, R. (2001), *Critics not Caretakes: Redescribing the Public Study of Religion*, Albany: SUNY Press.

Mello, P. C. (2013), "Angola proíbe operação de igrejas evangélicas do Brasil," *Folha de São Paulo*, April 27. Available online: http://www1.folha.uol.com.br/mundo/2013/04/1269733-angola-proibe-operacao-de-igrejas-evangelicas-do-brasil.shtml (accessed June 17, 2017).

Mendonça, A. G. (2007), "Protestantismo no Brasil," *REVISTA USP* 74: 160–73.

Mendonça, A. G. and Filho, P. V. (2002), *Introdução ao protestantismo no Brasil*, São Paulo: Loyola.

Ministry of Tourism. (2016), "Turismo religioso continua em alta no Brasil," January 12. Available online: https://goo.gl/6oHaa7 (accessed August 23, 2020)

Mittleman, J. (2000), *The Globalization Syndrome: Transformation and Resistance*, Princeton: Princeton University Press.

Modino, L. M. (2018), "Bolsonaro, Sobre os Bispos Brasileiros: 'Eles são a Parte Podre da Igreja Católica'," *Instituto Humanitas Unisinos*, October 17. Available online: http://www.ihu.unisinos.br/78-noticias/583781-bolsonaro-sobre-os-bispos-brasileiros-eles-sao-a-parte-podre-da-igreja-catolica (accessed August 26, 2020).

Mori, L. (2019), "Punir universidade por conhecimento que não convém ao governo é inconstitucional, diz diretor do Direito da USP," *BBC*, May 2. https://www.bbc.com/portuguese/brasil-48130548 (accessed June 12, 2019).

Myscofski, C. (1998), *When Man Walk Dry: Portuguese Messianism in Brazil*, Atlanta: Scholars Press.

Navarro, E. de Almeida. (1997), "Vida e obra de José de Anchieta," in E. de Almeida Navarro (organizer), *Anchieta, Vida e Pensamentos*, São Paulo: Ed. Martin Claret. Available online: http://tupi.fflch.usp.br/sites/tupi.fflch.usp.br/files/Vida%20e%20obra%20de%20Jos%C3%A9%20de%20Anchieta.pdf (accessed March 2, 2017).

Navarro, E. de Almeida. (2006), "Anchieta, um humanista e um gramático na Babel do Renascimento," *Revista Philologus* 35: 7–19. Available online: http://www.filologia.org.br/rph/ANO12/35/001.pdf (accessed March 2, 2017).

Nielssen, H., Okkenhaug, I. M., and Hestad-Skeie, K., eds. (2011), *Protestant Missions and Local Encounters in the Nineteenth and Twentieth Centuries: Unto the Ends of the World*, Leiden: Brill.

Nogueira-Godsey, E. (2013), "A History of Resistance: Ivone Gebara's Transformative Liberation Theology," *Journal for the Study of Religion* 26 (2): 89–106.

O'Brien, J. M. (2010), *Firsting and Lasting: Writing Indians out of Existence in New England*, Minneapolis: University of Minnesota Press.

O'Connell, G. (2020), "What's in Pope Francis' Apostolic Exhortation on the Amazon Synod," America, February 12. Available online: https://www.americamagazine.org/faith/2020/02/12/whats-pope-francis-apostolic-exhortation-amazon-synod (accessed September 6, 2020).

O'Neill, K. L. (2015), *Secure the Soul: Christian Piety and Gang Prevention in Guatemala*, Berkeley: University of California Press.

Okedara, J. T. and Ademola Ajayi, S. (2004), *Thomas Jefferson Bowen: Pioneer Baptist Missionary to Nigeria, 1850–1856*, Ibadan: John Archers.

Oosterbaan, M., van de Kamp, L., and Bahia, J., eds. (2019), *Global Trajectories of Brazilian Religion*, London: Bloomsbury.

Orsi, R. (2005), *Between Heaven and Earth: The Religious Worlds People Make and the Scholars Who Study Them*, Princeton: Princeton University Press.

Orsi, R. (2016), *History and Presence*, Cambridge: The Belknap Press of Harvard University Press.

Osborn, C. (2019), "The Christian Coalition that Elected that Helped Elected Bolsonaro Has Started to Crumble," *Foreign Policy*, April 6. Available online: https://foreignpolicy.com/2019/04/06/the-christian-coalition-that-helped-elect-bolsonaro-has-started-to-crumble/ (accessed April 26, 2019).

Otten, A. (1990), *Só Deus é grande: a mensagem religiosa de Antônio Conselheiro*, São Paulo: Loyola.

Pessar, P. (2004), *From Fanatics to Folk: Brazilian Millenarianism and Popular Culture*, Durham: Duke University Press.

228   Bibliography

Peterson, A. L. (1997), *Martyrdom and the Politics of Religion: Progressive Catholicism in El Salvador's Civil War*, Albany: SUNY Press.

Peterson, A. L. and Vásquez, M. A. (2008), *Latin American Religions: Histories and Documents in Context*, New York: New York University Press.

Pew Research Center (2013), "Brazil's Changing Religious Landscape." http://www.pewf orum.org/2013/07/18/brazils-changing-religious-landscape/#fn-14966-5 (accessed April 23, 2017).

Phan, P. (2012), "World Christianity: Its Implications for History, Religious Studies, and Theology," *Horizons* 39 (2): 171–88.

Phillips, R. (2006), "Rethinking the International Expansion of Mormonism," *Nova Religio: The Journal of Alternative and Emergent Religions* 10 (1): 52–68.

Pierucci, A. F. (2004), "Bye, bye, Brasil—o declínio das religiões tradicionais no censo 2000," *Estudos Avançados* 18 (52). https://goo.gl/uKiAI2 (accessed April 16, 2017).

Pierucci, A. F. (2006), "Cadê a nossa diversidade religiosa?" in F. Texeira and R. Menezes (eds.), *As Religiões no Brasil: Continuidades e Rupturas*, Petrópolis: Vozes.

Pierucci, A. F. and Prandi, R. (1996), *A realidade social das religiões no Brasil*, São Paulo: Hucitec.

Pietz, W. (1987), "The Problem of the Fetish, II: The Origin of the Fetish," *Anthropology and Aesthetics* 13: 23–45.

Pinheiro, A. 2004. *A dádiva no ritual da procissão do fogaréu na cidade de Goiás*, M.A. Thesis (Religious Studies). Goiás: Universidade Católica de Goiás. https://goo.gl/BjkG1q (accessed 16 April 2017).

Pinto, P. H. G. R. (2009), "Arabs with Christ," *Revista de História*. http://www.revistade historia.com.br/secao/capa/arabes-com-cristo (accessed December 17, 2016).

Pires, B. (2020), "Igrejas Desafiam Recomendação de Suspender Missas e Cultos Diante da Pandemia do Coronavírus," *El País*, March 19. Available online: https://brasil.elpais.com/brasil/2020-03-20/igrejas-desafiam-recomendacao-de-suspende r-missas-e-cultos-diante-da-pandemia-do-coronavirus.html (accessed August 25, 2020).

Pires, M. (2014), "Templo of Solomon—Special Documentary of Inauguration," August 15. Available online: https://www.youtube.com/watch?v=4arL8q-tsCM (accessed August 23, 2020).

Pissolato, E. (2013), "'Tradições indígenas' nos censos brasileiros—Questões em torno do reconhecimento indígena e da relação entre indígenas e religião," in F. Teixeira and R. Menezes (eds), *Religiões em movimento: o censo de 2010*, 235–52, Petrópolis: Vozes.

Pitta, M. and Fernandes, S. (2006), "Mapeando as rotas do trânsito religioso no Brasil," *Religião & Sociedade* 26: 120–34.

Poletto, I. (2015), "Churches, the Pastoral Land Commission, and the Mobilization for Agrarian Reform," in M. Carter (ed.), *Challenging Social Inequality: The Landless Rural Worker's Movement and Agrarian Reform in Brazil*, 90–112, Durham: Duke University Press,

Bibliography

Portela, G. (2014), "Quantos São os Usuários do Crack no Brasil," *Fundação Oswaldo Cruz*, February 9. Available online: https://www.icict.fiocruz.br/node/1336 (accessed August 23, 2020).

Postma, J. (2003), *The Atlantic Slave Trade*, Westport: Greenwood Press.

Prado, F. (2015), *Edge of the Empire: Atlantic Networks and Revolution in Bourbon Río Plata*, Berkeley: University of California Press.

Prandi, R. and Valentin, F. F. (1998), "A renovação carismática e a política," in R. Prandi (ed.), *Um Sopro do Espírito: A renovação conservadora do catolicismo carísmatico*, 171–8, São Paulo: Edusp & Fapesp.

Premack, L. (2016), "'The Coca-Cola of Churches Arrives': Nigeria's Redeemed Christian Church of God in Brazil," in A. Edogame (ed.), *The Public Face of African New Religious Movements in Diaspora: Imagining the Religious Other*, 215–32, New York: Routledge.

Prezzi, L. (2017), "Novas Comunidades, Números e Desafios," Instituto Humanitas Unisinos, April 5. Available online: http://www.ihu.unisinos.br/566507-novas-comunidades-numeros-e-desafios (accessed August 23, 2020)

Provai e Vede. (2014), "Documentário da História dos 150 Anos da Igreja Presbiteriana no Brasil," January 29. https://www.youtube.com/watch?v=bjmbdP9_z3o (accessed August 23, 2020).

Queiroz, M. I. P. de (1965), *O messianismo no Brasil e no mundo*, São Paulo: Edusp.

Radding, C. (2005), *Landscapes of Power and Identity: Comparative Histories in the Sonoran Desert and the Forests of Amazonia from Colony to Republic*, Durham: Duke University Press.

Ramos, R. (2020), "Pastores, Preguem! As Pessoas Precisam, Pede o Mandetta," *Pleno.News*, March 27. Available online: https://pleno.news/fe/pastores-preguem-as-pessoas-precisam-pede-mandetta.html (accessed August 25, 2020).

Rangel, L. H. V. (2008), *Festas juninas, festas de São João: origens, tradição e história*, São Paulo: Publishing Solutions.

Rapoza, K. (2016), "A Look at Brazil's Poverty Rate After 14 Years of Workers' Party Rule," *Forbes*, September 12. Available online: https://www.forbes.com/sites/kenrapoza/2016/09/12/a-look-at-brazils-poverty-rate-after-14-years-of-workers-party-rule/#e514edd7703e (accessed April 27, 2019).

Reily, D. A. (1980), "Os metodistas do Brasil (1889–1930)," *Estudos Teológicos* 20 (2): 100–22.

Renovação Carismática Católica - Brasil. (2012), *Cartilha de conscientização do Ministério Fé e Política*, Pelotas, Rio Grande do Sul: CCR Brasil.

Rial, C. (2013), "'The Devil's Egg': Football Players as Missionaries of the Diaspora of Brazilian Religion," in C. Rocha and M. A. Vásquez (eds.), *The Diaspora of Brazilian Religions*, 91–115, Leiden: Brill.

Ribeiro de Oliveira, P. (1979), "Romanization of Catholicism and Agrarian Capitalism in Brazil," *Social Compass* 26 (2–3): 309–29.

Ribeiro de Oliveira, P. (1985), *Religião e dominação de classe: Gênese, estrutura e função do catolicismo romanizado brasileiro*, Rio de Janeiro: Vozes.

Richard, P. (1987), *Death of Christendom, Birth of the Church*, Maryknoll: Orbis Books.

Rivera, D. P. B. (2013), "Brazilian Pentecostalism in Peru: Affinities Between the Social and Cultural Conditions of Andean Migrants and the Religious Worldview of the Pentecostal Church 'God is Love,'" in C. Rocha and M. A. Vásquez (eds.), *The Diaspora of Brazilian Religions*, 117–36, Leiden: Brill.

Roark, D. (2016), "How the Hillsong Cool Factor Changed Worship for Good and for Ill," *Christ and Popular Culture*. https://christandpopculture.com/how-the-hillsong-cool-factor-changed-worship-for-good-and-for-ill/ (accessed June 13, 2019).

Robertson, R. (1992), *Globalization: Social Theory and Global Culture*, London: Sage.

Robertson, R. (1995), "Glocalization: Time-Space and Homogeneity-Heterogeneity," in M. Featherstone, S. Lash, and R. Robertson (eds.), *Global Modernities*, 25–44, London: Sage Publications.

Rocha, C. (2013), "Transnational Pentecostal Connections: An Australian Megachurch and a Brazilian Church in Australia," *PentecoStudies* 12 (1): 62–82.

Rocha, C. (2017a), "'God is in Control:' Middle-Class Pentecostalism and International Student Migration," *Journal of Contemporary Religion* 34 (1): 21–37.

Rocha, C. (2017b), *John of God: The Globalization of Brazilian Faith Healing*, New York: Oxford University Press.

Rocha, C. (Forthcoming), "Cool Christianity: The Fashion-Celebrity-Megachurch Industrial Complex," *Material Religion*.

Rocha, C. and Vásquez, M. A., eds. (2013), *The Diaspora of Brazilian Religions*, Leiden: Brill.

Rohter, L. (2007), "Brazilian Pentecostal Leaders Caught in a Scandal," *The New York Times*, March 19. http://www.nytimes.com/2007/03/19/world/americas/19iht-brazil.4958717.html

Rohter, L. (2014), "Exposing the Legacy of Operation Condor," *The New York Times*, January 24. Available online: https://lens.blogs.nytimes.com/2014/01/24/exposing-the-legacy-of-operation-condor/ (accessed April 27, 2019).

Rolim, F. C. (1985), *Pentecostalism no Brasil: Uma interpretação socio-religiosa*, Rio de Janeiro: Vozes.

Roller, H. (2014), *Amazonian Routes: Indigenous Mobility and Colonial Communities in Northern Brazil*, Stanford: Stanford University Press.

Romancini, R. (2018), "Do 'kit gay' ao 'monitor da doutrinação': A reação conservadora no Brasil," *Contracampo* 37 (2): 1–23.

Romero, S. (2013), "Missteps by Brazil Mar the Visit by Pope," *The New York Times*, July 24. Available online: http://www.nytimes.com/2013/07/25/world/americas/popes-visit-to-brazil-is-marred-by-missteps.html (accessed January 1, 2018).

Romero, S. (2014), "Temple in Brazil Appeals to a Surge of Evangelicals," *The New York Times*, July 24. Available online: https://www.nytimes.com/2014/07/25/world/americas/temple-in-brazil-appeals-to-a-surge-in-evangelicals.html?_r=0 (accessed March 10, 2017).

Roudometof, V. (2016), *Theorizing Glocalization: A Critical Introduction*, London: Routledge.

Sanneh, L. (2005), *The Changing Face of Christianity: Africa, the West, and the World*, New York: Oxford University Press.

Sanneh, L. and McClymond, M. J., eds. (2016), *The Wiley Blackwell Companion to World Christianity*, Hoboken: John Wiley & Sons.

Sansi-Roca, R. (2007), "The Fetish in the Lusophone Atlantic," in N. P. Naro, R. Sansi-Roca, and D. Treece (eds.), *Cultures of the Lusophone Black Atlantic*, 19–40, New York: Palgrave MacMillan.

Santiago-Vendrell, A. (2010), *Contextual Theology and Revolutionary Transformation in Latin America: The Missiology of Richard Shaull*, Eugene: Pickwick Publications.

Santos, M. (2020), "Pastores Criticam Jejum Convocado por Bolsonaro Contra a Covid-19," *Rede Brasil Atual*, April 4. https://www.redebrasilatual.com.br/politica/2020/0 4/pastores-criticam-jejum-convocado-por-bolsonaro-contra-a-covid-19/ (accessed August 25, 2020)

Scheper Hughes, J. (2012), "Mysterium Materiae: Vital Matter and the Object as Evidence in the Study of Religion," *Bulletin for the Study of Religion* 41 (4): 16–24.

Schreiber, M. (2019), "Como o apoio evangélico ajudou a aproximar Israel e governo Bolsonaro," *BBC*, January 9. https://www.bbc.com/portuguese/brasil-46790185 (accessed April 26, 2019).

Selka, S. (2007), *Religion and the Politics of Ethnic Identity in Bahia, Brazil*, Gainesville: University Press of Florida.

Serbin, K. (2006), *Needs of the Heart: A Social and Cultural History of Brazil's Clergy and Seminaries*, Notre Dame: University of Notre Dame Press.

Shalders, A. (2019), "Por que a 'Agenda de Costumes' de Bolsonaro Deve Continuar Parada no Congresso em 2020," *BBC News*, December 26. Available online: https://www.bbc.com/portuguese/brasil-50898836 (accessed September 5, 2020).

Shaull, M. R. (1963), "Ashbel Green Simonton (1833–1867): A Calvinist in Brazil," in H. T. Kerr (ed.), *Sons of the Prophet: Leaders of Protestantism from Princeton Theological Seminary*, 100–22, Princeton: Princeton University Press.

Shaull, M. R. (1966), "The Revolutionary Challenge to Church and Theology," *The Princeton Seminary Bulletin* 60 (1): 25–32. http://scdc.library.ptsem.edu/mets/mets.aspx?src=PSB1966601&div=7 (accessed June 23, 2017).

Shor, I. and Freire, P. (1987), "What is the Dialogical Method?" *Journal of Education* 169 (3): 11–31.

Silva, G. (2006), *Encontros de mundos: o imaginário colonial brasileiro refletido nos sermões do padre Antonio Vieira*, Canoas: Ulbra.

Silva, L. D. (2005), *Holandeses em Pernambuco (1630–1654)*, Recife: Instituto Ricardo Brennand.

Silva, R. Lima da (2008), *Os Mórmons em Santa Catarina: Origens, conflito e desenvolvimento*, Master's Thesis in Religious Studies, São Paulo: MacKenzie Presbyterian University.

Silva, R. S. (2001), *Antônio Conselheiro: a fronteira entre a civilização e a barbárie*, São Paulo: Annablume.

Sims, S. (2018), "Far-Right Populist and the Women who Like Him," *The Atlantic*, October 4. Available online: https://www.theatlantic.com/international/archive/2018/10/brazil-bolsonaro-election-far-right-lula-election/572203/ (accessed April 28, 2019).

Slater, C. (1986), *Trail of Miracles: Stories from a Pilgrimage in Northeast Brazil*, Berkeley: University of California Press.

Soloway, B. (2014), "Brazilian Bishop Urges Ordination of Married Community Elders as Priest Shortage Grows," *The National Catholic Reporter*, November 24. https://www.ncronline.org/news/world/brazilian-bishop-urges-ordination-married-community-elders-priest-shortage-grows (accessed April 30, 2021).

Souza, A. et al. (2020), "Mandetta Contraria Bolsonaro e Pede Manutenção de Restrições Impostas pelos Estados," *O Globo*, March 30. Available online: https://oglobo.globo.com/brasil/mandetta-contraria-bolsonaro-pede-manutencao-de-restricoes-impostas-pelos-estados-24339323 (accessed August 25, 2020).

Souza, L. A. Gómez de (1984), *A JUC: Os estudantes católicos e a política*, Petrópolis: Vozes.

Souza, L. A. Gómez de (2000), "As CEBs vão bem, obrigado," *Revista Eclesiástica Brasileira* 60 (237): 93–110.

Souza, L. A. Gómez de (2002), "The Origins of Medellín: From Catholic Action to the Base Church Communities and Social Pastoral Strategy (1950–68)," in J. O. Beozzo and L. C. Susin (eds.), *Brazil: People and Church(es)*, 31–7, London: SCM Press.

Steil, C. A. and Toniol, R. (2013), "O Catolicismo e a igreja católica no Brasil à luz dos dados sobre a religião no censo de 2010," *Debate do NER* 14 (24): 223–43.

Stoll, D. (1990), *Is Latin America Turning Protestant? The Politics of Evangelical Growth*, Berkeley: University of California Press.

Swyngedouw, E. (2004), "Globalisation or 'Glocalisation'? Networks, Territories and Rescaling," *Cambridge Review of International Affairs* 17 (1): 25–48.

Teixeira, F. (2013), "O Censo de 2010 e as religiões no Brasil: esboço de apresentação," in F. Teixeira and R. Menezes (eds.), *Religiões em movimento—o censo de 2010*, 17–35, Petrópolis: Vozes.

Tornielle, A. (2017), "'Arautos do Evangelho,' O Fundador Renuncia Enquanto o Vaticano Investiga," *Instituto Humanitas Unisinos*, June 13. Available online: http://www.ihu.unisinos.br/568623-arautos-do-evangelho-o-fundador-renuncia-enquanto-o-vaticano-investiga (accessed August 26, 2020).

Tran, J. Y. and Tran, A. Q., eds. (2016), *World Christianity: Perspectives and Insights*, Maryknoll: Orbis Books.

Tremura, W. (2004), *With an Open Heart: Folia de Reis, A Brazilian Spiritual Journey Through Song*, PhD Thesis. Tallahassee, FL: The Florida State University.

Tsuriel-Harari, K. (2014), "Brazilian Evangelical has a Grandiose, Jewish Path to Salvation," *CALCALIST*. Available online: https://worldcrunch.com/culture-soc iety/brazilian-evangelical-has-a-grandiose-jewish-path-for-salvation/sao-paulo-j erusalem-king-solomon-solomon-039-s-temple-dilma-rousseff/c3s17067 (accessed February 20, 2021).

Tunes, G. (2019), "Bolsonaro participa do ato de consagração do Brasil ao Coraçao de Maria," *Correio Braziliense*, May 21. https://www.correiobraziliense.com.br/app/not icia/politica/2019/05/21/interna_politica,756186/bolsonaro-consagra-o-brasil-ao-i maculado-coracao-de-maria.shtml (accessed June 16, 2019).

Tunes, S. M. (2009), *O pregador silencioso: Ecumenismo no jornal Expositor Cristão (1886–1982)*, Master's Thesis in Religious Studies, São Bernardo do Campo, SP: Universidade Metodista de São Paulo.

Turner, S. (2013), "Take the Church to the Streets, Pope Tells Young Faithful," July 25. https://www.christiantoday.com/article/take-the-church-to-the-streets-pope-tells -young-faithful/33387.htm (accessed August 22, 2020).

Tweed, T. (2006), *Crossing and Dwelling: A Theory of Religion*, Cambridge, MA: Harvard University Press.

Tylor, E. B. (2010 [1871]), *Primitive Culturem*, Cambridge: Cambridge University Press.

United Nations Population Fund. (2014), *Annual Report: A Year of Renewal*, New York: United Nations.

Uribe, G. and Carvalho, D. (2020), "Brasileiro Mergulha no Esgoto e não Acontece Nada, Diz Bolsonaro ao Minimizar Coronavírus," *Folha de São Paulo*, March 23. Available online: https://www1.folha.uol.com.br/poder/2020/03/brasileiro-mergulha -no-esgoto-e-nao-acontece-nada-diz-bolsonaro-ao-minimizar-coronavirus.shtml (accessed August 25, 2020).

Vainfas, R. (2010), *Jerusalém Colonial: judeus portugueses no Brasil holandês*, Rio de Janeiro: Civilização Brasileira.

Vainfas, R. (n.d.), "Rituais indígenas que não se apagam: a catequização frustrada," *Diversitas*—Universidade de São Paulo. http://diversitas.fflch.usp.br/rituais-indige nas-que-nao-se-apagam-catequizacao-frustrada (accessed February 21, 2021).

Valle, R. and Pitta, M. (1994), *Comunidades eclesiais católicas*, Petrópolis: Vozes.

Van de Kamp, L. (2011), "South-South Transnational Spaces of Conquest: Afro-Brazilian Pentecostalism, *Feitiçaria* and the Reproductive Domain in Urban Mozambique," Presentation at the 13th General Assembly, CODESRIA. Rabat, Morocco, December 5–9.

Van de Kamp, L. (2015), "Transatlantic Pentecostal Demons in Maputo," in W. C. Olsen, & W. E. A. van Beek (eds.), *Evil in Africa: Encounters with the Everyday*, 344–363, Bloomington: Indiana University Press.

Van de Kamp, L. (2016), *Violent Conversion: Brazilian Pentecostalism and Urban Women in Mozambique*, Suffolk: Boydell and Bower.

Van de Kamp, L. (2017), "The Transnational Structures of Luso-Pentecostal Mega-Cities," *New Diversities* 19 (1): 1–17.

Van Wyk, I. (2014), *The Universal Church of the Kingdom of God in South Africa: A Church of Strangers*, Cambridge: Cambridge University Press.

Varga, I. (2012), "Detraditionalization and Retraditionalization," in M. Juergensmeyer and W. C. Roof (eds.), *Encyclopedia of Global Religion*, 295–8, Los Angeles: SAGE.

Vargas Llosa, M. (1981), *La guerra del fin del mundo*, Barcelona: Seix Barral.

Vásquez, M. and Knott, K. (2014), "Three Dimensions of Religious Place Making in Diaspora," *Global Networks* 14 (3): 326–47.

Vásquez, M. A. (1998), *The Brazilian Popular Church and the Crisis of Modernity*, Cambridge: Cambridge University Press.

Vásquez, M. A. (2017), "Toward a Transnational, Postcolonial Phenomenology of the Spirit: Pneumatic Religions and Cosmopolitics in the Americas," *Emisférica*. https://hemisphericinstitute.net/es/emisferica/emisferica-122/4520-toward-a-transnational-post-colonial-phenomenology-of-the-spirit-pneumatic-religions-and-cosmopoli tics-in-the-americas-es.html (accessed May 27, 2017).

Vásquez, M. A. and Alves, J. C. S. (2013), "The Valley of Dawn in Atlanta, Georgia: Negotiating Incorporation and Gender Identity in Diaspora," in C. Rocha and M. A. Vásquez (eds.), *The Diaspora of Brazilian Religions*, 313–37, Leiden: Brill.

Vásquez, M. A. and Marquardt, M. F. (2003), *Globalizing the Sacred: Religion across the Americas*, New Brunswick: Rutgers University Press.

Ventura, R. (1997), "Canudos como cidade iletrada: Euclides da Cunha na *urbs* monstruosa," *Revista de Antropologia* 40 (1): 165–82.

Verger, P. F. (2018), *Orixás: Deus Iorubas na África e no Novo Mundo*, Salvador, Bahia: Fundação Pierre Verger.

Vieira, A. (1966), "Sermon Condemning Indian Slavery," in E. Bradford Burns (ed.), *A Documentary History of Brazil*, New York: Knopf.

Vilaça, A. and Wright, R. M., eds. (2016), *Native Christians: Modes and Effects of Christianity among Indigenous Peoples in the Americas*, London: Routledge.

Vingren, I. (1985), *O diário do pioneiro: Gunnar Vingren*, Rio de Janeiro: Casa Publicadora das Assembléias de Deus (CPAD).

Vingren, I. (2008), "The Pioneer's Diary," in A. L. Peterson and M. A. Vásquez (eds.), *Latin American Religions: Histories and Documents in Context*, 170–6, New York: New York University Press.

Viveiros de Castro, E. (1992), *From the Enemy's Point of View: Humanity and Divinity in an Amazonian Society*, Chicago: University of Chicago Press.

Watts, J. (2013), "'Pope Francis' Final Mass in Brazil 'Attended by 3m'," *The Guardian*, July 28. Available online: https://www.theguardian.com/world/2013/jul/28/pope -frances-rio-brazil-millions (accessed August 22, 2020).

Weber, M. (1963), *The Sociology of Religion*, Boston: Beacon Press.

Wilde, G. (2015a), "The Political Dimension of Space-Time Categories in the Jesuit Missions of Paraguay (Seventeenth and Eighteenth Centuries)," in G. Marcocci et al. (eds.), *Space and Conversion in Global Perspective*, 175–213, Leiden: Brill.

Wilde, G. (2015b), "Imagining Guaranis and Jesuits—Yesterday's History, Today's Perspective," *ReVista: Harvard Review of Latin America*. https://archive.revista.drclas.harvard.edu/book/imagining-guaranis-and-jesuits (accessed February 20, 2021).

Wilkinson, D. (2017), "Is There Such a Thing as Animism?" *Journal of the American Academy of Religion* 85 (2): 289–311.

Willeke, V. (1974), *Missões Africanas no Brasil*, Petrópolis: Vozes.

Willems, E. (1967), *The Followers of the New Faith. Cultural Change and the Rise of Protestantism in Brazil and Chile*, Nashville: Vanderbilt University Press.

Williams, R. (1977), *Marxism and Literature*, Oxford: Oxford University Press.

Wimmer, A. and Glick Schiller, N. (2003), "Methodological Nationalism, the Social Sciences, and the Study of Migration: An Essay in Historical Epistemology," *International Migration Review* 37 (3): 576–610.

Winant, H. (2001), *The World Is a Ghetto: Race and Democracy since World War II*, New York: Basic Books.

Winter, B. (2018), "Jair Bolsonaro's Guru," *Americas Quarterly*, December 17. Available online: https://www.americasquarterly.org/content/jair-bolsonaros-guru (accessed on April 26, 2019).

Wright, R. M. (2017), "The State of the Arts in the Study of Indigenous Religious Traditions in South America," *International Journal of Latin American Religions* 1: 42–56. https://link.springer.com/content/pdf/10.1007%2Fs41603-017-0002-9.pdf (accessed June 24, 2017).

Xavier, A. B. and Županov, I. (2015), *Catholic Orientalism: Portuguese Empire, Indian Knowledge*, New Delhi: Oxford University Press.

Zanotto, G. (2010), "Tradição, família e propiedade (TFP): Um movimento católico no Brasil (1960–1995)," *Locus: Revista de História* 30 (1): 87–101.

Zawiejska, N., ed. (2018), *Pentecostalism in the Lusophone World*, special issue of *PentecoStudies* 17(1).

Županov, I. G. (1999), *Disputed Mission: Jesuit Experiments and Brahmanical Knowledge in Seventeenth-Century India*, New Delhi: Oxford University Press.

Index

abertura   158

abortion   37, 98–9, 137–8, 149, 150, 166, 167, 174, 203 n.8, 210 n.18

Acre   101–2, 193 n.35, 198 n.1, 199 n.11, 202 n.1

Africa   3, 13, 16–18, 22, 42, 51, 111, 138, 147, 148, 150, 186, 189 n.5, 198 n.2, 204 n.17, 211 nn.22–3

African-based religions   3, 5, 17, 18, 38, 40, 41, 45, 52, 58, 105, 108–9, 111, 118, 129, 139–41, 148, 173, 185, 193 n.35, 199 n.9, 200 n.12, 201 n.14, *see also* Candomblé; Umbanda

African Pentecostals in Brazil   211 n.23

Afro-Brazilians   16, 18, 51, 108–9, 111, 120, 126, 133, 147–8, 152, 154, 166, 178, 190 n.6, 199 n.9, 201 n.14

aggiornamento (updating)   33, 77, 135, 156, *see also* Second Vatican Council

aldeias   19

Alternative Christianity   37, 50–1, 129, 140

Alves, José Claudio Souza   204 n.15

Amaral, Rita   105

Amazons   179, 186–7, 193 n.35, 199 n.10

Anchieta, José de   19, 58, 60–3

Anderson, Benedict   20, 124

Anglicans and Episcopalians   122, 124, 126

animism   40–2, 174, 194 n.4

anti-clericalism   26–7, 75

Aparecida, São Paulo   174, 175

apocalypticism   43, 105

Araújo, Ernesto   155, 187, 206 n.28

Arcoverde, Joaquim   75

Arns, Paulo Evaristo   34, 91, 92, 158

Assemblies of God (AG)   36, 52, 53, 82, 83, 126–7, 130–1, 149, 150, 170, 175, 203 n.4, 203 n.6

Ave de Jesus   73, 180

ayahuasca religions   109–10, 193 n.35, 199 nn.10–12

Azusa   81, 82, 126, 130

Azzi, Riolando   23, 191 n.15, 192 n.23

Bahia   14–16, 18, 22, 23, 28, 42, 44, 45, 63, 64, 69, 102, 108, 117, 121, 143, 183, 199 n.9

Baixada Fluminense   168

bancada evangélica (Evangelical caucus)   87, 149, 151, 162, 203 nn.6–8

bandeirantes   25

Baptists   37, 81, 82, 120, 122, 142, 149, 150, 205 n.21

base ecclesial community (Comunidade eclesial de base, CEB)   8, 33–5, 48, 54, 90, 93, 95, 135–6, 149, 154, 156, 158–60, 162, 202 n.22, 203 n.3

Bastide, Roger   195 n.13

Bauman, Zygmunt   5, 154

beatos (as)   24–5, 28, 29, 43, 73, 191 n.17

Beck, Ulrich   180, 210 n.13

Belém   82, 84, 101, 108, 126, 203 n.4

Benedict XVI   37, 90–1, 93, 157, 164, 165, 174–5, 182

Berg, Daniel   36, 81–5, 102, 108, 116, 126

Boff, Clodovis   47, 91, 92, 97, 156–7

Boff, Leonardo   35, 49, 91–6, 98, 136, 156–7, 163, 187, 198 n.27, 207 n.33

Bolsonaro, Jair   8–9, 12, 44, 136–8, 142, 150–5, 165–72, 176–8, 183, 187, 189 n.6, 204 n.12, 204 n.16, 205 nn.18–21, 206 n.24, 206 nn.26–7, 207 n.29

Bourdieu, Pierre   193 n.1, 195 n.14

Brandão, Carlos Rodrigues   195 n.9, 199 n.5

Brasília   101, 104, 166, 193 n.35

brasilidade (Brazilianness)   105–6

Brasil Para Cristo (Brazil for Christ)   130, 131, 203 n.6

Brazil

history 13–38
politics 141–3, 146–72
regions 101–5, 152–3, 180–1, 202 n.21
religious field 6, 9, 32, 37, 40, 56, 109, 111, 117–19, 128, 139, 140, 176, 178, 182, 185, 193 n.35, 202 n.23
society 141–6, 152
Brazilian Apostolic Catholic Church 73, 127
Brazilian Christianity 14–23, 170, 172, 173, 178
characteristics 18
and income distribution/ inequalities 203 n.2
and its global influence 185–7, 211 nn.21–4
origins 14–23
south-south flows 186, 201 n.18, 211 nn.22–4
Brazilian Society for the Defense of Tradition, Family, and Property (TFP) 183, 210 n.18
brotherhoods 17, 24, 29, 44–5, 108, 110–11, 116, 143
Bruneau, Thomas 76
Burdick, John 147–8, 158, 160, 181, 193 n.33, 201 n.14
Bynum, Carolyn Walker 194 n.6

Calvinists 61, 63, 65–7, 78, 121, 124–5
Câmara, Hélder 31, 36, 91, 97
caminhada 48, 162, 173
Campos, Roberta 73, 180–1
Camurça, Marcelo 5, 46, 117, 139, 184
Canção Nova (New Song) 5, 24, 38, 54, 138, 185
Candomblé 3–5, 17, 40, 45, 103, 108, 117, 148, 186, 198 n.2, 199 n.9, 201 n.14, 203 n.3
Canudos 12, 28, 68–71, 125, 143, 173, 183, 191 n.21, 197 n.10
capitalism 5, 27, 32–3, 53, 55, 67, 68, 95–6, 139, 143–6, 150, 157, 161, 163–5, 183, 184, 192 n.28, 204 n.17
capitanias (captancies) 16
Capuchins 23, 73, 77
Cardijn, Joseph 31
Cardoso, Fernando Henrique 192 n.28

Carnival 109, 203 n.8, *see also* festivals and feasts
Carranza, Brenda 5, 54–5, 138, 161, 193 n.36
Carter, Miguel 160
Carvalho, Olavo de 206 n.25
casa grande 16–18, 27, 43, 102, 190 n.6, *see also senzala*
Casaldáliga, Pedro 34, 91
Catholic Action 31, 33, 47–8, 55, 75, 77, 192 n.25
Catholicism 1–2, 75–6, 136, 147–8, 169, 170, 192 n.24
Charismatic 5, 37–8, 51–6, 88, 90, 110, 136–8, 140, 149, 161, 162, 165–6, 167, 171, 176, 180, 182, 185, 203 n.3, 207 n.32, 210 n.16
conservative 135–8, 153–4, 166–7, 183, 208 nn.37–8, 210 n.18
customized 139–40, 181
decline 112–14, 116–17, 128, 144, 178–9, 209 n.9
global 30, 163, 186–7
Iberian 11–14, 111, 173, 194 n.6, 208 n.37
mineiro 110–11
numbers in Brazil 1–2, 102, 112–18, 128, 176, 200 n.12
penitential aspects 43, 68, 73, 105–7, 109
progressive 8, 21, 23, 34–6, 46–9, 70, 75, 91–2, 96, 135–6, 137–8, 147, 148–9, 158, 160, 163, 164, 167, 175–8, 182, 187
resilience 73, 112, 116, 144, 180–2
rural 180–1
traditional (Luso-Brazilian) popular 23, 24, 29, 37, 39–45, 52, 68, 71, 73, 74, 83, 105, 106, 116, 138, 171, 179–83, 185, 187, 194 n.2, 199 n.5, 201 n.14
Catholic Parliamentary Front 166
celibacy 73, 127, 136, 187
census 85, 127
Chesnut, Andrew 48, 146–8, 203 n.4
Christian Congregation of Brazil (Congregação Cristã do Brasil) 36, 126, 131
Church: Charism and Power 93, 136, *see also* Boff, Leonardo

238   *Index*

church-state relations and conflicts 14, 20, 25–8, 75, 141, 142, 155, 156, 170–1, 209 n.49

Cícero Romão Batista (Padre Cícero) 28, 29, 40, 71–4, 85, 102, 107, 180, 183, 194 n.3, 197 n.15

civil society 8, 34, 76, 124, 142, 154, 158–60, 177, 183, 192 n.25, 206 n.27

class 29, 31–3, 44, 47, 48, 55, 76, 85, 86, 98–9, 133, 138, 147, 157, 161, 168, 176, 186, 201 n.18

Clossey, Luke 190 n.8

colonialism 12, 15, 18, 21, 23, 27, 30, 38, 41, 43, 63–4, 102, 119, 121, 141, 143, 191 n.18, 194 n.4

Comaroff, Jean and John 204 n.17

Comblin, José 91, 96, 97

concordat 30, 33, 77, 155, 192 n.25

conscientização (consciousness-raising) 32, 162, 163

Conselheiro, Antônio 25, 42–3, 67–73, 85, 196 n.9, 204 n.12

conservatism 149–54, 161–2, 166–8, 203 n.8, 204 n.12

Constitution of 1891 142

Constitution of 1934 30

Contestado 143, 191 n.21

conversos 64

"Cool Christianity" 132, 139

coronelismo 68, 73, 141–3, 197 n.10

corruption 12, 28, 48, 69, 88, 150–2, 165, 166, 171, 175, 176

Council of Trent (1545–1563) 13, 28, 29, 40, 43, 142, 194 n.3

COVID-19 167–72, 177, 199 n.6, 208 n.44

crente (believer, Evangelical Protestant) 128, 146, 147, 153

crime 12, 32, 103, 152, 154, 166–7, 171, 177, 204 n.15, 210 n.13

Cristo Redentor 30–1, 77, 87, 155

Crivella, Marcelo 203 nn.8–9

Cunha, Euclides da 197 n.11

cura divina (divine healing) 52, 53, 83, 136, 173, 180

Davila, Manuela 208 n.38

deacons 179–80, 187

Della Cava, Ralph 72, 158, 191 n.21, 192 n.24, 194 n.3

democracy and democratization 34, 35, 92, 124, 142, 145, 156, 160, 166

denominations 8, 120–6, 129, 140

dependency theory 33, 192 n.28

Descola, Philippe 40, 195 n.17

desobriga (unburdening) 24

De Theije, Marjo 54, 162, 195 n.11

detraditionalization 111–12, 116, 119, 154, 178–81, 183, 185, 199 n.15, *see also* re-traditionalization

Deus é Amor (God is Love Church) 130, 131, 186, 201 n.15, 203 n.6, 211 n.24

Diacon, Todd 191 n.21

dictatorship 30, 32, 34, 50, 92, 97, 151, 157–8, 177

diversity 9, 79, 104, 132, 135, 140, 144, 154–5, 184

   channeled (*acanhada*) 184

domination 6, 29, 57, 143, 156

dominion theology 150, 155–6

Dom Vital Center 31, 77

Drogus, Carol 159–60

Droogers, Andre 46

drugs and drug addiction 3, 133, 148, 152, 164, 166, 184, 202 n.21, 204 n.15, 210 n.13

Durkheim, Emile 40, 144

Dutch presence and influence on Brazilian Christianity 13–14, 63, 121–2, 200 n.2

ecumenism 50, 105, 125, 176, 185

Edinburgh (World Missionary Conference 1910) 123, 125

empadrinhamento (godparenthood) 142

engenhos (sugar cane plantations) 16

Entre Nós (Between Us) 204 n.10

Estado Novo 76–7, 143, *see also* Vargas, Getúlio

favelas 133, 165, 171, 202 n.20

feitiçaria (sorcery/witchcraft) 41–2, 82, 194 nn.5–6

Fernandes, Sílvia 55, 88, 89, 129, 132, 135, 137, 139, 180, 181, 184, 189 n.1, 195 n.33, 197 n.20, 198 n.32

festivals and feasts 43, 44, 105–7, 139

firsting 191 n.18

Index

Foucault, Michel 20, 57, 204 n.17
Francescon, Luigi 36, 126–7
Francis, Pope 1–2, 37, 62, 73, 96, 99,
  136, 163–4, 169, 170, 174–6, 182–3,
  187, 189 n.1, 196 n.31, 207 n.34,
  210 n.16
  Laudato Si 49, 96, 163–4
  Lumen Fidei 164
Franciscans 22–3, 44, 55, 92, 174,
  191 n.14, 191 n.16
Franciscan Theological Institute 92
Francis of Assisi 49, 55, 163, 164,
  189 n.1, 199 n.13, 210 n.19
Frei Damião 73
Freire, Paulo 31–2, 34, 47, 50, 136,
  206 n.25
French Antarctic 61, 109, 121, 196 n.4
Frente Parlamentar Evangélica
  (Evangelical Parliamentary
  Front-FPE) 149–50, 170
Freston, Paul 130, 149, 201 n.16, 203 n.7,
  210 n.15
Freyre, Gilberto 190 n.6
Friar Galvão 174
Frigerio, Alejandro 117–18
funk gospel 133, 202 n.19

Gebara, Ivone 92, 96–9, 163, 187
gender 98–9, 147, 148, 152, 154–5,
  192 n.22, 203 n.8, 204 n.12,
  206 n.28
globalization 5, 7, 9, 130, 143–5, 150,
  154–5, 160, 167, 173, 174, 178–9,
  183–5, 189 n.7
glocalization 7, 173, 186, 189 n.8
glossolalia 2, 42, 52, 82, 130, 173
Gracino, Paulo 2, 134, 144, 147
Great Commission 4, 150, 165
Guaranís 14, 21, 23, 26, 191 n.14
Gutiérrez, Gustavo 34, 50, 96, 97, 163,
  192 n.28

Haddad, Fernando 151, 166, 167,
  205 n.18, 205 n.21
Heralds of the Gospel 182–3
Hervieu-Léger, Danièle 199 n.15
Hillsong Church 132, 201 n.18
Hobsbawm, Eric 197 n.10
Holy Spirit 2, 37, 51–2, 83, 86, 89, 94,
  110, 128, 130, 136, 146, 147, 161,
  173, 183

Hoornaert, Eduardo 14, 16, 18, 22, 23,
  121, 190 n.7
Hourtart, François 198 n.30
Human Development Index (HDI) 104–
  5, 114, 118, 199 n.4
human rights 158, 207 n.29
hybridity 6, 11, 13, 29, 40, 105, 119,
  183–4, 190 n.6
Hypólito, Adriano 193 n.32

Iglesia y Sociedad en América Latina
  (Church and Society in Latin
  America) 50
Igreja Internacional da Graça de Deus
  (International Church of God's
  Grace) 132
Igreja Mundial do Poder de Deus
  (World Church of God's Power-
  IMPD) 52–3, 132, 156, 211 n.22
Igreja Renascer em Cristo (reborn in
  Christ Church) 132–3, 165,
  196 n.25
immigration and immigrants 27, 36, 77,
  81, 92, 101, 103, 117, 120, 122–4,
  126, 130, 133, 142, 154, 155, 178,
  184, 186, 193 n.35, 200 n.6
Imperial Constitution of 1824 122
inculturation 190 n.13
independence 26, 67, 69, 75, 102, 122,
  125, 142, 156
Indigenous Brazilians 14–15, 58, 59,
  61, 105, 109–10, 120, 136, 154,
  166, 171, 177, 183, 187, 189 n.6,
  190 n.13, 191 n.14, 191 n.18
Indigenous Missionary Council 35,
  136
Indigenous religions 15, 40–2, 109, 173,
  185, 195 n.17, 199 nn.11–12
Ingold, Tim 41
Ireland, Rowan 147–8, 153, 181,
  195 n.16

Jehovah's Witnesses 50, 129, 130, 140
Jesuits 19–22, 25–6, 37, 58–64, 77,
  109, 190 n.11, 191 n.14, 191 n.20,
  196 n.3
Jews 12, 88, 121, 155
John of God 193 n.35
John Paul II 35, 37, 89, 90, 92, 157, 159,
  161, 163, 165, 182, 208 n.38
Johnson, Sylvester 59

240 *Index*

Juazeiro 71–3, 107, 180, 194 n.3
Judaism 88, 129, 141

Kalley, Robert Reid 78–81, 124–5
Kalley, Susan 80–1, 124
Kardecist Spiritism 40, 77, 117, 122,
 129–30, 139, 193 n.35, 199 n.12,
 200 n.3, 203 n.3
karma 200 n.3
Keane, Webb 200 n.1, 209 n.2
Kirschke, Paulo 160
Kloppenburg, Boaventura 93
Kramer, Eric 146

Lalive D'Epinay, Christian 144–5
Landless Workers Movement (Movimento
 dos Trabalhadores Sem Terra,
 MST) 136, 160, 164, 207 n.30
Langfur, Hal 59–60, 190 n.12
Leme, Cardinal Sebastião 30–1, 74–7,
 155
Levine, Daniel 159, 196 n.2
Levine, Robert 191 n.21, 195 n.8
LGBT Rights 149–51, 154, 166, 204 n.11
liberation theology 8, 34, 47–9, 54, 70,
 92, 93, 95–9, 135, 149, 154, 156,
 157, 160, 162–3, 174, 175, 187,
 207 n.33
 ecological aspects 49, 95–7, 163–4,
 187, 207 n.33
 feminist 49, 97–9
Lima, Alceu Amoroso 31, 77
lived religion 57, 195 n.2
Louvain 97, 98, 198 n.30
Lutherans 37, 103, 120, 123, 142, 149,
 170

McAlister, Robert 85, 86
Macedo, Edir 2–3, 84–8, 90, 131, 150,
 165, 187
Machado, Maria das Dores 147, 162
McCutcheon, Russell 57
macumba 186
Maduro, Otto 198 n.30
Mafra, Clara 81, 131, 150, 189 n.4,
 211 n.22
Mainwaring, Scott 193 n.32
Malafaia, Silas 150–1, 170
Mandetta, Luiz Enrique 168–70

Marian devotions 37, 43, 45–6, 49,
 55, 74, 105, 108, 139, 173, 179,
 197 n.14, 199 n.11, 208 n.38
Mariano, Ricardo 52, 53, 86, 134, 146,
 203 n.3
Mariz, Cecília 134, 138, 147, 158, 161,
 185, 195 n.17
Maronites 127
Martin, David 145–6, 203 n.3
Marxism 33, 35, 70, 94, 154, 157,
 198 n.30, 206 n.25, 206 n.27
masculinity 98, 147, 204 n.12
materiality 40–42, 46, 52–3, 105, 119,
 139, 173, 194 n.6, 200 n.1, 209 n.2
Medellín (1968) 8, 33–4, 135, 156, 157,
 177
media 5, 8, 84, 86, 89–91, 131, 132, 138,
 139, 150, 168, 183, 193 n.35
 electronic 5, 9, 37, 55, 91, 132, 138,
 150, 151, 153, 157, 161, 167, 168,
 174, 178, 181, 183, 184
 social 132, 139, 151, 155, 169, 181,
 201 n.18
Mendes, Chico 198 n.1
Mendonça, Antonio Gouvêa 120
messianism 12, 125, 153, 172, 204 n.12,
 205 n.20
Methodists 37, 79, 124, 126, 142, 149
milícias (para-military gangs) 204 n.15
military 32, 157–8, 163, 167, 176, 177
millenarianism 27–8, 42, 51, 67, 125,
 153, 172, 174, 180, 189 n.1
"minimal Brazilian religiosity" 46, 140,
 195 n.17
missions 38, 51, 61–2, 64, 78, 110, 114,
 122–4, 185
modernity 9, 49, 70, 74, 96, 109, 143,
 154, 156, 181, 183, 187, 193 n.35,
 210 n.13
Mormons (Saints of the Latter Days) 37,
 51, 120, 125, 126, 129, 130, 140,
 201 n.13
Moro, Sérgio 171
Mother Teresa of Calcutta 164
Movimento de Educação de Base (Base
 Education Movement) 31, *see also*
 Freire, Paulo
Müller, Cardinal Gerhard 163
mysticism 40, 95, 193 n.35, 194 n.2

"Não Religião" (religiously unaffiliated) 103, 112, 114, 118, 128–9, 182, 210 n.14
National Conference of Brazilian Catholic Bishops (Conferência Nacional dos Bispos do Brasil, CNBB) 34, 62–3, 92, 136, 166, 176–7, 179, 209 n.6
nationalism 6, 9, 28, 151, 154, 167, 169, 177, 187, 192 n.24, 206 n.28
New Christendom 29–30, 155
New Evangelization 35, 37, 89, 161, 162, 165
New Religious Movements 104, 129, 173, 185, 193 n.35
Nóbrega, Manoel da 19, 58–60
Nossa Senhora Aparecida 3, 25, 40–2, 45–6, 52, 106, 166, 194 n.3
Nosso Senhor do Bonfim 44, 108–9
novas comunidades de vida e aliança (New Communities of Sacred Life and Covenant) 5, 24, 54–6, 138, 140, 182–3
nuns 5, 23, 29, 33, 34, 96, 135, 161, 192 n.22, 198 n.1, 209 n.10

O'Brien, Jean 191 n.18
Oliveira, Pedro Ribeiro de 29–30, 192 n.23, 195 n.10, 198 n.30
Operação Lava Jato (operation car wash) 151–2, 171
orders
    clerical 18, 22–3, 28–9, 191 n.16
    tertiary (lay) 24, 191 n.16
orientalism 19, 41, 57, 60, 194 n.4
orixás 18, 45, 108, 198 n.2, 210 n.19
Orsi, Robert 173, 196 n.2
Otto, Rudolf 195 n.15
Our Lady of Fatima 166, 187, 208 n.38
Ouro Preto 111, 199 n.13

pajés 15, 24, 195 n.17
Palmares 17–18
Pará 36, 82, 83, 101, 108, 126, 198 n.1, 202 n.1
pastoral do negro 201 n.14
Pastoral Land Commission 136, 149, 198 n.1, 207 n.30
patriarchy 8, 17, 43, 57, 97, 102, 142, 145, 151, 158, 168, 187, 191 n.15, 197 n.10

patronage 43–4, 172
Pedro I 26
Pedro II 27, 79, 92, 123
pelourinho 17
Pentecostalism 2–4, 9, 32, 36–7, 46, 48, 51–6, 70–1, 80, 81, 83, 89–90, 102, 103, 105, 108, 111, 114, 126–8, 130–6, 139, 140, 143–51, 158–9, 161, 162, 165, 178, 179, 181, 182, 185, 186, 189 n.4, 199 n.15, 202 n.19
    in Africa 3, 211 nn.22–3
    and class 3–4, 145–6, 159, 203 n.2
    first wave 81–4, 127, 130–1
    fourth wave 132–3, 139, 181
    and gender 147, 203 n.8, 204 n.11
    in Latin America 4, 127, 145, 186, 210 n.14, 211 n.24
    Neo-Pentecostals 4, 42, 49, 52–4, 84, 88, 130, 137, 146, 150–2, 155, 171, 180, 186, 204 n.17, 211 nn.22–3
    numbers in Brazil 2, 129, 134, 181, 185, 202 n.1
    and politics 146–7, 149–51, 159, 204 n.10
    and race 147–8
    second wave 130–1
    third wave 130–1
    and urbanization 117, 144–5
Pessar, Patricia 191 n.21, 195 n.7
Pierucci, Antonio 111–12, 138, 184
Pietz, William 194 n.5
pilgrimage 28, 43, 68, 72, 73, 105–7, 116, 201 n.15
pluralism 8, 9, 37, 84, 140, 142, 167, 176, 178, 185
Pombal, Marquis of 26, 191 n.20
poor, the 1, 22, 32–4, 37, 47, 49, 55, 67, 69, 90, 92, 94, 96, 98, 135, 136, 156–9, 161, 163–5, 175, 176, 178, 186, 191 n.14, 193 n.30, 205 n.21, 207 n.33
popular culture 132–4
populism 6, 9, 150–1, 154, 177, 187
Portella, Joel 177, 209 n.6
Portugal and the Portuguese 11–14, 16, 24–6, 29, 42, 44, 58, 60, 62, 64, 86, 106, 108, 120–2, 124, 166, 191 n.15, 191 nn.18–20, 208 n.38
poverty 32, 48, 55, 73, 96, 137, 146–7, 153, 154, 157, 164–5, 176–7, 189 n.1, 206 n.22, 207 n.33

Prandi, Reginaldo 138, 161
preferential option for the poor 22, 34, 49, 94, 135, 156, 161, 163, 165–6, 178, 193 n.30
Presbyterians 37, 50, 78, 124–7, 140, 142, 149
priests 67–8, 72, 76, 89–91, 98, 106, 110, 116, 143, 158, 161, 179–80, 187, 192 n.24, 209 n.11
  singing (cantores) 89–90, 184
processions 107–9, 116
progressive Evangelicals 204 n.10, 205 n.21
promessas (vows) 46, 107
prosperity theology 49, 52, 84, 85, 130, 146, 165, 186, 196 n.26, 204 n.17
Protestantism 2, 27, 37, 64–7, 72, 76–8, 80, 140, 141, 178, 187
  Evangelical 2, 37, 102, 103–4, 110, 112, 114, 116, 127, 129, 134, 140, 149, 153, 162, 167, 170, 171, 173, 178, 179, 182, 200 n.5, 207 n.32
  historic (mainline) 27, 37, 49–50, 64–7, 78, 103, 122–5, 127, 148, 149, 181, 200 n.3
  numbers in Brazil 2, 37, 102, 112–18, 128, 178, 182, 200 n.12, 209 n.9, 210 n.15
  origins in Brazil 27, 64–7, 120–2, 123

quilombos 17, 21, 25

race 17, 18, 63, 70, 86, 88, 101, 111, 147–8, 155, 190 n.3, 190 n.6, 201 n.14, 203 n.5
rationalization 48, 117, 139
Ratzinger, Joseph 93, 94, 198 n.26, *see also* Benedict XVI
Recife 12, 13, 18, 30, 31, 36, 75, 80, 97, 98, 121, 125
Rede Globo 86, 90, 91, 169, 186
Rede Record 86, 90, 151
reductions (*reduções*) 20, 26, 190 n.10, 190 n.13
religious affiliation and mobility 9, 103, 114, 140, 181–2, 184, 201 n.14, 202 n.23, 210 nn.14–15
resistance 6, 15, 17–18, 21, 29, 57, 119–20, 143, 164, 171, 197 n.10
re-traditionalization 183–4, 185, 187, *see also* detraditionalization

rezadeiras 24
Rial, Carmen 133
Rio de Janeiro 1, 61, 69, 75, 79, 83, 84, 87–8, 103, 112, 117, 121, 122, 126, 143, 144, 166, 169, 180, 181, 199 n.9, 203 n.8
Rivera, Dario Paulo Barrera 211 n.24
Rocha, Cristina 5, 132, 181, 185, 193 n.35, 201 n.18
Roller, Heather 20
Romanization 28–30, 49, 72, 74–5, 124, 143, 192 nn.23–4, 197 n.14
Rossi, Marcelo 5, 88–91, 182
Rousseff, Dilma 142, 149–51, 169, 171
Royal Patronage (Padroado Real) 13–14, 27, 28, 141, 156

Saints 24, 37, 43–6, 85, 105, 106, 109, 139, 141, 179, 191 n.17, 198 n.2
Salvador 16, 18, 44, 58, 60, 61, 63, 108, 117, 169, 199 n.9
Santidade 15
Santo Daime 109–10, 193 n.35, 199 nn.11–12
São Paulo 1, 61, 69, 75, 83, 87–90, 96, 103, 112, 117, 126, 132, 143, 144, 158, 169, 180, 201 n.15
Scheper-Hughes, Jennifer 195 n.17
Scherer, Odilo 170
Sebastianism 12, 42, 64, 69, 153, 173, 190 n.1, 204 n.12, 205 n.20
Second Great Awakening 125
Second Vatican Council (Vatican II, 1962–1965) 8, 30, 33, 77, 94, 97, 135, 136, 143, 156, 157, 162, 177, 198 n.30
secularization 8, 27, 50, 67, 69, 72, 103, 112, 117, 118, 161, 166, 168, 174, 180, 183
see-judge-act (*ver-julgar-agir*) 31, 33, 34, 47–8, *see also* Catholic Action
Selka, Stephen 148, 201 n.14
senzala (slave quarters) 16–18, 27, 43, 102, 190 n.6, *see also casa grande*
Serbin, Kenneth 15, 20, 28
Serra, Raimundo Irineu 199 n.11
sertão (hinterland) 42, 68, 74, 110, 144
Seventh-Day Adventists 50, 125–7, 140
shamans and shamanism 109–10, 195 n.17, 211 n.24
Shaull, Richard 50

Silva, Benedita da 149
Silva, Luíz Inácio (Lula) da 35, 44,
    149–50, 160, 171, 206 n.22
Silva, Marina 149
Sister Dulce 169–70, 183
slavery 5, 6, 16–18, 22, 68, 110, 122, 142
Soares, Romildo Ribeiro 85
Solomon's Temple (UCKG) 2–3, 5, 87,
    88, 90, 150, 181, 187
Souza, Luiz Alberto Gomes de 192 n.25,
    202 n.22
space 6–7, 20, 58, 108, 124, 148, 173,
    180, 184, 186, 191 n.18
spirit exorcism 52, 53, 84, 130, 148, 152,
    173, 180, 184
sports and Christianity 132–3
Stang, Dorothy 198 n.1
Steil, Carlos 116–17, 145, 179
Steiner, Leonardo Ulrich 166, 177,
    209 n.6
Stewart-Gambino, Hannah 159–60
Stoll, David 210 n.14
structural sin 157
structures of feeling 7, 39, 41, 44, 56, 57,
    84, 139, 153, 167, 179, 195 n.17,
    201 n.14, *see also* Williams,
    Raymond

Távora Affair 26, 191 n.20
Temer, Michel 176–7
Theological Institute of Recife (ITER) 97
Theotokos Sanctuary 5, 90
Third Great Awakening 126
Toca de Assis 5, 24, 54, 138, 182
Toniol, Rodrigo 116–17, 179
transnationalism 4–5, 37, 81, 118, 124,
    131, 133, 136, 138, 150, 152, 157–8,
    174, 184–7, 193 n.35, 201 n.16,
    210 n.13
    South-South flows and networks 186,
        201 n.18, 211 nn.22–4
Trump, Donald 154, 206 n.24, 206 n.28,
    208 n.44
Tupis 59–62, 66, 191 n.18
TV Globo 86, 90
Tylor, E. B. 40

Umbanda 3–5, 17, 40, 85, 103, 117, 130,
    134, 148, 152, 183, 186, 198 n.2,
    199 n.9, 199 n.12, 201 n.14, 203 n.3

Universal Church of the Kingdom of
    God (Igreja Universal do Reino
    de Deus) 3–4, 25, 37, 42, 52, 53,
    84–87, 90, 131–2, 148, 150, 156,
    165, 181, 185–7, 195 n.25, 201 n.16,
    203 n.6, 203 n.8, 211 n.22
urbanization 8, 32, 46, 67, 102, 104, 115,
    116, 131, 144–5, 178

Valle, Rogério 136, 158, 193 n.31
Valley of Dawn (*Vale do
    Amanhecer*) 104, 183–4, 193 n.35,
    210 n.19
Van de Kamp, Linda 4–5, 186, 189 n.4,
    201 n.16, 211 n.22
Vargas, Getúlio 30, 44, 76, 87, 127,
    143
Vásquez, Manuel A. 7, 42, 159, 173, 181,
    183–5, 189 n.1, 189 n.8, 193 n.31,
    193 n.35, 195 n.19, 196 n.33,
    209 n.1
Verger, Pierre Fatumbi 195 n.13
Vieira, Antônio 21, 62–3, 168, 196 n.6
Villegagnon, Nicholas de 61, 65–7, 121,
    196 n.7
Vingren, Gunnar 36, 81–5, 102, 116,
    126
Viveiros de Castro, Eduardo 109

Weber, Max 40, 145, 146, 152, 194 n.2,
    204 n.17
Wilde, Guillermo 20–2, 190 n.10
Willems, Emilio 144–5
Williams, Raymond 7, 39, 193 n.1
women 23, 24, 80, 92, 98–9, 147, 148,
    152, 155, 160, 162, 178, 186, 187,
    191 n.15, 192 n.22, 198 n.32,
    204 n.16
Workers' Party (Partido do
    Trabalhadores) 35, 104, 149,
    151–2, 160, 165, 167, 168, 171
World Youth Day 1, 5, 165
Wright, Robin 110, 195 n.17

youth 5, 132–3, 138, 139, 146, 152, 161,
    165, 178, 180, 181, 184–5, 189 n.5,
    193 n.35, 211 n.21

Zumbi 17–18, 148
Županov, Ines 19

Printed in the USA
CPSIA information can be obtained
at www.ICGtesting.com
LVHW010325090324
773943LV00001B/141